EDDIE
JONES

EDDIE JONES

RUGBY MAVERICK

Mike Colman

ALLEN&UNWIN

First published in Great Britain in 2018 by Allen & Unwin
This updated paperback edition published in Great Britain in 2019
by Allen & Unwin

Allen & Unwin
c/o Atlantic Books
Ormond House
26–27 Boswell Street
London WC1N 3JZ

Phone: 020 7269 1610
Fax: 020 7430 0916
Email: UK@allenandunwin.com
Web: www.allenandunwin.com/uk

A CIP catalogue record for this book is available from the British Library.

Paperback ISBN 978 1 91163 045 6
E-Book ISBN 978 1 76063 595 4

Printed and bound in Great Britain by Clays Ltd, Elcograf S.p.A.

10 9 8 7 6 5 4 3 2 1

CONTENTS

Maverick: A person who thinks and acts in an independent way, often behaving differently from the expected or usual way.

(*Cambridge English Dictionary*)

Prologue

THE EX-SON-IN-LAW

Eddie Jones is the ex-son-in-law who has gone away and made good. Now he's back and wants to buy the big house across the road. Every time you open the front curtains he wants you to see him driving in and out in his Rolls Royce, and he wants you to think, 'We never should have let him go.'

Courier-Mail, 10 June 2016

When Eddie Jones brought his team to Australia six months after being appointed England coach he scoffed at suggestions he was seeking revenge over the country that had cast him aside. Not too many believed him. As one columnist noted: 'Eddie Jones has a long memory.'

Sacked as Wallaby coach in 2005, Eddie had endured an at-times torturous climb back to the top of world rugby over the following decade. Humiliated during an abortive one-season stint at the Queensland Reds, he was then roundly criticized in Australia for assisting South Africa in its successful 2007 Rugby World Cup campaign. Another disheartening term cut short with English club Saracens saw him coaching corporate rugby in Japan, a far cry from the glory days of leading Australia to the final of the 2003 World Cup. It was only the stunning upset win by his Japanese 'Brave Blossoms' over the Springboks at the 2015 World Cup that saw him back in the frame and appointed to coach England, the best-resourced team in world rugby.

With the English scheduled to embark on a three-Test tour of Australia in June 2016, well before his appointment, the series against the World Cup finalists could not have provided a better opportunity for Eddie to prove a point to his many detractors down under.

Rarely has there been a character in Australian sport who has polarized opinion to the degree of Eddie Jones. His most favoured ex-players and staff members avow that while a perfectionist workaholic and hard task-master, he can be warm, funny and loyal. Those in the opposing camp are just as vehement that he is despotic, cruel and unreasonable. Former Wallabies such as Elton Flatley and Wendell Sailor describe him as the best coach they ever had. Others, including former Australian Rugby Union boss John O'Neill, are quick to label him almost impossible to work with.

None of this is a secret to Eddie, who knows that there were many, past and present, in the corridors of power at ARU headquarters who all but rejoiced in his very public fall from grace following the 2003 RWC final.

All of this combined to make the 2016 mid-year series the most eagerly anticipated for years. Since the heady days of the 2003 World Cup, which netted hosts Australia an unprecedented $43 million windfall, the stock of the Wallabies had fallen alarmingly. With Eddie sacked after eight losses from nine Tests, former Queensland coach John Connolly was given the task of mounting Australia's campaign at the 2007 World Cup. It ended in the quarter-finals, with the Wallabies' nemesis Jonny Wilkinson kicking four penalty goals in England's 12-10 win. Eight months later, John O'Neill took the unprecedented step of hiring Australia's first-ever foreign-born head coach in former All Blacks assistant Robbie Deans.

Deans, who had enjoyed great success as coach of the Canterbury Crusaders, taking them to five Super Rugby titles, was seen as the man to halt the disturbing slide in rugby's popularity in Australia. Just prior to Deans' appointment, O'Neill had commissioned a report on the game's health. In summary it read: cash down, crowds down, TV ratings down and participation rates down 1.8 per cent – the first drop in ten years.

The hoped-for Deans-led revival never came. Live TV coverage on Channel 7 of his first Test in charge, an 18-12 win over Ireland in Melbourne, was out-rated by a rerun of the movie *Richie Rich* on rival network Channel 9. In the lead-up to the Wallabies' next match, against France at Sydney's 80,000-seat ANZ Stadium a fortnight later, ticket sales were so slow that stadium management offered them free to anyone who spent more than $80 at a local shopping centre. An ambitious national second-tier competition proved little more than a money pit, draining the ARU 'war-chest' down to just $8 million.

High hopes had been held for the 2011 Rugby World Cup in New Zealand, but it too was a disappointment. Deans placed enormous faith in his precocious backline stars James O'Connor, Kurtley Beale and Quade Cooper – dubbed 'The Three Amigos' by the Australian press corps – but they failed to live up to his expectations. Mercurial fly-half Cooper was hounded from one end of New Zealand to the other by crowds and local media, who labelled him 'Public Enemy Number One'. His confidence shot, he fell apart, and the team's attack imploded with him. The Wallabies lost their pool match against Ireland and were shown the exit door 20-6 in the semi-final by eventual Cup winners the All Blacks. Deans followed eighteen months later after a series loss to the British and Irish Lions.

If things were bad they were going to get worse. Replacing Deans was former Wallaby front-rower Ewen 'Link' McKenzie whose tenure ended controversially three years later following a much-publicized clash between Beale and a team manager.

With the public image of Australian rugby at its lowest ebb, the dubious honour of coaching the Wallabies was handed to Eddie's former Randwick team-mate Michael Cheika.

The playing styles of Eddie and Cheika could not have been more different: Eddie a diminutive hooker as renowned for his ceaseless chatter as high work-rate, Cheika a hard-boiled back-rower who preferred to let his take-no-prisoners physicality do his talking for him.

It is the same with their coaching styles. Eddie has a reputation for ripping into his players and coaching assistants with his razor-sharp tongue, his sarcasm and straight-out abuse known to reduce even hardened Test forwards to tears. Cheika is more likely to use his powerful body language to get the message across, as Eddie noted: 'We played four or five years together. He was pretty rough and tough. He was always smart, always a thinker, but he definitely had a temper. I think maybe he's got control of that now that he's got older, but he still has that aura that allows him to impose his personality on his players.'

As Wallaby scrum-half Nick Phipps put it, 'Sometimes if someone makes a mistake Cheik will rub it in with a bit of a laugh. Other times . . . well, there's no laughing.'

Stories of Cheika's toughness during his playing days are legendary. Long-time Randwick player and coach Jeff Sayle tells the story of Cheika copping a boot to the head that required thirty-eight stitches and showing up at training four days later determined to play the following weekend. Sayle took one look at the festering wound and told him to get to a doctor.

'If the doctor says you can play, you can play,' Sayle said, knowing the chances of that were nil. The doctor did a quick examination and booked him into hospital for immediate treatment. The scar is still evident, although not as prominent as the cauliflower ears Cheika earned in over three hundred club games.

But while on-field they might have been poles apart, off-field Eddie and Cheika had followed a similar road to get to the top of international coaching. When Eddie, the son of an Australian father and Japanese mother, described Cheika to a reporter during the 2015 Rugby World Cup, he could have been talking about himself.

'I think he was always a bit of an outsider, a Lebanese kid in what was then an upper-class private-school game. I think that's why he was so determined to make it.'

And make it he did, at just about everything he put his mind to. When his playing career ended in 1999, Cheika moved into coaching at Italian club Padova. In 2001, when his father fell ill, he returned to Australia and coached Randwick, taking them to the Sydney premiership in 2004. The following year he joined Leinster, in 2009 coaching the Irish club to its first-ever European title with a 19-16 Heineken Cup victory over Leicester Tigers at Murrayfield. In 2014 he coached NSW Waratahs to the Super Rugby title, becoming the first coach to win major professional competitions in both northern and southern hemispheres.

At the same time as playing and coaching rugby, Cheika was establishing a highly successful wholesale fashion operation in Australia and Europe. A millionaire many times over and fluent in English, Lebanese, French and Italian, Cheika has a rough exterior that belies a shrewd business mind, as ARU officials found when they faced him over the negotiating table.

Three months after the Waratahs' historic Super Rugby victory, with the sudden departure of Ewen McKenzie, he was appointed Australian coach. Four days after that, he was introducing himself to Wallaby players at the airport as they headed to England to start their four-Test spring tour. With just one win, over Wales, and losses to Ireland, France and England, the tour was not successful on the scoreboard but in terms of laying the first foundation stones for Australia's 2015 Rugby World Cup campaign it was invaluable.

A year after being handed control of a team in turmoil, Cheika took the Wallabies all the way to the World Cup final, in the process dealing a killer blow to Stuart Lancaster's England side and opening the door to the biggest career opportunity of Eddie Jones' life.

Upset by Wales in their second pool match, England had to beat Australia at Twickenham in their next game in order to make it through to the quarter-finals. Instead, the Wallabies produced their best World Cup performance since Eddie's side had beaten New Zealand in the semi-final of the 2003 tournament, belting England 33-13 and handing them the unwanted title of first World Cup hosts to be eliminated in the pool stage. The loss rendered England's next game against Uruguay meaningless and ended Lancaster's tenure in failure. With Eddie given the job, and handed a blank cheque by England's Rugby Football Union to turn things around, the stage was set for a series to remember in Australia.

Rarely do the stars align as they did when Eddie and his men arrived at Brisbane airport on Thursday, 2 June 2016. The machinations behind the scenes couldn't have been more perfect if they had been scripted by Rugby Australia's marketing department. There was Eddie, the disgruntled former coach, riding into town at the head of the white-shirted Poms, who had snatched the World Cup from Australia's grasp back in 2003; the confident Wallabies, who had brushed England aside on their way to the RWC final just eight months earlier; an England side still smarting from the embarrassment dealt to them by Australia on their own ground; and two fiercely competitive ex-team-mates, outwardly friendly, but desperately keen to finish the series with bragging rights. To add even more spice to the mix, if England won they would leap-frog Australia to the number two world ranking behind New Zealand. There was also the matter of the World Rugby Coach of the Year award bestowed on Cheika after the World Cup. Many believed it should have gone to the All Blacks' Steve Hanson or even, after the heroics of the Brave Blossoms, Eddie. Given how many times he alluded to it throughout the tour, it would appear that Eddie fell into the latter group.

A lot had changed in Australian rugby since Eddie had left under a cloud over ten years earlier, but there was still one direct link to his time as national coach. Captaining the Wallabies was hooker Stephen Moore, the last remaining player from Eddie's time in charge of the team. Moore, who had made his Test debut in 2005, could well have ended up playing for Ireland if not for Eddie's intervention.

'It was in 2003 just after the World Cup. I was nineteen at the time, studying at Queensland University and playing for the university club. I was in the Australian Under-21 squad but I hadn't played any senior representative football at that stage. My parents are both Irish, and there was a bit of interest from the Irish Rugby Union asking if I'd be interested in going over and playing for one of the provinces and maybe playing for Ireland. I remember I was at uni waiting to go into a lecture one day and my phone rang, and it was Eddie. It was, how can I put this . . . an animated conversation. He was like, "Mate, we want you to sign with the ARU. You need to sign straight away." It was my first interaction with him, but I remember at Under-21 camps I'd see Wallabies standing around sweating bullets waiting to go in for meetings with Eddie and they'd come out soaked in sweat, so he was a pretty daunting character. It was pretty intimidating. I was scared to be honest. I got off the phone and rang my mum and dad straight away. I signed the next day, and it was 100 per cent the right thing to do. I've never regretted it for a moment. That's just the way Eddie was, big on detail, very professional. He taught me a lot about trying to be the best in the world at what you do. I knew that playing against a team coached by Eddie would be hard. I was pretty young when I played under Eddie, first at the Wallabies and then the Reds, but I've always thought I would have loved to play under him as a senior player. He knows what is important when it comes to winning. He has a good grasp of that; it's something I've always admired about him.'

When Eddie's flight touched down, the only people happier than ARU officials with their looming financial bonanza were the Australian rugby media. Nobody gave better copy than Eddie, and Cheika was no slouch either, as evidenced by his outburst after the *New Zealand Herald* printed a caricature of him dressed as a clown ahead of an All Black Test. Even so, Cheika refused to be drawn into a war of words with Eddie throughout the series. Not that it mattered. Eddie did enough stirring for both of them. Even before he'd left the airport to head to the team hotel he made his theme for the tour clear: he would be playing the role of the victim.

'I just went through immigration and I got shunted through the area where everything got checked. That's what I'm expecting, mate. Everything that's done around the game is going to be coordinated. All coordinated to help Australia win. We've got to be good enough to control what we can control. Australia are second in the world. They've got the best coach in the world. They're playing in their own backyard; they're going to be strong favourites for the tour. Our record in Australia is three Tests since Captain Cook arrived, so it's not a great record, is it?'

Perhaps not, but the England side Eddie had shaped since taking on the job was very different from the one that the Wallabies had destroyed at Twickenham in their previous meeting. Different, in fact, from any England side that had ever toured Australia. Recently crowned champions of Europe following their Grand Slam win in the Six Nations, they were fit, strong, fiercely combative and, just like their coach, had plenty to prove against the Wallabies.

Before announcing his touring squad, Eddie made a statement that he, more than anyone, knew would incite Australians. A great lover of cricket and well versed in the game's history, he invoked memories of the infamous 1932–33 Ashes series, during which the England leg-side tactics sparked a diplomatic crisis between the two countries.

'We've got to take a side down there to play Bodyline. If we're going to beat Australia in Australia, we've got to have a completely physical, aggressive team.'

Eddie later claimed that by 'Bodyline rugby' he meant England would have to be inventive, rather than violent, if they were to upset the Wallabies.

'It's a figure of speech. The whole thing is, we've got to do something different here. We can't do what's been done by previous English teams. We've got to have a different mindset, a different way of how we play the game against Australia to change history.'

Regardless of the semantics, the result was the same. England ran out for the first Test determined to overpower the Wallabies in the forwards, and that is exactly what they did. After Australia had shot out to a two-try 10-0 lead after fifteen minutes, it looked like England's six-Test unbeaten run under Eddie was about to come to an inglorious end. Instead, the boot of Owen Farrell drew them within a point, 9-10, before the English forwards, led by flankers James Haskell and Chris Robshaw, the Vunipola brothers, front-rower Mako and number eight Billy, and exciting lock Maro Itoje, took control. The scoresheet showed that Australia scored four tries to three and had another disallowed in going down 28-39, but no one who saw the game was in any doubt: this was a win to England every bit as comprehensive as the loss they had suffered at the hands of the Wallabies eight months earlier.

It was England's first-ever win in Brisbane and the most points they had ever scored against Australia. It also gave Eddie a perfect six-from-six Test record at Suncorp Stadium after five wins with the Wallabies. The joy it gave him was evident from the way he jumped to his feet, arms raised above his head, before 'high-fiving' his friend and assistant coach Glen Ella as wing replacement Jack Nowell ran onto a perfectly weighted George Ford kick to score the win-clinching try.

So happy was Eddie, in fact, that even he might have struggled to find a reason to continue his victim routine if not for the untimely intrusion at the post-match media conference of a camera crew led by former Wallaby back-rower Stephen Hoiles.

Hoiles, who had been handed his first Test jersey by Eddie in 2004, was working for *The Other Rugby Show*, a new 'alternative' cable TV programme on the Fox Sports network, official broadcasters of the Test series. With its premiere episode airing the following week, the producers had concocted a supposedly humorous segment in which Hoiles would be given a list of unrelated words and have to include them in a question to Eddie. It backfired horribly. Not only were legitimate journalists appalled and angry at having their workplace invaded by a second-rate comedy act, it gave Eddie ammunition to use as motivation for his team in the lead-up to the second Test.

Hoiles' question was: 'You seem to be in the press a bit more than Donald Trump this week, and the lads were pumped up. There was a bit of moisture out there, and I think you and Glen had a good moment, looked lubed-up and a fair bit of shrinkage. How did you enjoy that moment with your old mate Glen up in the box?'

Caught off guard, Eddie answered: 'Sorry? Repeat the question, mate. I don't like the tone of the question, mate . . . Are we not allowed to enjoy a win, mate?'

There was an awkward silence before a serious question was asked by a member of the working press, but after the media conference had broken up and he had regained his composure, Eddie was quick to get stuck into Hoiles and also the Fox Sports promotional campaign that featured former Wallabies turned Fox commentators Tim Horan, Phil Kearns, Greg Martin and Rod Kafer making fun of English rugby failures. Asked if Hoiles had disrespected him, he replied: 'Without a doubt. You get that sort of ridiculous question from Hoiles. You've seen the Fox promos, they are disgusting. All I am saying is there's been quite a disrespectful way in which the team has been treated in the media here. It is quite demeaning, disrespectful to the team, so we're not going to let this opportunity pass.'

The segment never aired, with host Sean Maloney instead offering an apology to Eddie, the England team and the working media for any offence caused. Hoiles also contacted Eddie personally to apologize. It was an apology that Eddie accepted, but he still milked the situation for all it was worth, before moving on to Melbourne with a parting dig at Cheika.

'They've got the world's best coach, and the expectation's high for them. The pressure's on them next week.'

If Eddie was starting to irritate his old team-mate with continued references to his Coach of the Year award, Cheika wasn't showing it, telling reporters who asked why he wasn't returning serve, 'He hasn't called me fat or bald or anything.'

Besides, it wasn't snide comments from Eddie that Cheika was concerned with. It was his team's inability to beat England.

The second Test was another win to the visitors, this time 27-3, an astonishing result given Australia's dominance everywhere except the scoreboard. Incredibly, the Wallabies had 70 per cent of possession, ran the ball 172 times to England's 53, and gained 962 run metres to England's 282. Most telling of all, England were forced to make 217 tackles against Australia's 81.

It was a series-clinching win that defied logic, but Eddie gave reporters one of his best lines of the tour, claiming that giving the Wallabies so much ball that they ran out of steam was a move borrowed from Muhammad Ali's famous tactic against George Foreman in 1974's 'Rumble in the Jungle': 'We had to play Rope-a-Dope today,' he said.

Wallaby fly-half Bernard Foley isn't too sure about the Ali–Foreman analogy, but he does know that England were well prepared that night and followed Eddie's instructions to a tee.

'That was very smart the way they changed their game plan from the first Test. That had been our first match since the World Cup, and we expected the momentum to continue, which was poor judgement on our part. We were both different teams to what we had been at Twickenham. We had four players making their debuts on a week's preparation, and England were a different beast to what they had been. They had a new strategy and they implemented it well. We underestimated what needed to be done. In saying that, we couldn't have started that first game better. We scored some good tries and then we made an error, and they capitalized. They got on a roll, and we struggled to stop the flow. That changed everything for the next game in Melbourne. The expectation was all on us. We were the ones in a must-win situation to keep the series alive. Eddie knew we would be throwing everything at them and they changed their structure so they were defending more in a line. They kept tackling, we kept chasing the win, and when they got a chance they scored.'

For Eddie it was proof positive that all the hard work he and the team had been doing for the previous six months had paid off. Not only had England beaten their European rivals, they had also been able to adapt to Southern Hemisphere conditions and tactics.

'We have to be tactically flexible in Test rugby,' Eddie said. 'That's why I'm so pleased. They had all the ball, and then we had the opportunity to score a try and we took it. That's the sign of a good side.'

A side that, with the series and world number-two ranking safely locked away, now had another goal: a 3-0 whitewash.

'The boys started talking about it on the field, and we're committed to doing that. We want to be the best team in the world. If the All Blacks were in this situation now, what would they be thinking? They'd be thinking 3-0. If we want to be the best team in the world, we have to think 3-0.'

And 3-0 it was. The record highest score against Australia of 39 that England had posted in the first Test lasted just two weeks, with Eddie's men ending their tour with a 44-40 victory. It was the first 3-0 series drubbing the Wallabies had suffered since they went down to the Springboks in 1971. Eddie resisted the opportunity to gloat at the post-match media call, describing the banter throughout the series as 'all a bit of fun', and allowed himself only one minor dig at the country of his birth.

'It's been great to be in Australia,' he said. 'Obviously, being an Australian, I'm always grateful to Australia for what they've done for me in rugby . . .' He then flashed the tiniest of cheeky smiles. '. . . but it's certainly nice beating them 3-0.'

He then twisted the knife ever so slightly, making special mention of the work Australia's long-time tormentor Jonny Wilkinson had done with the England kickers Owen Farrell and George Ford prior to the tour. Farrell, whose goal-kicking Eddie described as 'solar-system class', had been the difference in the third Test, booting a Wilkinson-like twenty-four points.

Australian captain Stephen Moore, who retired in 2017 with 129 caps, believes the Wallabies, playing their first Tests of the season, weren't in the right mental place to withstand the battle-hardened Englishmen.

'There's no doubt we took things for granted after 2015. We thought the spirit and culture that we'd built up through the World Cup would just follow over. On the flip side, England had a lot to prove after being bowled out of their own tournament. It was a hell of a series, though. Both sides played good footy. They were some of the best opposition I ever encountered in my career and they showed what a good team they were over the next couple of seasons. Given the way Eddie left the Wallabies, I'm sure he would have enjoyed it, but Eddie is a proud Australian and he has never shied away from that.'

The question over Eddie's allegiances has long been a matter of debate. Many believe that a former national coach should not be coaching another country against his old team. Eddie always makes it clear that there is a distinction between one's country of birth and their country of employment, and whoever pays him will have his loyalty.

At the media conference after the final Test of the series he was asked by an Australian journalist if he believed the success of England's defence against Australia's policy of all-out attack had proved the Wallabies needed to be more flexible.

'They're well coached,' he answered. 'They'll work it out for themselves. I'm not coaching Australia. I'm coaching England, and it's an honour for me to coach England. If I was coaching Australia, I'd tell you.'

A year later he gave a more telling insight into his feelings at the time when recounting an experience he had had at the start of the first Test in Brisbane.

'I'm Australian and I love Australia, but any semblance of a conflict was destroyed when I walked up the grandstand and sat in the box, and there was this woman sitting outside. She was immaculately dressed. She had the Yves Saint Laurent shoes on, the nice scarf, everything. And she turns after the national anthems and starts giving me the finger and an assortment of words, and I thought, "Maybe I'm not in love with Australia any more."'

And even more so back in 2015, when the ex-son-in-law was asked, the day after he had been appointed England coach, how he would feel preparing a team to beat the Wallabies.

'I didn't divorce Australia,' he answered. 'Australia divorced me.'

1

LARPA BOYS

Eddie Jones was nine years old when he first saw the face of racism up close. Eddie had always known he was different, but he lived in a rarefied little world where everyone was different, and that difference was embraced rather than suppressed or rejected.

But not on this day in 1969, with his father away with the Australian armed services in Vietnam and his mother left alone with Eddie and his two sisters at their home in the Sydney southeastern suburb of Little Bay.

It was customary for members of the local Returned Services League to help out the families of soldiers serving overseas. A roster would be drawn up, and RSL members, many veterans of conflicts in the Second World War or Korea, would arrive unannounced for a few hours' gardening or handyman work. Eddie remembers well the day a man from the RSL pushed a lawnmower up their garden path.

When Eddie's Japanese mother opened the front door, the man took one look at her, growled, 'I'm not mowing *your* lawn,' and headed back down the path. Eddie's mother shrugged, said calmly, 'Looks like we'll have to mow our own lawn,' and shut the door.

It wouldn't be the last time Eddie would be subjected to racist attitudes or slurs. He would hear them from time to time on sporting fields around Sydney, but like his mother he learned to stay calm and move on.

'If she had said, "Oh, they are racist," then it would have been embedded in me, but it wasn't,' he says. 'I never grew up feeling isolated. My mother was dead against us having any sort of Japanese characteristics because of the environment, so we were brought up dinky-di Aussies.'

Eddie's father Ted was a career soldier who had served as part of the British Commonwealth Occupation Forces in Japan after the Second World War. It was there that he met Nellie, who was working as a translator at BCOF headquarters at Eta Jima, 8 kilometres west of the major port of Kure. Having spent much of her life in the US, Nellie spoke perfect English. Her father had moved from Japan to California before the war and established an orchard in the Sacramento Valley. The future looked bright in his new country, and then came 7 December 1941 and Japan's attack on Pearl Harbor. Nellie's family, along with an estimated 120,000 other US residents of Japanese descent, were rounded up and relocated. The fruit in the orchard rotted on the trees as for four years they were split up and shunted between a series of internment camps. Nellie's father never went back to California. At war's end, angered and humiliated by the treatment they had received at the hands of the US authorities, he returned to Japan and arranged for his family to join him.

By then twenty-one years old, Nellie had to learn a new culture and a second language all over again. She may have looked Japanese, but her life experiences and thought processes were very much American. It made assimilation difficult, but her knowledge of western ways and language skills made her a valuable acquisition when she began work at BCOF headquarters. It also made it easier for her and Ted Jones to communicate and fall in love.

Fraternization between members of the occupying forces and local girls was inevitable and, while officially frowned upon, the longer the occupation lasted, the more accepted it became. But the sight of Australian servicemen walking down the street or dining with Japanese women in Kure was one thing. The idea of them marrying, and returning to 1940s Australia, quite another altogether.

When Australian forces arrived in Kure in 1946, many straight from the former battlefields of the Southwest Pacific, Australia was still reeling from four years of bitter conflict with the Japanese. Newsreel vision of returning prisoners of war being stretchered off ships in shocking physical condition, and newspaper reports of the cruelty and deprivation they had been subjected to at the hands of the Japanese, were still very fresh in the minds of the Australian public. Over the ten years that the occupation continued, the attitudes of many of the occupying soldiers towards the Japanese may have mellowed, but for many back home they remained as bitter and intractable as ever.

In October 1947 Corporal H. J. Cooke became the first Australian soldier to apply for permission to marry a Japanese bride and bring her back to Australia when his deployment ended. In rejecting the application, Australia's minister for immigration, Arthur Caldwell, spoke for many of his countrymen when he said, 'It would be the grossest act of public indecency to permit a Japanese of either sex to pollute Australia.'

By the time Ted and Nellie made their application to marry, the prevailing attitudes had softened. The peace treaty between the Allied Powers and Japan was signed in September 1951, and seven months later legislation was passed in the Australian parliament to allow Australian servicemen to bring their Japanese wives and children home to Australia.

The first to do so was Sapper Gordon Parker, who arrived with his wife Nabuko, known as Cherry, and their two children in June 1952. By the time the last Australian occupying troops left Japan in November 1956, another 650 couples had joined them, including Ted and Nellie Jones.

In 1960, Ted, Nellie and their two daughters, Diane and Vicky, were living close to the city of Burnie, Tasmania, as Ted worked at Kokoda Barracks in nearby Devonport. It was at Burnie, on 30 January, that Eddie was born. Soon afterwards Ted was posted to Sydney's Randwick Barracks, and the family moved to Little Bay, a working-class suburb in the Randwick municipality. Bounded by Matraville, Malabar and Chifley, it is also a short walk to La Perouse, a bayside suburb that would have enormous significance for Eddie and the sport of rugby union itself.

Although it was only a few minutes' drive to some of Sydney's most expensive waterfront suburbs, La Perouse was far from affluent. In fact, it has been described as 'Sydney's Soweto'. Known as 'Larpa', in the early 1800s it became a dumping ground for the city's Aborigines, who were herded together in a government-run mission to keep them isolated from the fast-growing white settlement. As the years went on, Aborigines from country areas who came to the city would also gravitate to Larpa and live in crudely built shacks and lean-tos outside the mission gates.

Among these non-mission families were Gordon and May Ella and their twelve children, including twin boys Mark and Glen – born in 1959 – and brother Gary, younger by one year. Like the dozens of other youngsters growing up in Larpa, the Ellas were active, spirited and sporty. They made their own fun outdoors, on the streets, playing in spare lots and fishing or swimming in the bay. They had little choice. Their ramshackle two-bedroom home was not a place in which to spend time. It had no hot running water or sewerage connection. There were only two power points, and the family would bathe outside in a copper tub using water heated in a kettle. Cooking was done on a fire stove fuelled with wood collected by the children from nearby scrub. The family ate in the kitchen, so small that meals were served at the four-seat table in shifts, and Mark, Glen and Gary slept together on a single mattress on the floor of their parents' bedroom.

It was a world devoid of comforts, but full of family, friends and fun, a world that seemed like boy heaven to Eddie Jones, and one that the Ellas were more than happy to share.

The day that Nellie took five-year-old Eddie a few minutes' walk to the local pre-school would prove to be one of the most fortunate of his life.

'I was very lucky,' he says. 'The first day I went to kindergarten at La Perouse, sitting next to me on the mat were the Ella brothers, three of the greatest athletes ever to play rugby. They changed the way the game was played and the expectation of how it could be played.'

For the next thirty years in local junior teams, then at La Perouse State School, Matraville High School and Randwick Rugby Club, Eddie would have a front-row seat as the Ellas put on a show those lucky enough to witness it will never forget. He saw them do things with a rugby ball in their hands never done before or since – much as Eddie has tried to replicate it in the teams he coaches.

'That's always been my dream, to go back to those days and to see the game played the way they played it.'

Rugby union would bring Eddie and the Ella brothers fame and – in his case – fortune, but it wasn't the only game that they played together in the early days. In fact, it wasn't even their major sporting interest.

'Rugby league was probably our favourite back then,' says Glen Ella, whose uncle Bruce 'Larpa' Stewart was an exciting and popular league player for South Sydney and Eastern Suburbs in the 1960s. Stewart also played A-grade league for the La Perouse All Blacks, and it was the ambition of every Larpa youngster to do the same.

The Ellas, and Eddie, played junior rugby league for La Perouse on Saturdays, and union for Clovelly Eagles on Sundays.

'Whatever we were into, he was too,' Glen says. 'Union, local league, cricket . . . and we were always playing touch footy. Whenever and wherever we could we'd be playing touch; on the oval, on the asphalt playground at school, it didn't matter. If we had a ball we'd use it, if we didn't, we'd use a can or a bottle or something.'

In summer the sport of choice was cricket, and it was as captain of his local junior team that Eddie first began to show the character traits for which he would become renowned.

'I probably spent the most time with Eddie in the early days because even though all four of us were in the same grade at school, Mark and Glen were older,' says Gary Ella. 'That meant I was in the same age group for local sports as Eddie. He was very popular because his Dad had a car, and he'd drive us to all the games. He seemed pretty quiet when we first met him, but that's probably because he was concentrating more on his studies than us. He was always smart, and not just in the classroom. He was a smart footballer, a very clever dummy-half at rugby league for La Perouse and a good flanker and then hooker at rugby, but cricket was where he really came into his own.

'He was captain, opening batsman and off-spin bowler for our junior side and as captain he took it very seriously. He was always a thinker, always a planner. We were playing in a local suburban competition, so you'd play against the same kids a lot. Eddie would work out their strengths and weaknesses and have a game plan to beat them. The rest of us would just show up for a game, but Eddie would have it all mapped out. He knew exactly what he wanted us to do.'

And if they didn't do it, he'd let them know about it.

'That was when the sledging started. He was so quick-witted, and the sarcasm would come out. Eddie's never been too scared to let people know what he thinks, and it wasn't just the players on the other sides. Eddie would always put himself in the most difficult position. He'd be the one fielding closest to the bat. That way he could get into the opposition batsmen's face, but if someone in our team did something wrong he'd let them have it too.

'That's just the way he is. If he puts the time in, he demands it of others.'

While he and his friends continued to play cricket throughout their school days and, in Eddie's case, beyond (he joined Randwick Cricket Club and rose through the grades to the Second XI), rugby union would usurp rugby league as their major sport once they started at Matraville High School in 1972.

At the time, rugby union in Sydney was seen very much as a blue-blood sport, with its roots firmly in the private-school system. Then an amateur code, unlike professional rugby league it offered no financial incentive and so was not considered an attractive sporting option for young men of limited means.

And Matraville High was a school full of young men of limited means. With its proximity to La Perouse, the school had a high percentage of Aboriginal students. A cruel and racist joke of the period suggested that when the boys graduated from Matraville High they could simply walk straight across Anzac Parade to begin their new life at Long Bay Jail.

It was a slur typical of the prevailing attitudes of the time, with Indigenous Australians treated as second-class citizens legally and socially. The feeling of marginalization had a flow-on effect, leaving many young Aborigines frustrated and without hope. What was the point in going to school, they asked themselves, when they would never get a decent job because of the colour of their skin? From the day the school opened in 1964 truancy at Matraville High was a major problem, as teachers struggled to keep pupils motivated. The solution they came up with was sport. If the kids were keen to play in school teams, they reasoned, they would at least show up for classes.

The obvious winter sport for Matraville High to play was rugby league, with the school in the heart of the giant South Sydney Rugby League catchment area, and for the first four years of its existence that was the game it played. That changed in 1968 with the arrival of deputy principal Geoff Mould. A physical education teacher who had played both league and union in his youth, Mould was convenor of the Combined High Schools rugby union programme and so pushed for Matraville to change over to the fifteen-a-side game. It was a suggestion that did not please the school's parents, many of whom saw professional rugby league as a way for their boys to get a start in life. There was also an element of reverse snobbery. Rugby union, they felt, was the domain of the toffee-nosed private-school set. How could little Matraville with only 900 students – half of them girls – hope to compete with rugby powerhouses like Sydney Boys' High, Cranbrook, North Sydney Boys' High or, the grand-daddy of them all, St Joseph's College, Hunters Hill?

It was a valid concern, but rather than being put off by rugby's cultural traditions, Mould was attracted to them.

'I found that among the various school sports, rugby was one of the few which was devoted to an amateur philosophy. The game's traditional approach appealed to me. The old school tie can be ridiculed at times but it can also be a valuable asset.'

Mould had another reason for wanting to promote rugby union at the school. Soon after he arrived at Matraville, he was approached by Bob Outterside, coach of Randwick's first-grade side, to help with the club's pre-season fitness campaign. Although in his mid-thirties at the time, as he ran and worked out with the players Mould felt himself drawn back into the rugby club environment and signed up to play for Randwick in the unofficial fifth-grade competition. For two years until he finally retired from the game, Mould embraced everything that rugby and Randwick had to offer. Like many before and since, he was smitten by the club's playing style, which relied on the backline standing flat in attack, quick ball movement through the hands, backing up and daring counter-attack from anywhere on the field. Randwick's commitment to running rugby, which earned the club the nickname 'The Galloping Greens', traces its origins to the legendary Waratahs side that toured the UK, France and Canada in 1927–28. Unable to call itself an Australian side because the Queensland Rugby Union had collapsed and so the game was run entirely out of New South Wales at the time, the Waratahs were led by Sydney University's Arthur Cooper 'Johnnie' Wallace, who, as a Rhodes Scholar, had won rugby Blues at Oxford from 1922 to 1925, and played nine Tests in the centres for Scotland.

It was Wallace who instilled in the Waratahs the philosophy of running rugby that would thrill crowds as they won thirty-one of thirty-seven games on tour, including Tests against Ireland, Wales and France. The Test against England, in which the Waratahs came back from an 18-5 deficit to lose 18-11, was described at the time as the greatest match ever seen at Twickenham. Randwick had two representatives in the Waratahs, halfback Wally Meagher and Wallace's centre partner Cyril

Towers, who would spread the running rugby gospel with almost religious zeal on their return.

'They actually first saw it being played in New Zealand,' says former Randwick and World Cup-winning Wallaby coach Bob Dwyer, who played back row in first-grade sides coached by Towers.

'Their captain, Johnnie Wallace, said, "This is the way to play the game," and they latched onto it. They all brought it back to their clubs, but it was only Randwick that fully embraced it. When Wally Meagher died, Cyril continued to coach that style. He wasn't the best explainer. One night at training he shouted at me, "I'll never coach another team that you're playing in." When I started coaching Randwick I kept pestering him to re-explain his theories until finally one night I told him, "Okay, okay, I get it."'

It wasn't just first-grade players that Towers tutored on what he believed was the only way to play the game. He would carry a jar of old coins in his pocket and line them up on the clubhouse bar to demonstrate backline formations to anyone who showed an interest. One such person was Geoff Mould, who, when he introduced rugby to Matraville High, put everything Towers had taught him into practice.

It helped that amongst his small playing group he unearthed one of the greatest schoolboy talents to ever play the game.

Russell Fairfax, with blond hair falling halfway down his back and a spindly physique that suggested a decent tackle would break him in half, looked like he would be more at home on a surfboard than a rugby pitch, but appearances were deceiving. Talked into joining Mould's first Matraville side, Fairfax was a sensation. Playing at fullback, but popping up wherever the ball was, Fairfax embraced the running rugby credo with spectacular results. In 1969 he was chosen in the first-ever Australian Schoolboys side that toured South

Africa. The following year, while still at school, he was playing first grade for Randwick when picked for the Sydney representative team to play against Scotland. If any Matraville parents still had doubts that Mould was on the right track, they had only to look at Fairfax.

When Eddie and the Larpa boys arrived at Matraville High in 1972, Fairfax had moved on to bigger things, including eight Tests for the Wallabies before attracting cult-star status with the Eastern Suburbs rugby league side, but his influence remained. In four short years Matraville, in no small way through its association with the Fairfax name, was fast becoming a respected force in high-school rugby.

Schoolboy rugby in NSW is split into several groups, the major organizations being the privately funded Greater Public Schools (GPS), Combined Associated Schools (CAS), NSW Combined Catholic Colleges (NSWCCC) and government-funded Combined High Schools (CHS). Each organization runs its own competition, the most prestigious being that of GPS, but there was one tournament open to all schools in the state: the Waratah Shield. For the most part the elite GPS schools chose not to enter the knock-out tournament, but it still attracted around a hundred teams each year and was regarded as one of the ultimate school sporting competitions in the country.

As Eddie and his friends began their high-school education at Matraville, there was no question about who were the biggest men on campus. The whole school would turn out to cheer on the 1st XV each Wednesday afternoon as they knocked over one opponent after another on their way to the Waratah Shield final and, ultimately, lifting the shield for the first time.

'They were great players,' says Mark Ella, who would go on to captain the Wallabies in ten of his twenty-five Tests and score a try against each of the four Home Nations on the 1984 'Grand Slam' Tour.

'It was inspiring to watch them. They would run onto the field immaculately dressed in the school's colours, and the crowd would go wild every time they scored a try. It made a big impression on us, and the only thing we wanted to do was play in the firsts and win the Waratah Shield.'

Before that could happen they had to work their way up through the age divisions. It didn't take long for the newcomers to make their mark. When Matraville High mathematics teacher Allan Glenn looked at the motley collection of boys who showed up for the first practice of his Under-13 team, he wondered what he was getting into. When he handed them the ball and told them to throw it around, he couldn't believe what he was seeing. At first glance they seemed an eclectic group; a mish-mash of different ethnic and cultural backgrounds, shapes and sizes, but on a football field they meshed together like few school teams before or since.

The backline was made up entirely of Aboriginal players, apart from red-headed winger Greg Stores – earning it the nickname 'the blackline with the red tip'. Outside halfback Darryl Lester were four future Wallabies in the three Ellas and silky-skilled centre Lloyd Walker. The only forward with any size was second-rower Warwick Melrose, who, like many of the team, would become a regular first-grader at Randwick. Eddie Jones was the smallest, but punched well above his weight.

'He was small, but it didn't faze him,' says Glen Ella. 'We scored a lot of tries, but you can't do that if you don't have possession. It was amazing how many times Eddie would go into a maul and come out with the ball.'

At a time when a try was worth four points they would regularly put fifty, sixty or more points on the opposition. Allan Glenn's half-time speeches often consisted of little more than 'Do you think you can double it?', and usually they would.

Glen Ella says what they did in organized matches was simply an extension of what they had been doing in games of touch footy for years. The only difference was they now always had a football to play with instead of a can.

'It was just basic catch and pass, use the open field. We were a small team so when we got the ball we made the most of it. The forwards would fill in like backs.'

In 1974 the NSW Rugby Union started an Under-15 version of the Waratah Shield, the Buchan Shield, named after long-time junior administrator and referee Arthur Buchan. Early in the season, Buchan was at one of Matraville's matches. When Allan Glenn pointed him out to his players, Glen Ella marched up to him and said, 'Hey Mister, we're going to win your shield.' He was right. Matraville beat St Ives High 33-11 in the final.

The shield win, played at the Sydney Cricket Ground as curtain-raiser to an Australia–England school international won 28-9 by England, did wonders for the boys' confidence and esteem. The true personality of the once quiet, shy Eddie Jones emerged.

'He was a ratbag,' says Mark Ella. 'That's the funny thing. Everyone thinks that Eddie is so serious now, but at school level he was just as crazy as everyone else. He was probably more academically attuned than the rest of us but he was out there. There's this image of him now being something of an outsider, a loner, but he was just part of the gang back then.

'No one treated him any different from anyone else, and I can't recall him copping any racial taunts when we played footy for our school. We had five Aborigines in the backline, a half-Japanese hooker and a redhead on the wing. If anyone had anything to say it was levelled at all of us, and anything Eddie copped he could give back with interest.

'He was fairly competitive at rugby and cricket, but the biggest thing about him was his quick tongue. He'll never die wondering. He and [former Matraville High, Randwick, Brumbies and Wallabies five-eighth] David Knox were the best sledgers I ever played with.'

But it wasn't fear of being 'out-sledged' by Eddie that stopped opponents from making racist comments about him or any of his team-mates, according to Gary Ella.

'We were winning just about everything during that period, and the opposition didn't want to stir us up.'

It is a viewpoint that Eddie subscribes to, and one that has stayed with him.

'I copped a little bit of racist stuff through my career. There was a game when I was playing for NSW against Queensland, and their prop called me a Chinese so-and-so. I told him, "Mate, you're too stupid to know the difference between Chinese and Japanese." Back then in Australia you were either white or Aboriginal. There weren't any Asians. When you're young you want to be liked and you have to be good at something. The only thing I could be good at was sport, and the racial thing wasn't too bad because I came through with the Ellas. They were just unbelievable sportsmen, so we won everything, and because you are winning, you tend to get less people mouthing off. If you are winning, there's not much that people can say, is there?'

Winning became a habit for the Matraville High teams in which Eddie played. Allan Glenn believes their for-and-against in the years he coached them would have been in the vicinity of 1000 points for, fifty against. When they graduated to the 1st XV and the coaching of Geoff Mould, the success continued. It could be argued that the natural talents of players such as the Ellas and Lloyd Walker meant they didn't require any tutoring, but Mould refined and polished the skills they'd been born with. To do so he called on the experience of the man who knew more about Randwick-style running rugby than anyone: Cyril Towers.

Aged in his early seventies, Towers would walk several kilometres from his home in South Coogee each week to help with the team's preparation. It was the start of a coaching education that would have a lasting effect on Eddie as he moved through the ranks at Randwick.

'I remember Cyril coming up and helping coach my high-school team. The Ella brothers were in that side, so he had a huge part in the way we played. Then when we went to Randwick it was a natural progression.

'Cyril coached Bob Dwyer. Bob coached me and Ewen McKenzie and Michael Cheika, and we all coached the Wallabies. Ewen moved away from the Randwick style a bit, but Michael and I have tried to stick with that flat-ball game. It's the way we were brought up to play.'

Towers, who died in 1985 aged seventy-nine, called that Matraville High side the best schoolboy team he had ever seen. It won the Waratah Shield in 1976 and 1977, but it was an unofficial pre-season match that cemented its reputation in the minds of those who really know Sydney rugby. In the lead-up to the 1976 season Mould extended an invitation to play a trial match to the mighty St Joseph's College.

At that time the GPS premiership had been contested on fifty occasions. 'Joeys' had won thirty of them and would add title number thirty-one in that season. The school has produced more Wallabies than any other, and it is compulsory for all students to attend all matches in full uniform, creating an intimidating wall of sound at their Hunters Hill oval. Few casual observers would have given the Matraville boys a ghost of a chance against the thoroughbreds of schoolboy rugby. The Joeys side that day included future Wallabies lock Steve Williams and hooker Bruce Malouf, who would keep Eddie in reserve grade when he arrived at Randwick. The Joey's players and supporters arrived in a fleet of eight buses. Eddie and his team-mates ran onto the field wearing an odd assortment of different-coloured shorts and socks. In the crowd, getting his first look at the players he would later coach, was Bob Dwyer.

'When I watched the two teams come out, it looked like a scene out of an American movie. We were seeing the kids from the wrong side of the tracks trying their hand against the superstars. One team ran out beautifully attired, fit and strong and healthy. Then Matraville emerged, half of them looking like members of the Jackson Five, with skinny legs and socks around their ankles.

'While Joeys played strong, quick rugby full of initiative and aggression, the little Matraville guys would just tackle and tackle, until their opponents coughed up possession. Their approach was, bang, bang, zing, zing, twenty passes, tackle, contest, keep the ball going, try. They won by twenty points, back in the era when a try was only worth four.'

In actual fact the final score was 15-9 to Matraville, but in terms of sending shockwaves through the stodgy schools rugby community, it seemed far greater.

The following year Matraville won a second consecutive Waratah Shield in an unbeaten twenty-four-match season that saw eleven of its players selected for Combined High Schools and nine, including Eddie, chosen for the two NSW teams to contest the Australian Schools Championship. With the championship doubling as trials for the 1977–78 Australian Schoolboys tour of Japan, The Netherlands, Britain and Ireland, there was plenty on the line. Gary Ella was selected for NSW 1st XV, with Eddie and the twins in the seconds. Such was the strength of the Matraville connection that both NSW sides made the final, with Eddie's team winning 6-3.

A few days later the names of the twenty-nine players who would take part in one of Australia's most celebrated sporting tours were read out by coach Geoff Mould. Eddie Jones was not amongst them. While five Matraville High boys made the side – the Ellas, Darryl Lester and Warwick Melrose – the selectors went with NSW first's Tony Ryan and Queenslander Merrick Illett as the two hookers.

'Eddie was unfortunate not to make that tour,' says Gary Ella. 'He was in the side that won the Australian championship and usually that would count for a lot. It must have been close.'

Close or not, missing the chance to tour the world with his three closest mates was a bitter blow for Eddie, and it would not be the last. A stunning selection snub that would temporarily end his love of rugby – before setting him on the path to becoming the number one coach in the game – was waiting up the road at Randwick.

2

LITTLE GREEN MAN

Eddie Jones embarked on the 1989 season thinking it was going to be his year. He was number one hooker at both Randwick and NSW following the retirement of club-mate Bruce Malouf in 1983 and had played in five first-grade grand finals, winning three. His former Randwick coach and mentor Bob Dwyer was back in charge of the Wallabies and, with long-serving Test hooker Tom Lawton headed to South Africa to finish his career, it seemed a fait accompli that Eddie would finally get to wear the green and gold.

It was not to be, with Dwyer instead making an audacious selection that would stun the rugby community and shatter Eddie Jones.

For six years Eddie had been a vital part of a Randwick side that is recognized as the best ever seen in Sydney club rugby, and arguably the best Australia has produced. Between 1977 and 1992, the club made an unprecedented sixteen consecutive grand finals, winning all but four.

The 'Wicks' were beaten 17-9 by Parramatta in the 1977 decider, but with the three Ella brothers slotted straight into the grade ranks after the Australian Schoolboys tour the next year, they would win the next five.

'All the other Matraville boys went into Randwick Colts (Under-20s), and we wanted to play with our mates,' says Gary Ella. 'We got talked into playing in the grade trials very late in the piece.'

Dwyer, who had taken over as Randwick first-grade coach the previous season, needed all the persuasive skills honed as a successful real estate agent to sell the Ellas on the idea of playing in the senior competition. They were still in their teens and skinny as rakes. The thought of continuing to play with school friends Eddie, Darryl Lester, Warwick Melrose , Lloyd Walker and Greg Stores in the Colts was appealing, and there was always the fear of being broken in half by one of the old hard-heads of the Sydney grade ranks. But Dwyer was adamant. He had seen the Ellas in action for Matraville against Joeys and their feats with the Australian Schoolboys – who went through their nineteen-match tour undefeated, scoring 110 tries and conceding six – had made them household names. Dwyer figured, correctly as it turned out, that the grizzled forwards of opposition sides wouldn't hurt the Ellas because they wouldn't be able to lay a hand on them.

Visiting them at their home at La Perouse, along with Randwick stalwart and Wallaby back-rower Gary Pearse, he made them an offer they couldn't refuse: if they played in the grade trials and felt uncomfortable or overawed, they could go back and play Colts. They never looked back.

'In those trials they tore the opposition to shreds,' Dwyer recalled. 'They would ghost their way through gaps, back each other up, do run-arounds and cut-outs. They ran like emus. They didn't look like they were going fast, but no one could touch them.'

The three brothers were graded in reserves but didn't stay there long. Due to an injury, Gary made his top-grade debut at outside centre in the first round, scoring a try in the win over Eastern Suburbs. With Wallaby five-eighth Ken Wright away on representative duty the next week, Mark joined his younger brother in the match against Gordon. When Wright returned, the selectors moved him to inside centre and kept Mark at number ten. The three brothers finally played first grade together when Glen was a late call-up for a fourth-round grand final replay against premiers Parramatta. They won 36-10, Gary scoring three tries and Mark one. A week later, their names appeared together on the official team sheet for the first time against the undefeated Northern Suburbs at North Sydney Oval.

The previous week Norths had won a thriller over Manly and were co-leaders of the competition with Randwick. They had every right to fancy their chances, but the Ella-inspired Galloping Greens beat them 63-0 in a game televised nationally. Overnight the Ellas were in the cross-hairs of cashed-up rugby league clubs, hoping to entice them across from the amateur rugby code. The next day the back-page headline on the rugby league-centric Sydney *Daily Telegraph* boomed, '$100,000 for Ellas'.

Eddie and the rest of the former Matraville High players joined their illustrious schoolmates in grade after two years in Colts, but none would have the meteoric rise experienced by the Ellas. Eddie's apprenticeship through the lower grades was long and hard-earned. At around 162 cm (5 feet 3 inches) and 80 kg (12½ stone), his slight stature was more obvious in senior rugby than it had been at school and Colts level, but as Randwick club historian John Brewer put it, he was 'a tigerish forward who played well above his weight, supplementing good tight play by operating as a third flanker'.

Eddie played around fifty lower-grade games in Randwick's famous myrtle green before cementing a first-grade position, but soon earned the respect of senior club players and officials. In 1982, his second year in grade, he won the club's best and fairest award, and the first of two most improved player trophies. The following year, Eddie played in Randwick's reserve-grade grand final-winning side. In 1984, with representative hooker Bruce Malouf retiring after seventy-five top-grade games and four winning grand finals, he inherited the first-grade number two jersey that he would proudly wear on 147 occasions.

Bob Dwyer, who had coached the Wallabies with mixed results in 1982 and 1983, had returned to Randwick after losing the national job to Manly's Alan Jones. He would take the club to the next five grand finals, with Eddie playing a major role. He may not have been the stereotypical 'third prop' style hooker in vogue at the time – Alan Jones' Wallaby hooker, Queenslander Tom Lawton, was a hulking 186 cm (6 feet 1 inch) and 118 kg (18½ stone) – but he cleverly used his lack of size to his advantage. His energetic mobility and expertise at burrowing his way under and between the bigger forwards at the breakdown earned him the nickname 'Beaver' amongst his club-mates.

'He understood his gifts and his shortcomings,' said Dwyer. 'His running skills, agility and balance all negated his slight physical presence. He tackled cleanly and low. He stayed away from the direct impact and just cut the ball-carrier down. In possession he was like a whirling dervish, spinning out of hits and tackles, stepping right, left and keeping a very low body position. By and large, people couldn't get a proper shot at him.'

But Eddie could always get a 'proper shot' at anyone in his sights. While he might never make a Wallaby side, he was world-class as a sledger. When aimed at club-mates, Eddie's sharp tongue was seen as humorous banter.

'He used to do this thing where he would do a commentary when we were running at training,' recalls Glen Ella. 'You'd be playing touch to warm up or running team drills and you'd hear Eddie's voice in the background, chirping away like, "And out it goes along the backline, Ella to Ella to Ella . . . oh, this is Ella magic, folks . . ." It was pretty funny.'

If any Randwick player had a characteristic that Eddie could exploit for a laugh or a dig, he wouldn't hold back, regardless of their stature. Wallaby back-rower Simon Poidevin was regarded as a true warrior of the game. The flame-haired former country boy played fifty-nine Tests and 125 first-grade games for Randwick, earning an unmatched reputation for toughness and durability. He was superbly built and incredibly fit, and the only possible chink in his otherwise impeccable all-round game was the occasional handling error. That was enough for Eddie, who labelled the club's most respected forward 'Venus' – as in Venus de Milo, great body, no hands.

There was no offence taken with Eddie's off-field wise-cracking amongst his Randwick team-mates, but on the field it was a different matter. His use of insults and sarcasm was a tactic to upset his opponents and put them off their game.

And that meant any game, regardless of the stakes. Mark Ella recalls Eddie imbuing social indoor cricket fixtures with the importance of Test matches.

'At one point I had to walk away, saying, "You've got to stop sledging people. We're supposed to be mucking around."'

Former Randwick team-mate Michael Nethery was another who on occasions was less than impressed with that side of Eddie's game.

'Eddie was a very good player. He had a sharp intellect and an even sharper tongue. In fact, he was an embarrassment at times to many of us who played with him. He learned this behaviour from his days playing club cricket with some rather unsporting types who had quite a reputation for sledging in Sydney grade cricket circles. There was one in particular who played grade cricket for the Randwick club. Eddie was heavily influenced by that culture.'

In 1988 Randwick played a mid-week game against the touring All Blacks. It was a match of historical significance for several reasons: the fact that it was the first and only time a New Zealand team had played an Australian club side, and because the Randwick pack contained three future Wallaby coaches in Eddie, prop Ewen McKenzie and number eight Michael Cheika. For Simon Poidevin the game was memorable for something else: the way Eddie Jones stood up to the All Blacks' legendary number two Sean Fitzpatrick.

'There was Eddie, this little half-Japanese hooker, giving it to Sean Fitzpatrick. Sledge, sledge, sledge throughout the whole game. He would give an absolutely executing one-liner.'

On most occasions any angst caused by Eddie's on-field verbal sprays was forgotten once the full-time whistle sounded, although it would be fair to say he was not popular amongst players from other clubs, who labelled him a 'pest'.

'Anything you've ever heard about him sledging and carrying on is true,' says former Manly hooker Rod Crerar, who had many on-field tussles with Eddie. 'From kick-off to full-time he never stopped. He was a good player, but the thing anyone who ever played against him will always remember him for is his mouth. He was always whingeing, always complaining about what we were doing, complaining about the referee's calls. On and on and on. It was quite funny really.

'It was part of the game in those days. Blokes used to have a bit to say, and Eddie was one of the best, but I never worried about anything he said. As far as I was concerned, it was always forgotten at full-time.'

But on one notable occasion the barb was not forgotten over a beer. Nor the night after the game. Not ever. As Mark Ella put it, 'Eddie has an extremely witty, at times vicious sense of humour. His tongue could be lethal.' One day, he finally went too far. He sledged the wrong player.

In 1983 a whirlwind had blown across the Sydney rugby scene, leaving in its path a scene of destruction: upturned sacred cows, strewn tweed jackets with leather elbow patches muddied and torn and septuagenarian club administrators grumbling into their scotch and sodas. Its name was Alan Belford Jones.

Originally from Queensland, Oxford graduate Jones was a former high-school teacher who had never coached higher than GPS 1st XV level. Active in conservative politics, in 1978 he left teaching and worked for a time as a speechwriter for Australian Prime Minister Malcolm Fraser before accepting a job as executive director of the NSW Employers Federation. Like his namesake Eddie Jones, Alan was intelligent, quick-witted and sharp-tongued. A perfectionist workaholic and brilliant orator who survived on only a few hours' sleep per night, in 1978 Jones' political aspirations had brought him into the orbit of Liberal Party heavyweight Ross Turnbull, a former Wallaby back-rower who was chairman of the NSW Rugby Union. Through Turnbull's patronage Jones became manager of the 1982 NSW side that toured New Zealand. And not just any manager. As one journalist wrote, 'The force of Jones' personality marked him as more than someone who counted the players on and off the bus. Confronting groundkeepers, arguing with hoteliers, Alan was unusual.'

It was on the NSW tour of New Zealand he was convinced by Manly players Ross Reynolds, Steve Williams and Bill Calcraft to make himself available to coach their club.

'I certainly didn't crave the job,' he says. 'I had plenty on my plate, but I relented and I was appointed.'

A strong and well-supported club in the Sydney competition, Manly was also an under-achiever, having won just four Sydney premierships in its seventy-seven-year existence, and none for thirty-three years.

Newly appointed as club coach, Alan Jones left nothing to chance. He prepared for weekly matches with an intensity and attention to detail unprecedented in the Sydney club competition. Each game was a step up the ladder to the ultimate goal: winning the grand final or, to be more precise, beating Randwick in the grand final. Even though Randwick's recent dominance had revolved around the skills of three Aboriginal brothers from La Perouse – the ultimate example of the kind of downtrodden suburb Jones would famously label 'Struggle Street' in his later role as an influential talk-back radio host – he still saw the Galloping Greens as representative of all that he felt was wrong with Sydney rugby: cronyism, elitism and favouritism at the representative selection table.

'I was concerned then, as I am now, that the administration of the game was not representative of the components of the game,' he says. 'Randwick had the presidency of Australian Rugby, the coach of Australian Rugby, the captain of Australian Rugby, the staff at Australian Rugby. I didn't regard that as healthy then and I've written recently that I don't regard it as healthy now. I don't get into this hating or deep dislike stuff but I was concerned then, as I am now, with the administration of the game.'

Back-rower Tim Sheridan, a member of the Manly first-grade squad who would later become a well-known television journalist, says Jones' animosity towards Randwick was palpable.

'Alan definitely felt that Randwick ran rugby in Australia. If you look at who held the offices of power at NSW and Australian Rugby at the time and the sway that Bob Dwyer held over the whole scene it was not such an outrageous claim. They were incredibly powerful on and off the field.'

Jones was not alone in his view. In the pre-Super Rugby days there were only two major provinces in Australian rugby: New South Wales and Queensland. Their annual interstate clashes were fiercely contested, no-holds-barred battles for national supremacy and Wallaby selection. From the mid-1970s the once-underdog Queenslanders had dominated NSW and turned their home ground Ballymore into a fortress. In May 1976 Queensland beat NSW 42-4. Three years later, they equalled that winning margin with a 48-10 thrashing and in 1980 they downed the touring All Blacks 9-3 to earn the title of best provincial side in the world.

In 1982, after a disappointing tour of Britain in which the Wallabies won just the one Test against Ireland, national coach Bob Templeton – a Queenslander – was replaced by Bob Dwyer for the upcoming home series against Scotland. Dwyer's tenure in the job could not have got off to a worse start. Untested as a representative coach, he stuck to what he knew and planned to initiate the Wallabies in the art of Randwick-style running rugby. Unfortunately he moved too fast, too soon. In the lead-up to the first Test in Brisbane, Queensland beat NSW 23-16 in Sydney and 41-7 at Ballymore, before downing Scotland 18-7, with five-eighth Paul McLean and dashing fullback Roger Gould prominent. Even so, when Dwyer named his Test team, McLean and Gould were missing, replaced by the Ella twins, Mark and Glen. There is no more parochial sports fan than a Queenslander, and the perceived favouritism by Dwyer for his Randwick pets over the local heroes was met with shock and anger amongst the rabid Queensland rugby public.

When the Wallabies ran onto Ballymore to face Scotland on 4 July 1982, the Queenslanders in the crowd did the unthinkable and booed two of their own country's players. The biggest cheer of the afternoon came when an obviously rattled Glen Ella spilled the first of many high balls put up to him by Scottish five-eighth John Rutherford. When Mark Ella hit his brother on the shoulder with a mistimed pass and a certain try was bombed, the disgraceful abuse intensified. The chant of 'We want Gould, we want Gould' rang out from kick-off to full-time. Scotland won the Test 12-7. McLean and Gould were recalled for the second Test, won 33-9 by Australia, and Bob Dwyer and Glen Ella would have nightmares of Ballymore for years to come.

Whether that debacle had something to do with Queenslander Alan Jones' animosity towards Randwick or whether he was simply employing the age-old tactic of creating an 'us against them' mentality amongst his players is unknown. What is certain is that Jones made no secret of his deep dislike of the Sydney rugby superpower, or his delight at dethroning them 12-10 in the 1983 grand final.

Respected rugby writer Greg Growden was one of the first into the winners' dressing room at the Sydney Sports Ground after Manly's historic win and witnessed a bizarre scene.

'They were all jumping up and down and shouting, but they weren't going, "You beauty, we've won the premiership." It was more, "You beauty, we beat those Randwick bastards." They needed someone to hate, and Alan gave it to them.'

Manly hooker Rod Crerar says Jones would 'do anything to upset Randwick'.

'They'd won the last five grand finals and they always used the same dressing room. We beat them in the semi-final so we went straight into the grand final while they had to beat Eastwood the next week to get there. Jonesy got on to the Rugby Union and told them as the first team into the grand final we had the right to choose which dressing room we wanted. Randwick arrived at the game thinking they'd have their usual dressing room, and we already had it. They weren't happy. We were in front before the game even started.'

Eddie would never have admitted it at the time, but it was the sort of move he would have been proud to implement himself. After all, this was the man who, when he coached Australia, would pace out the width of Murrayfield before a Test match against Scotland and complain to the referee that it was 5 metres short, try to shame England coach Clive Woodward into changing his tactics with talk of a 'responsibility to the game' and continually taunt Michael Cheika over his Coach of the Year award. In fact, if they had ever worked together, Eddie and Alan Jones would have made a formidable partnership. Instead, they remained rivals every bit as bitter as the Manly and Randwick teams that lined up in the 1983 grand final.

In the days following his side's momentous victory Jones was glowing in his praise of his team of 'young men, not just of great capacity, but also of great will', and dismissive of the opposition. While it is customary for the winning coach to acknowledge the efforts of the losing grand finalists, Jones was having none of it.

Writing in Manly's 1983 annual report, he began his summation of the season with, 'Manly's defeat of five-time premier Randwick, for the third time in as many weeks, put paid to those who sought to argue Manly's inadequacy and Randwick's invincibility. On that day at the Sports Ground, a super Manly side laid many myths to rest with a display of character, courage and skill.'

In actual fact, Manly hadn't beaten Randwick three times in as many weeks. The result of their match in the last premiership round of the competition was a draw, although Jones wrote that the 20-20 final score 'surely flattered Randwick'.

Minor details aside, and forgetting that a late field-goal attempt from Mark Ella that would have given Randwick its sixth consecutive premiership just brushed the outside of the upright, there was no denying that Manly's win was the result of an astonishing coaching display from Jones. Virtually unknown twelve months earlier, he was now seen and heard everywhere. No invitation to speak was turned down; no crowd was too small, no rugby clubhouse too far from the beaten track. If someone wanted to be educated by the wisdom of Alan Jones' eloquently delivered views on just about anything, he would be there. It was almost as if he was running for public office. In effect, he was. When Bob Dwyer was asked to reapply for the position of national coach after two years in the job, Alan Jones stood against him. With the support of his old Liberal Party friend Ross Turnbull, and despite just one season's first-grade coaching experience on his resumé, Jones won the biggest job in the game.

His first task was to take a team to Fiji for a short tour before the arrival of the 1983 All Blacks for a three-Test series. The side was chosen in the empty grandstand at Sydney's Concord Oval after the interstate match won 12-6 by Queensland, captained by Andrew Slack. NSW was led by Mark Ella, the incumbent Wallaby captain. Jones says he showed a list of his preferred players to co-selectors John Bain and Bob Templeton, who rubber-stamped them without discussion.

'I said, listen I've got to go. I was halfway down the steps, and they called out and said, "What about a captain?" Oh God, a captain. I said Mark Ella. They said, "Mark Ella? You're talking about new discipline in Australian rugby and you're talking about a bloke . . ." and I got this great lecture. I said, "Look I don't care who the captain is." Mark hadn't played for Sydney, he'd come back for the interstate game and he was overweight, but they'd made him captain, and so there were two captains. Mark was one and Andrew Slack was the other so I said, "If Mark's not the bloke, pick Andrew, it doesn't matter to me," so Andrew became the captain, and all hell broke loose.'

It is a version of history that Randwick supporters have great difficulty accepting. They will always believe that Ella was shafted by Jones, despite his continued protestations.

'It wasn't my decision. There was strong feeling amongst my other two colleagues about Mark's lack of discipline.'

Regardless of the reasons behind Ella's demotion, Jones and Slack proved a winning combination. The Wallabies had great initial success under Jones, achieving Australia's first 'Grand Slam' against England, Wales, Ireland and Scotland in 1984 and two years later lifting the Bledisloe Cup – the symbol of Trans-Tasman rugby supremacy – with a series win over the All Blacks in New Zealand, a feat not achieved since 1949.

The Wallabies went into the first Rugby World Cup in 1987 with high expectations, but by then the Alan Jones magic was starting to lose its gloss. Mark Ella was already out of the picture, having retired aged twenty-five after the 1984 tour. Roger Gould, injured in the opening match of the tournament, a 19-6 win over England, walked out of the team hotel one morning and never returned, labelling it 'the unhappiest time of my rugby career'. The team's training schedule had to be fitted around Jones' daily morning radio commitments, and some in the squad were becoming increasingly frustrated at their coach's perceived favouritism of certain players.

One of these was Brian Smith. A precociously talented twenty-year-old, Queenslander Smith was the latest in a long list of players for whom Jones prophesied greatness and then did everything in his power to make that happen. To the chosen ones, the support of

Jones was an invaluable boost to their careers both on and off the field. He was a sport and life coach whose patronage and loyalty were appreciated and reciprocated. Those outside the Jones inner circle saw his closeness to certain players as a means to diminish his reputation and influence.

Says Jones: 'As to playing favourites, it was the first question I was asked when I became coach: "Will you be favouring people?" because Dwyer had favoured Randwick players. I said I would. I'd be favouring the best. I believe Brian Smith was gifted and capable of playing in any position. His subsequent record speaks for itself.'

The coach's unflinching support for his latest protégé stunned followers of the game on the Wallabies 1987 tour of Argentina, when Smith was chosen at halfback in the first Test ahead of Grand Slam hero and future World Cup-winning captain Nick Farr-Jones, although Jones says there was more to it than a simple 'shock selection'.

'If memory serves me correctly, and I could stand corrected, I think that Nick was injured or not fully fit for that first Test in Argentina.'

After the Argentina tour, which would prove the nadir of Jones' Wallaby tenure, Smith moved from Brisbane to Sydney to further his career. It was there, in a club match against Randwick, that he found himself in Eddie Jones' sights. As Smith lined up a kick at goal Eddie did what he had done to dozens of opponents over the years: he gave him an unrelenting verbal spray. Zeroing in on Smith's closeness to Alan Jones, as the Randwick players stood behind the goal line, he launched a torrent of insults and graphic innuendo.

On it went, from the time Smith stepped up to take the kick, through placing the ball on the mound, pacing out his run-up and moving in, Eddie didn't let up. The kick taken, Eddie followed Smith back to the halfway line, never stopping the abuse for a moment. What

Eddie didn't realize was that, standing behind the fence, listening to every word, was Alan Jones.

Alan Jones has an expression for those who are loyal to him and to whom, in return, he is equally loyal. He calls them the Pick and Stick Club. Members of that select band know just what a valuable friend he can be. Whether it be Wallaby jerseys, entry into Oxford, help with property purchases or employment opportunities, Alan has the means and influence to make things happen. Likewise, those who have offended Jones in some way and earned his enmity – from prime ministers down – will attest that he can be a very powerful enemy. That day at a suburban rugby ground in Sydney, Eddie joined the second group. Some would say he captained it. Alan Jones would never forget what was said by the little man in green. Whether on the air, speaking to his supporters within the rugby hierarchy or in the private letters he would regularly send to influential friends, he wouldn't miss an opportunity to voice his lack of regard for Eddie's coaching ability and personal qualities.

'Eddie Jones, when it suited him, could be the master of filth, in particular filthy language,' Jones says. 'I learned that day the character of the man. And it's something with which I can't and won't identify.'

Eddie, typically, remains unrepentant.

'It's true. It didn't make me popular with Alan. Actually I find it funny that he still carries a grudge. I've spoken to him once in my life. It did happen, but that was club rugby in those days. I admit I was a good sledger. Probably a better sledger than I was a player.'

Eddie had never been a chance to play for Australia when Alan Jones was coach. Even though he had established himself as the top-choice NSW hooker, representing his state on thirteen occasions, former Manly coach Jones wouldn't consider adding another Randwick player to his squad, always preferring the two Queensland hookers Tom Lawton and Mark McBain. But in 1989, that was no longer an issue. Alan Jones was out, and Bob Dwyer was back in. After the Wallabies had lost that season's series to the British and Irish Lions 1-2 in heartbreaking fashion – winger David Campese throwing an ill-conceived pass to his fullback Greg Martin that was pounced on by Lions' wing Ieuan Evans for the clinching try – Dwyer went back to the drawing board.

With Tom Lawton heading overseas after the Lions loss and Dwyer making no secret of the fact that he saw the upcoming one-off Test against the All Blacks as an opportunity to inject some new blood into the side, Eddie was confident that his time had come. What Eddie didn't see – what no one saw – was the threat standing right behind him.

Phil Kearns had played 2nd XV at Sydney GPS school Newington and spent two years in Randwick Colts before moving up to grade. By 1989 he had made his way from thirds to reserve grade, occasionally playing firsts when twenty-nine-year-old Eddie was absent representing NSW. A solid but mobile hooker with a high work-rate, Kearns was obviously a player with huge potential. In 1988 Mark Ella had come out of retirement to play for Randwick at the same time that his brother Glen had moved across the harbour to play fly-half at Manly. The game in which the twins would first oppose each other was big news, and a large contingent of sports writers converged on Coogee Oval. As they sat on timber seating on the sideline watching the reserve-grade game, one reporter couldn't help but be impressed by the dominant performance of Kearns.

'Who's the Randwick number two?' he asked the colleague sitting next to him. Told it was Phil Kearns, he answered, half-joking, 'He'll play for Australia.' The comment brought a laugh, but no one was laughing twelve months later. Least of all Eddie Jones.

When Bob Dwyer sat down with Wallaby selectors Bob Templeton and John Bain to choose the team to play the All Blacks on 9 August 1989, he was looking further ahead than the Bledisloe Cup match at Eden Park. The British and Irish Lions had strong-armed the Wallabies pack a month earlier, and Dwyer realized he needed a better platform up front if Australia were to be serious contenders for the 1991 Rugby World Cup. The props he had in mind were Randwick's Ewen McKenzie and Australian Under-21 loose-head Tony Daly. McKenzie was injured and would have to wait until the next year's tour of France to make his Test debut, but the selectors were happy to give Daly a chance. There was also unanimous consent for inexperienced but prodigiously talented eighteen-year-old centre Tim Horan.

It was the next player on Dwyer's wish list that he felt would create the most discussion. In fact, he says he was unsure of how to raise his name without being either laughed at or accused of Randwick bias.

Instead, when the panel got to the hooking position, he recalls saying, with some trepidation, 'The bloke I feel has enormous potential is Phil Kearns.'

To which Bob Templeton replied, 'Who's that?'

'Phil Kearns,' repeated Dwyer, adding, 'he's currently playing second grade.'

John Bain, known for pushing through some rather unusual selections in his time, advised Dwyer, 'If you think he's the best, then why don't you propose him?'

'Okay . . . I propose Phil Kearns.'

Bain and Templeton both said, 'Done,' and a sixty-seven-Test career was launched.

The selection of Kearns from reserve grade caused headlines around the country and in New Zealand. For Eddie Jones, it caused despair. This wasn't just a missed opportunity; it was a very public humiliation. To be overlooked for national selection was one thing, to be overlooked for your club understudy – and by your former coach and mentor to boot – was another entirely.

In the words of Simon Poidevin, 'Eddie is an ultra-competitive guy. Being left out by Australia was pretty chastening for him.'

Which is one way to describe it. Eddie puts it more strongly.

'I was filthy for twelve months. I had my worst year in the game. I didn't want to play. I was just going through the motions, but in the end it taught me a lot. I learned that you are going to have disappointments and you have to move on.'

Eddie did eventually move on, but it didn't happen overnight. His heart might not have been in it, but he was still a respected member of the club. First-grade coach Jeff Sayle, a Randwick legend who played 379 games in the myrtle green before moving into coaching, stayed loyal to Eddie. When Australia's latest hooker Phil Kearns returned from Test duty, he went straight back into reserve grade. Eddie held his spot right through to the first-grade grand final, in which he won his fourth top-grade premiership with a 19-16 victory over Eastwood. Even so, the writing was on the wall. Kearns was part of the Wallaby front row that would soon establish itself as the best in the world, and Eddie was relegated to reserve grade midway through 1990. The blow was softened when he was named captain of the 1991 side and told, in his words, 'to pretty much run the show'.

It was the first time Eddie had captained a side since his under-age cricket days at La Perouse, but nothing had changed. He still worked incredibly hard and expected his players to match his commitment. In setting the highest standards and coming down hard on anyone who failed to meet them, he was emulating a role model he had adopted some twenty years previously: former Australian cricket captain Ian Chappell.

In 2004 journalist and author Greg Growden edited a book called *My Sporting Hero*. With a portion of the proceeds going to the Salvation Army, Growden approached an eclectic mix of athletes, politicians, celebrities and media personalities to write about a sporting hero who had influenced their life. The request brought forth a collection of memoirs ranging from the humorous to the poignant. The 'heroes' included well-known professional athletes and those who never rose above the level of schoolyard legend. There were rugby players and tennis stars; the Australian synchronized swimming team even got a mention. Marathon swimmer Susie Maroney wrote a beautiful memorial to her twin brother Sean, who was killed in Honolulu aged twenty-seven while training for the Hawaii Triathlon.

Eddie began his piece: 'I will never forget watching Ian Chappell captaining Australia in his first Test in the Ashes Series of 1970–71,' and then proceeded to describe Chappell in terms that could just as accurately describe Eddie himself, as a captain, coach and person.

'My memory of Ian Chappell that day, as I sat in the grandstand with my father, was an image of defiance, restlessness and unconventionality. He stood at first slip, shirt unbuttoned, gesticulating and encouraging the downbeat Australian team to follow his lead. He didn't look comfortable leading a team that seemed to be accepting defeat.

'It seemed to me that Ian Chappell from his first day was changing the culture within the team. Performance was everything, and he would strive to find any way possible to get his team to perform at their best. Convention would not stand in his way. From that day I watched and admired Ian Chappell as he transformed the Australian team. Over time they developed a certain hardness. They became tactically smart, and high quality performances began to flow consistently. They were criticised for being arrogant, but it was a belief in themselves that shone through.

'He turned the Australian team from one that was hopelessly beaten by England in 1970–71 into the best team in the world. Players played for him, and played for him day in and day out at nothing less than 100 per cent. The culture changed significantly in the team. It was a culture based on hard work and a positive attitude. Winning was everything but it was done through hard work and commitment to excellence.

'Ian Chappell certainly influenced my thinking on sport. I have been lucky enough to coach a number of teams. I want the teams that I coach to be tough and uncompromising. I want them to play positive rugby. I want our team to play entertaining rugby that sets standards of play. And I want to make sure that our team and team members are selfless in pursuit of excellence. These attributes are the attributes of Ian Chappell.

'Ian Chappell was a strong believer in being absolutely totally committed. He made you want to play. A pretty good hero.'

Eddie's last appearance in a Randwick jersey, after 210 grade games for the club, was captaining his team to a win in the 1991 reserve-grade grand final. At thirty-one years of age he would never wear the myrtle green again, but his playing days were not quite over. At that time Randwick had an exchange programme with English club Leicester Tigers. In recognition of the great service he had given over a decade Eddie was asked if he wanted to spend six months in Leicester, while Tigers' forward Matt Poole gained experience with Randwick. It was an opportunity he jumped at and soon found himself working in a furniture warehouse run by Poole's father, while training and playing with Leicester.

At the Tigers at that time was someone who would be a key player in the rollercoaster of his life: future England World Cup captain Martin Johnson.

Eddie played three first-team matches for Leicester, all wins over Bedford, Oxford University and Nuneaton. Front-row partner Wayne Richardson recalled: 'He was not your typical rough-and-tumble type of hooker. He played almost more as a back row. He was an excellent tackler – he had to be at his size – he was not the biggest guy that God put breath into. He enjoyed a beer. He would always stick about in the clubhouse and mix well with the lads. He was a nice bloke, quiet, unassuming, but gave the impression that he knew what he wanted from life. I guess that has been borne out by where he is now.'

Another team-mate was veteran forward Graham Rowntree, whom Eddie sacked as assistant coach when he took over as England coach.

Eddie's stint in the UK was never intended to advance his playing career – in fact he had planned to retire on his return to Sydney – but back home was talked into one last season as player-assistant coach by Glen Ella, who was coaching Southern Districts. The Tigers did, however, leave a lasting impression.

When he took over as England coach in 2016 Eddie told the story of his first game at Leicester. The ball had gone over the sideline in a good attacking position, and Eddie raced up and took a quick lineout throw in typical Randwick style to keep the game flowing and catch the opposition on the hop.

'One of the forwards came over, grabbed me on the jersey and said, "We don't do that here, son." That was the culture.'

A culture that one day Eddie, just like Ian Chappell, would have to change.

3

SCHOOL OF HARD KNOCKS

Reg St Leon never played a game of rugby in his life; it is doubtful he even watched one, but his influence on the making of Eddie Jones was as great as anyone who ever kicked a ball or packed a scrum. If Bob Dwyer, and by extension Cyril Towers, had introduced Eddie to the art of running rugby, it was Reg St Leon who taught him the power of belief.

Reg St Leon was a teacher and a visionary. Professor of Germanic Studies at Sydney University, he carried out an experimental programme at Paddington State School in the late 1970s which convinced him of the value of a type of teaching untried in the Australian education system. Under St Leon's system children as young as five would be taught to speak a second language. Half the day's lessons would be taught in English, half in another language. Some classes would be taught in two languages, simultaneously.

The thinking behind St Leon's revolutionary idea was two-pronged. He believed that the teaching of languages other than English in Australian schools started too late, and that when they were taught, they were taught the wrong way. Language, he felt, shouldn't be a separate subject; it should be integrated into the teaching of all subjects.

'The teaching of foreign languages started much too late – at the very worst time actually – when kids were just entering adolescence and they had all sorts of other things on their minds. Children who start learning languages very early, say at pre-school age, just absorb them, whereas later on it becomes sort of an academic chore, and that's counter-productive.

'I decided that the best way to teach the language was to use the language to teach the curriculum. I would go into classes that were being taught their normal daily lessons and I would ask the teachers to leave their work up on the blackboard, which of course was in English. I would then go through it with the children in German. Since they already knew what was there, they had no real trouble understanding it, but their German vocabulary just exploded. We realized that this is what the children expected us to do. You used a language to do things with. You talked and you did with the other language what you did with your own. They took to this quite automatically.'

Convinced that his system of bilingual teaching, combined with a greater emphasis on the study of music, would provide students with a better all-round education and expand their capacity for learning, in 1983 St Leon approached the NSW Department of Education with a proposal for starting his own school. In a short time the department and St Leon would find themselves on opposite sides of a courtroom, but their initial response was positive, and he pushed ahead with his plans. A public meeting was held, St Leon explained his concept to a room full of interested parents, and deposits of $250 each were taken for the enrolment of the first pupils of what would become International Grammar School.

It was the start of one of the most remarkable stories in the history of the Australian education system, and Eddie Jones was soon slap-bang in the middle of it.

When Eddie left Matraville High School at the end of 1977 he didn't, as the cruel joke went, walk straight across the road to Long Bay Jail.

He enrolled at Sydney University and savoured every moment of the university experience, dividing his time between campus life, study and playing rugby at Randwick. It was an idyllic, carefree time that he considers the most enjoyable of his life. He left with an honours degree in education majoring in physical education and geography. While he was committed to teaching and working with young people, Eddie's main priority remained rugby.

And then he answered an advertisement seeking teachers for the newly opened International Grammar School. Eddie went along to the interview hoping to sell himself to Reg St Leon. Instead, it was St Leon who did the selling – of his dream.

'It was nothing like a normal school. But it was a great place to work because it was something completely new. Reg was a fantastic sales person. He had a vision to create a kind of education that had never been done in Australia; where kids could not only do well academically but also do well academically through a second language. It was just so exciting.'

To the parents who sent their children to IGS, it was more than a school, it was a cause. To Eddie and the teachers who worked there it wasn't just a job. It was a calling.

If Eddie had started his teaching career at a traditional, conservative school, who knows? He might have ended up a traditional, conservative person. International Grammar School was anything but conventional. It strove to produce young adults who thought outside the box. It had a similar effect on Eddie Jones.

'The big thing for me is having vision. If you have a vision, something exciting, people generally will follow. Most people want to be part of something special. And there was – and still is – something very special at IGS. To create a school out of nothing, with no finances and no proper facilities . . . to be able to actually make a school out of that was amazing. Reg created that vision, and it's something I will remember the rest of my life.'

The school's first home was on a site close to Eddie's heart. St Leon entered into an agreement with the religious order Little Sisters of the Poor to move into their former convent at Randwick – just 2 kilometres from Coogee Oval – and buy the property after twelve months. With spacious grounds, lush grass, established trees, a tennis court and well-maintained buildings, it seemed almost too good to be true, recalled teacher Rita Morabito.

'The first day we arrived at Randwick, there were no desks, there were no pens, there were empty rooms – and a core group of us who were very excited at the prospect of creating a new type of school. There were forty students and a real buzz of excitement because it was something new in education. I was employed first as the Italian teacher. By second term the school had already grown enormously, and I had students from pre-school to year ten all in the one class, learning Italian. We were in beautiful grounds, and Reg lived there in the stone cottage. We would stay there till late and have gatherings, dinners, and parties. It was like a dream.'

A dream that would soon turn into an ongoing nightmare. Towards the end of the first year it became obvious that the school wouldn't have the funds to purchase the Randwick property. Rita Morabito recalls the feeling of devastation.

'Rita Fin [music teacher and vice principal] and I went to the Little Sisters of the Poor across the road and pushed through the clotheslines filled with black washing – the nuns' garments – found the front door and pleaded and cried to the nuns, begging them to let us stay. In that first year Reg had a capacity to make us feel calm and at ease, no matter what the reality of the situation. We truly believed that we would be safe and would return to Randwick the following year. It was not to be.'

Evicted from the former convent, during the holidays St Leon began a desperate search for an alternative site. What the students – and latest addition to staff twenty-five-year-old Eddie Jones – arrived to find on the first day of the 1985 school year was as far from the welcoming atmosphere of Randwick as imaginable. The only building St Leon could obtain was a disused former Elizabeth Arden cosmetics factory in the now-trendy, but then less than salubrious, inner-city suburb of Surry Hills.

'When we took over the building, it was at the stage where it should've been condemned,' St Leon recalled. 'I slept on a mattress on the floor for about two weeks, with rats running all over me. Once in the middle of the night I heard a noise at the back of the school, so I got up to see what it was. Apparently the Elizabeth Arden people had put in a back-to-base security system, which was operated by an electric current, and I had broken through it. The next thing I knew, the front doors opened and two blokes with pistols walked in. They asked, "Who are you?" and I said, "Well, I'm temporarily living here but I run the school." It took a lot of talking to convince them. Eventually they bought the story, put their pistols away and went back home.'

The building was cleaned, painted and reconfigured by teachers and parents in round-the-clock working bees, but it still fell well short of what was required. High-school classes were held in a stifling, windowless subterranean former car park called 'The Dungeon' by staff and students, and there were no outside areas. A tenet of St Leon's philosophy was that teachers should work across all grades, from pre-school to senior. Part of Eddie's duties was to take the school's youngest pupils to the nearby Ward Park for exercise and fresh air. A small oasis of open greenery amidst acres of tightly packed terrace houses and factories, the park was popular amongst local pet owners, earning it the nickname 'Dog Poo Park'. Children were warned to watch where they walked for fear of stepping on dog droppings or discarded hypodermic needles, and also not to talk to the many strange characters who lurked nearby.

Despite the sub-standard facilities (one former parent described the Surry Hills premises as 'appalling'), the school continued to grow and fulfil Reg St Leon's vision. There were those, however, who were determined that it should not be allowed to exist. The bureaucrats within the NSW Department of Education, who had at first supported St Leon's concept, were now totally opposed.

'If you start anything new, you've got problems,' said St Leon, 'but just how many problems we would have, I didn't know then. I suppose it's encapsulated in a phone call from someone I knew who warned me that the powers-that-be had said they were either going to break me or send me bankrupt.'

It was line-ball which would eventuate first. The financial problems that had beset the school at Randwick weren't eased by the move to Surry Hills. The department refused to grant the school certification, meaning it was not eligible for federal funding. For a period in 1985 teachers weren't paid, as St Leon struggled to meet the lease payments.

'Up until now I had been using my own money to keep our heads above water. I called a meeting of the parents one Saturday afternoon and I said, "I have to tell you this, and it's very hard for me to do, but because of the opposition we are striking with the NSW Department of Education, we're going to have to discontinue the school." I said that I was going to the bank on Monday but because I had no security to offer them, I was totally pessimistic about whether they would let us continue with our overdraft. I turned up at the bank, and there were three of our parents sitting there with deeds for their own houses to pledge to the bank. I still can't talk about that without having a lump in my throat. I mean, they were taking a terrible risk. They could have lost their own houses. I still find it unbelievable, but it's a story that should be told because it shows what lengths people are prepared to go to when they believe in something.'

With one of the parents committing to a second mortgage on his home as surety, the bank extended the loan, but the school was far from safe. The department continued to refuse certification. When the school's first students reached the age where they were required to sit their public leaving exams, they were refused permission by the department and threatened with prosecution if they continued attending IGS. In April 1986 the school initiated action against the department in the Equity Division in the NSW Supreme Court on the grounds of restraint of trade. The next month Justice David Yeldham ruled in favour of the school. The department immediately appealed the decision.

In September the students and teachers returned from holidays to find themselves locked out by the building's owners. With the rent months in arrears, the landlords had sent people to the school the previous morning to take possession. Reg had been sleeping there at the time and they had picked him up bodily in his chair, carried him outside and deposited him on the pavement before changing the locks. Only intervention by parents – and another second mortgage on a family home – saw the school reopen. The court cases continued, with six fought in twelve months, all going the school's way.

At the start of the 1986 school year, believing his relationship with the department had reached a point where it was harming the school's chances of certification and therefore financial security, Reg St Leon stepped down, and twenty-five-year-old Rita Fin was appointed principal, with Eddie as her deputy. They set themselves the task of fulfilling every possible requirement so that it would be impossible for the NSW Department of Education to deny them registration.

Many believe that Eddie's renowned round-the-clock work ethic is ingrained; a result of his Japanese heritage. They could be right, but it took the example of a young Sydney schoolteacher to ignite the flame that has since seen assistant coaches suffer burn-out around the globe.

'Rita Fin had this incredible work ethic,' Eddie said. 'The staff could be there from seven in the morning until eight or nine at night, but during that registration period there was so much to be done. We had to write the whole curriculum and make sure that everything was in place. It was a lot of hard work, but Rita and I would work fifteen to twenty hours a day trying to keep the school open, because it meant a lot to a lot of people.'

As well as battling the constant financial pressures, countless hours were spent by Eddie and Fin writing programmes, policies and procedures and putting together documentation and paperwork in a form that would be acceptable to the bureaucrats at the department.

'I can't recall how many inspections we had,' says Fin. 'But we had lots of them.'

If Eddie was in awe of Fin's work ethic, she was equally impressed with his.

'We worked our tails off for months,' she says. 'It was almost around the clock. I remember working on Christmas Day. I can't remember if Eddie was there with me, but you can rest assured that he would have been there the day before and the day after. He had an incredible work ethic. He was like a machine. If you gave him a job you never had to ask again. You knew it would be done, and done properly.'

There was another part of Eddie's personality that came in handy during that time as well, his ability to break the tension with a joke.

'Eddie has a very, very dry sense of humour. He would drop in these one-liners when you wouldn't expect it. Sometimes the jokes are not obvious, but then you realize what he is saying and he can be very funny. He was great with the kids that way. He would use his dry wit to bring them around. We were working with three-year-olds up to grade twelve. They loved him.

'He was never scared to speak his mind in staff meetings and was one of the most efficient guys I've ever worked with. Somehow, he managed a full-time teaching gig as well as all the rugby stuff.'

It was not just work and rugby that consumed Eddie. It was at International Grammar School that he met his wife Hiroko, who had left her job as a television researcher in Tokyo to backpack around the world. Landing in Sydney, she accepted a position teaching Japanese at IGS to earn some spending money before continuing on the next leg of her journey. Instead, just before she was planning to move on, Eddie asked her out, and plans changed. She and Eddie were married, and, in 1993, their daughter Chelsea was born.

At the end of 1986, with Rita Fin, Eddie and their staff finally meeting all the criteria that NSW Department of Education required, the school was granted registration, and therefore federal funding. Eddie continued as deputy principal until late 1991, when he and Hiroko spent six months in the UK while he played at Leicester. When they returned, Rita Fin announced she was reluctantly moving on to renew her passion for teaching music. Eddie was appointed acting principal.

The battle for registration over and the school's financial concerns eased, a sense of normalcy descended on International Grammar School. One of Eddie's responsibilities was to seek a more suitable site to accommodate the growing student numbers, but as there was no longer a daily struggle for the school's survival, he was able to follow a growing desire to coach rugby. In 1994, after hanging up the boots following a season playing and assisting Glen Ella at Southern Districts, Eddie applied for the job as coach of Randwick reserve grade.

His fellow coaches and players at the club were astonished by the hours and mental energy Eddie put into preparing his side each week, but after what he had been through at IGS for the previous nine years, nothing fazed him. It helped that he had some very talented players in his team, including future Wallaby outside backs Tim Kelaher, Peter Jorgensen and James Holbeck, and NSW scrum-half Adrian McDonald, who was flown to the UK as emergency back-up for injured Wallaby skipper Nick Farr-Jones late in the 1991 Rugby World Cup. Captain was front-rower Paul Cheika, brother of future Wallaby coach Michael, who also led Randwick's 1998 first-grade premiership-winning team. Not surprisingly, Eddie's side ran away with the competition, finishing the minor premiership clear leaders and going on to win the grand final.

At that time Eddie saw coaching as a hobby, a way to stay involved in the game that had been a part of his life for so long. His wife Hiroko, understanding the concept of amateur sport, but also knowing only too well the amount of time her husband was putting into the Randwick reserves, suggested that if he was planning to continue coaching perhaps he should be getting paid for it. 'It doesn't work that way,' he said, but over the next few months rugby was about to undergo the greatest revolution in its 175-year history. On April Fools' Day 1995, Rupert Murdoch's News Ltd, seeking product for its fledgling Australian Pay TV network, had launched an audacious raid on rugby league, signing up players and clubs in Australia, New Zealand and England for its breakaway Super League competition.

With the Australian Rugby League fighting back, financed by its own media billionaire in Kerry Packer, the 'Super League War' turned into a frantic cash-grab for the signatures of the hundreds of players needed to operate two competitions. Fearing that the warring parties would soon start eyeing off their elite players to fill the ranks, rugby union authorities pushed forward plans to turn professional. Following the 1995 Rugby World Cup in South Africa, a meeting of the International Rugby Board in Paris announced that 'the last bastion of amateurism' had fallen. Almost overnight, the world's best players became very wealthy young men. It would take several years before the real riches filtered down to coaches, but for Eddie, for the first time, there was a slight glimmer of hope. Who knows? He might be able to make a living out of coaching. All he needed was someone willing to pay him. The offer came from an unlikely direction that in retrospect seems obvious.

The previous season players from Tokyo's Tokai University Rugby Club had visited Randwick, and Eddie took them for a few training sessions. On their return to Japan the players were glowing in their praise of the half-Japanese coach who had been so knowledgeable and generous with his time. The university made Eddie an offer: join the staff as a lecturer in their School of Physical Education and coach the rugby team, first at a summer camp and then full-time. It meant resigning his position as acting principal at IGS and moving his wife and two-year-old daughter across the world to chase a dream, but it was also an opportunity that might never come his way again.

'The offer was only half my teaching salary, but Hiroko knew I wanted to coach, so she said, "Let's go."'

The eighteen months spent in Japan would prove to be a pivotal time. Not just professionally, but personally as well. To the Australians he grew up and played rugby with, Eddie might have looked Japanese but he never felt anything but dinky-di. His mother Nellie, mentally scarred from being ostracized by Americans during the war, and then by the Japanese when her family returned after the hostilities, was determined that her own children would not experience the same feelings of alienation in the country of their birth. They were raised as typical Aussies, with their mixed heritage rarely mentioned.

'I'm essentially Australian, mate,' Eddie says. 'There's not too many parts of me that are Japanese.'

Even so, from the moment he first stepped foot in Japan he couldn't help but feel an affinity with the country and its people.

'That was the first time I felt there was another part of me. It reinforced my work ethic. Everyone knows the way Japan rebuilt itself after the Second World War. It just further convinced me that to do something good you are going to have to work hard. The first six months was probably the hardest time of my life. Once a foreigner, always a foreigner over there. I speak Japanese, but not well. My wife won't let me speak it in the house because I'm so bad. I'm bilingual at rugby, but that's all.'

Like many before him, Jones had found Japan is a country apart. It isn't a copy of the US or anywhere else, more a parallel world to what he was accustomed to, but little by little he began to learn lessons which have stood him in good stead.

'One of the main things I learned there was patience. You have to line up and wait for everything. I also think Japan is a good example that you have to continually strive for improvement. You can't sit on your hands and hope things will get better. The Japanese are very good at taking other people's ideas and making them culturally specific. I suppose that is what coaching is all about, but most of all I have always found Japan a good place to think. Most of the best ideas I have ever had about footy have been over there. It is quiet there, and people can't contact me as easily, but even more than that it is a different environment. You see that things don't always have to be done a certain way, and that is very stimulating.'

Which is not to say that Jones was always accepting of the way things were done in Japan in a rugby sense.

'When I first came to Tokai University, the captain ran everything and the head coach had to follow everything the captain said.'

Not surprisingly, that soon changed. As players, assistant coaches and selectors would learn over the next twenty years or so, when Eddie Jones is head coach, there is only one person in charge, and that's him. Outside opinions are encouraged but rarely accepted, as Test great Tim Horan found when, along with former Randwick, Saracens and England backs coach Alan Gaffney, he was a selector for the Jones-coached Wallabies.

'I think I might have changed his mind once or twice, but it wasn't often. If ever you wanted to challenge Eddie about something you better have done your homework. I remember one time on the Europe tour at the end of 2005, Brendan Cannon was the number one hooker, but I thought we should play Jeremy Paul in the first game. There was a three-way telephone hook-up between me, Eddie and Alan Gaffney. I've said, "I think we should go with Jeremy Paul. He's hitting the line well, his lineout throwing is good, and his scrummaging is strong," and Alan has said, "Yeah I agree. Brendan has been playing well but Jeremy really deserves his chance." There's silence, and then Eddie says, "Okay, Brendan it is then."

'In saying that, in the two years I spent as selector we had a great rapport. His attention to detail was meticulous. Six months before the season started, he could tell me which games I would be going to and where he would be. Every Monday at 4 p.m. I would get all the tapes of the Super 12 games all cut up and ready to watch. First thing Tuesday morning he'd be on the phone asking what I thought.

'I found him a great bloke. He was terrific company over a beer but he just couldn't get away from rugby. I think he was like a doctor who loved his work. The type of bloke who could be operating at 1 a.m. and still be up doing his rounds at 5 a.m.'

That pedantic, single-minded, inexhaustible pursuit of the end-goal was nurtured in the battle to save International Grammar School and refined in Japan. Tokai was far from a dominant force in the twelve-team university competition, and Eddie's first instinct was to drive his new players with the intensity that had brought results in Australia.

They didn't know what hit them, Tokai fly-half and vice-captain Toshihiro Myano told British journalist Tom Cary from the *Telegraph* in 2017.

'The first thing he told us was: "This August will be the hardest August that you've ever had." He wasn't lying. All we did every day was train, train, train. There was no one else there. We all wanted to go home. We were only students. But Eddie-san's attitude was very much "no compromise".'

Not only did Eddie expect the Japanese players to train like his Randwick players, he wanted them to play the same way as well.

'His big idea was to ban kicking. As a stand-off I quite liked it, as it meant more time trying to run the ball. In some games, though, it might have been nice to relieve the pressure but Eddie-san never, never accepted it. Not even in our own 22-metre. The interesting thing, though, is that it was a blueprint for the way Japan later played. A Japan style. You could say he practised on us: pass the ball. No kicking. Don't give up possession. Keep moving the point of contact. Try to create a little chaos. Decoy runs.'

It was a style of play that would one day help pull off arguably the greatest upset in rugby history, but it wasn't quite as successful at Tokai, recalled Myano.

'We hardly won a game. I think the players were not up to the standard needed.'

As far as helping Eddie understand that coaching in different environments requires different approaches, though, it proved invaluable.

'You have to work out the fights you can win and the ones you can't. The Japanese hate conflict. Australians are quite direct. We like to say what we think and tell people what we think. I had to change that considerably in Japan, because it wasn't going to work.

'Conflict in any organization is important, because from conflict you get creativity. I had to find different ways to generate the right kind of conflict. The Japanese don't want to have any sort of conflict in front of people, so you can't do that. You get the person one-on-one, then you can have conflict.'

Many of the players who found themselves on the end of Eddie's sharp tongue during his long association with Japanese rugby would no doubt suggest that his determination to become less direct in his dealings is still a work in progress. His favourite Japanese phrase is *zenzen dame*, meaning 'absolutely useless' and his now infamous dressing-down of Japan captain Toshiaki Hirose at a media conference following a loss to the French Barbarians in 2012 is a cringe-inducing demonstration of public humiliation.

Regardless of the culture clashes, there is no question that from day one Eddie was good for Japanese rugby, and Japanese rugby was good for Eddie. He stayed with Tokai University for two seasons, and while they didn't manage championship success in that time, he helped them lay the foundations for reaching three successive All Japan University finals in 2015–17. It was also Tokai University that provided Eddie with his first experience of international rugby.

In 1996 Glen Ella had taken on the role of backs coach for the Japanese national team, known as the 'Brave Blossoms'. With Ella's easy-going, friendly nature and instinctive grasp of attacking rugby an instant hit with the players, he was asked if he could recommend an Australian forwards coach who might be interested in coming to Japan.

'The best forwards coach I know is already here,' he said, opening the door for Eddie to join him in the Japanese national set-up for two seasons.

Glen has always been the most laid-back and playful of the Ellas. On the Australian Schoolboys' tour of Britain in 1977, bored with sitting on the bench during a mid-week match, he sneaked onto the field at half-time, surreptitiously swapped jerseys with his twin brother Mark, and played the second half as fly-half without anyone noticing. It was the type of prank the cheeky, wise-cracking Eddie Jones would have been at the centre of in their younger days, but Glen found the laughs few and far between when reunited with his old mate in Japan. Rugby was no longer an interest for Eddie; it was an obsession.

The two Australians would often get away from the training field or meeting room for a coffee, but Eddie couldn't switch off, even for a few minutes. Just like Cyril Towers with his pennies on the bar at Randwick Rugby Club, Eddie would take the sugar sachets from the bowl on the table and move them around to demonstrate backline moves and defensive patterns.

'He was like, "This is the halfback, this is the five-eighth,"' Ella recalled. 'I'd have to tell him, "Mate, can you stop talking about rugby for one second?"'

Eddie readily admits that he gives an enormous amount of time and thought to his job, but makes no apologies.

'Yeah, I expect to work seventy to eighty hours a week but I meet taxi drivers who do that and they earn a lot less than a football coach. The head coach at the Philadelphia Eagles NFL team lives at the club Monday to Friday. What I do isn't abnormal or over the top. I actually think it is a fairly normal way to be.'

4

CLASS ACT

Eddie went from one rugby outpost to another when he moved from Japan to Canberra in the Australian Capital Territory in 1998. Not that rugby was unknown in the ACT. Its high-school system had produced such prodigious talents as dual internationals Michael O'Connor and Ricky Stuart, and future Rugby World Cup winners George Gregan and Stephen Larkham, but it was still seen very much as the poor cousin to the major powers of NSW and Queensland. Professionalism changed all that. With the advent of SANZAR – a company formed by the controlling bodies of South African, New Zealand and Australian Rugby to provide Pay TV product – a third Australian provincial team was required to fill the final spot in the new Super 12 competition.

Financial sense would suggest that the best location for such a team would be the major business centre of Melbourne, but with Victorians obsessed with their home-grown code of Australian Football, and, time being of the essence, the Australian Rugby Union instead opted for the stop-gap measure of an ACT-based franchise. The idea was that the side would make up the numbers for a year or two until the necessary groundwork could be laid in Melbourne, when it would then be closed down, or relocated to Victoria.

It was a reasonable plan, but the bean-counters at ARU headquarters in Sydney didn't take into account the ACT public's appetite for rugby, or the extraordinary talents and drive of the man chosen to usher in the new team.

Rod Macqueen was a Renaissance man. A no-nonsense forward for the Warringah club in Sydney and national title-winning surfboat rower, he was also a talented commercial artist and successful businessman whose innovative point-of-sale displays for companies such as Revlon and Taubmans Paints had been sold internationally. Meticulous in the planning and execution of his business concepts, Macqueen had long had the dream of implementing similar principles in coaching rugby teams. He had met with some success coaching the Warringah first-grade side and had taken NSW to an undefeated season in 1991, but in the days of amateurism and part-time footballers, there was only so far he could go in putting his ideas into practice. At the end of 1995 he had two offers: to continue coaching the NSW Waratahs in the new professional competition, or completely start afresh with the yet-to-be named ACT franchise.

After meeting with Waratahs management, Macqueen was convinced that the NSW Rugby Union was too set in its ways to embrace change. Having survived two near-fatal health scares over the previous decade, Macqueen was not inclined to sit around and wait for things to happen. He chose to go to ACT and build the new club to his own specifications, from the ground up.

Macqueen's fingerprints were all over Australian rugby's latest entity. He pushed for the name 'Brumbies', sketched the rough design that would become the club logo and nurtured an environment that would meld a group of disparate players, many of them rejects from NSW and Queensland, into the best-performing team in the country.

Macqueen was an innovator, always on the lookout for an edge over the opponents, no matter how minor or seemingly insignificant. To foster closeness amongst his players he arranged for them to live together in the one apartment block, nicknamed 'Melrose Place'. In order to ensure that not a moment was wasted in the half-time break, he put a stopwatch on every phase: the amount of time it took for the players to walk from the field, how long needed for a drink, medical checks and talks from the specialist coaches before Macqueen's final instructions. Each was recorded, streamlined, allocated and policed, to the point where the once-disorganized mishmash of players and coaches shouting over the top of each other and wandering off to various parts of the dressing room was replaced by an almost choreographed operation.

A graphic example of the kind of simple, yet inspired, thinking that Macqueen brought to his coaching came during his time with the Wallabies. Seeing the dual effect of the haka – pumping up the All Blacks and intimidating their opponents going into the kick-off – Macqueen instructed his players to wear their tracksuits during the pre-game war dance. They would then walk to the sideline and remove their warm-up outfits, the delay taking the emotion out of the moment. Whether 'defusing' the haka was a major factor or not can never be measured, but in the Macqueen era the Wallabies played the All Blacks seven times and lost only twice.

With the luxury of having his Brumbies players available on a full-time basis, Macqueen was able to successfully introduce the business principles that he had wanted to implement at the Waratahs. The most-used was SWOT analysis, with players and coaches spending hours detailing and discussing Strengths, Weaknesses, Opportunities and Threats of their opponents in preparation for upcoming matches. Macqueen was also a pioneer of the use of computer technology in rugby coaching, using his point-of-sale development experience to design an early version of a tablet to collect data on opponents' defensive patterns and attacking moves in different positions on the field. A long-held ambition of his was to program players to plan their moves four or five phases ahead, positioning themselves at each breakdown to execute the scoring play in the designated sequence. It was something he had tried to implement without success at the Waratahs, but through repetitive training on the field and at the whiteboard managed with the Brumbies.

It is all common practice today, but in 1996 it was breaking new ground in rugby union, although Macqueen did have the advantage of having ready access to the ideal blueprint for professional rugby – the Canberra Raiders rugby league club.

Like the Brumbies, the Raiders had been added to the NSW-dominated league competition almost as an afterthought in 1981, and by 1990, with back-to-back premierships, were the top club in the game. Unlike the set-in-their-ways NSW rugby officials who viewed the rugby league 'mungos' (a derogatory term, short for 'mongrels') as the enemy, Macqueen studied the professional set-up at the Raiders and learned from their experience – just like Eddie Jones was learning from Macqueen.

After his stint with the Japan national side ended, Eddie took over as head coach at Suntory Sungoliath, the rugby team fielded in corporate competition by the Suntory brewing conglomerate since 1980. Unlike the Tokai University side, Sungoliath wasn't made up of largely social players with more pressing matters than rugby on their minds. Even in the pre-professional days, the corporate rugby scene in Japan was far from amateur. Industrial giants such as Kobe Steel, Toyota, Sanyo, Toshiba and Ricoh saw their teams as an extension of their corporate identity. Success on the rugby pitch earned respect in the marketplace, and with no restrictions on the numbers of foreign players, companies were willing to pay well to recruit the best talent available. Former Wallaby winger Ian Williams, who played for Kobe Steel in 1994, estimated that during his time at the club there were 100 foreign players employed in the corporate league, earning twice as much as the local players. Of these only fifty performed any sort of duties for their employers other than training and playing rugby.

The professional players that Eddie coached at Suntory were far more receptive to his 'conflict produces creativity' style of coaching than the students at Tokai University, perhaps because several of them weren't Japanese or, more likely, because their weekly pay packets depended on success. Either way, the results came quickly. By the end of the 1997 season Suntory Sungoliath were premiers in the East Japan Company League, runner-up to Toshiba in the All Japan Company Championship, and finished third in the Japan Rugby Championship.

Eddie's time with the Japan national side and Suntory coincided with the formation of the Brumbies and, during off-season trips back to Australia, he was a regular at ACT training sessions. A teacher by profession, Eddie has always been a student in the art of coaching, voracious in his appetite for knowledge from any source. Former Queensland Reds coach Richard Graham, who worked with Eddie at Saracens in 2008–09, described him as 'one of the great sharers of information'.

'He's always hungry to learn. Whenever he meets anyone he's thinking, "What can I learn from you?", but at the same time he's very generous with his knowledge as well. I had been coaching in England for six years before Eddie arrived at Saracens. I learned more in one year with him than I had in the previous six. He's happy to let other coaches watch him work. He sees it as a two-way street.'

Over the years that street has taken Eddie to the doors of rugby league, Australian football, EPL, hockey and martial arts coaches.

A man who never switches off, he is always on the lookout for new ideas from other coaches, and other sports.

'We can always learn from each other. There's a constant interchange of ideas. If rugby does something good in sports science or in the way we train and people come and watch, they pass that back to their sport and make it better, and it works both ways. I've been to women's hockey, the Tour de France, Chelsea, Arsenal, Southampton, and from all of those teams I have found little things that I have brought back and customized. The thing is, as a coach, you can never think you know everything because you don't. I'm a student. I keep studying and learning about the game. There are always a lot of people out there who know more than you do. There's a lot of people who know more than me, so I go out there and seek the information and work out how I can make that information right for my team, and then you try to put it in your team and get better.'

In 1996–97 on his trips back from Japan, a key source of that information was Rod Macqueen and the Brumbies. The introduction had come through Eddie's former front-row partner at Randwick, Ewen McKenzie. Born and raised in Australian football-mad Melbourne, McKenzie had played under Macqueen at the Waratahs, and when he learned Macqueen was to become the inaugural ACT coach, he asked to join him, becoming one of the few big-name players in the first Brumbies squad.

Impressed with the way that Macqueen was introducing new ideas at the Brumbies, Eddie had contacted McKenzie to discuss the finer points. McKenzie had gone one better and asked Macqueen if his ex-team-mate could sit in on some training sessions. It was the start of a close relationship between the two coaches.

In taking on the job of creating the Brumbies Macqueen had committed to only two years, but the success of the team and the enjoyment it had given him encouraged him to agree to a third. Likewise, Eddie was considering a second year at Suntory when fate played a hand.

The first Wallaby coach of the professional era was Greg Smith from Sydney's Eastern Suburbs club. Despite an inability to beat the All Blacks, the Smith regime started strongly with the Wallabies going through their 1996 spring tour of Europe undefeated, beating Italy, Scotland, Ireland and Wales. There was also a 2-0 home series over Wales and a split series with the Springboks, but in 1997 things began to fall apart.

It was not so much the on-field performances of the team that concerned Australian Rugby officials, but Smith's increasingly erratic behaviour. Journalists would sit down at Smith media conferences unsure of what they would get. One day he would give an overly glowing endorsement of a player and, the very next, drop him from the side. His public assessment of players could be brutal, the most memorable being a stunning description of Wallaby fly-half David Knox as a 'non-tackler' and 'liability to any team'. He subsequently dropped, and then recalled, Knox for a Test against South Africa. Knox duly spearheaded Australia to a record 32-20 win, cheekily telling reporters, 'Luckily I had a couple of blokes to do my tackling for me.'

With the media and public harsh in their opinions of Smith, and the increasingly confused Wallabies crashing to an embarrassing 22-61 loss to the Springboks in the return match, Smith was shown the door. Four candidates, including Macqueen, were asked by Australian Rugby Union CEO John O'Neill to apply for the position. It was later discovered that Smith had been suffering from a brain tumour, which may have affected his thought processes. He died, aged fifty-two, on 3 September 2002, the day that O'Neill launched the ticket sales for the 2003 Rugby World Cup.

From the day he started at the Brumbies Macqueen had been considering who to endorse as his replacement. He worked with a number of assistant coaches who would have been logical candidates but his continued contact with Eddie convinced him that he was the man for the job. Eddie's visits to Brumbies training hadn't been one-offs; he had taken away what he had seen and kept in contact with Macqueen, asking for more information. Why had he done this? What was the benefit of that? Macqueen responded by inviting Eddie to attend the Brumbies' pre-season training camps and sending him videotapes of their matches during the Super 12 competition.

When Macqueen won the Wallaby position and told Brumbies officials he would not be returning for a third season in charge, the name he put forward as coach was Eddie Jones. In his autobiography *One Step Ahead* Macqueen wrote, 'I just felt more than anyone Jones understood the style of coaching and how the game of rugby was changing.'

The Brumbies team that Eddie inherited from Macqueen was a well-run, high-performing machine. In just its second year of existence it had gone down to Auckland in the Super 12 grand final after ending the previous season with a ten-try 69-30 drubbing of the touring Wales. Even so, Eddie was quick to put his own mark on the side. He wasn't a carbon copy of Rod Macqueen or any other coach, as his players were soon to find. Like Macqueen he was meticulous, businesslike and innovative, but that is where the similarities ended.

Macqueen once told a reporter, 'Rugby is not my life' – words that would never be spoken by Eddie – and was able to switch off when he wasn't in coach mode. He enjoyed the company of his players and would often have them and their wives and girlfriends to his home for barbecues and functions. He was a keen if not overly accomplished golfer and would join players for social rounds, joking that they won so much money from him he earned the nickname 'ATM'.

Eddie rarely mixes socially with his players. Asked about his relationships with players, he cites the example of New England Patriots NFL coach Bill Belichick and his star quarterback Tom Brady.

'It's all about business. They've got no personal relationship. They've been together umpteen seasons and they've never been out to dinner. They're not friendly at all, but they know what they've got to do. It's nice if people like you, but for us, our business is to win games of rugby.'

He stops short of calling himself a 'loner', but admits, 'I have a very small circle of friends that I feel comfortable with.' He also has a determination to keep his personal and professional lives separate, as an ARU colleague during his time as Wallaby coach recalled.

'If he wanted to watch a tape of a game during a day off he would come into the office at North Sydney and do it there. I think it was a Japanese thing: work was work and home was home, and the two shouldn't overlap.'

Eddie says the differentiation goes even further. Not only doesn't he take his work home, he doesn't even speak of it.

'I never talk to my wife about rugby. I don't have anything rugby-related in my house. If you walked in, you wouldn't know that I am involved in rugby. I don't keep anything. I give everything away. It means more to other people.'

Macqueen and Eddie were also very different personalities on the training paddock. Brumbies foundation player Stephen Larkham recalled that while Macqueen preferred a more English football manager-style role, supervising a team of specialist coaches, Eddie is hands-on in the extreme.

'Eddie is a great student of the game who likes to apply his own knowledge to what the team is doing, rather than delegate. It always seemed that he knew more than anyone else about the subject, so he would rather do it himself.

'Eddie likes to be in control of everything, whether it is the forwards' play or the backs' play. Even when he does delegate, he likes to know exactly what's going on. Rod took more interest in the forwards' play, having been a forward himself, but he was happy for the forwards' coach to run things at training, just as he was happy to let the backs train under the backs' coach. Rod stood back and kept an eye on everything but did not get overly involved. Eddie gets right into the nitty gritty. He watches the other coaches closely and quizzes them, "Why is he doing that? How come he's standing there?" Eddie has a thorough understanding of every position on the field and a detailed knowledge of the individuals who occupy these positions.'

On one occasion Eddie told Larkham, 'I know your game better than anyone else' – and Larkham had to agree.

'He probably knew it better than I knew it myself.'

And just as Eddie knew everything about his players, he expected them to know everything about each other as well.

At a Wallaby training session prior to the 2003 Rugby World Cup, league convert Wendell Sailor was bringing back a long kick-off when he stepped straight into the forwards who were running across field. Furious, Eddie screamed at them, 'What are you doing? Don't you know which foot he steps off? It's the left, always the left . . .'

There was another area in which Macqueen and Eddie differed, and that was in their concept of 'time and place' when it came to dealing with players and assistants. While Macqueen would never admonish a player in front of team-mates or onlookers, Eddie has no qualms about letting his feelings be known by all within earshot.

In *One Step Ahead* Macqueen told of the first training session attended by Brumbies newcomer Justin Harrison. An extroverted lock who would earn his fair share of headlines in coming years, Harrison stumbled, dropped the ball and fell over during a handling skills set. When it brought a laugh from his new team-mates, he kept doing it, exaggerating his clumsiness for maximum effect. Macqueen was not impressed.

'The more the players laughed, the more he played the fool, purposely tripping over and throwing the ball at their feet. I waited until the session was finished before I called him over. He had only been with the side an hour and he was about to be the shortest-lived Brumby ever. I suggested that if we had wanted a clown we would have paid for a clown and asked if he was really serious about playing football. To his credit he looked me in the eye and said, "It won't happen again." It didn't.'

In fact, it was Harrison who pulled off the match-winning lineout steal that clinched the match and series in the third Test against the Lions in 2001, Macqueen's final game as Wallaby coach.

It is fair to say that Eddie Jones would not have handled the situation the same way as Macqueen: he would never have waited for the session to end before blowing his top.

But the biggest difference the players noticed, according to Stephen Larkham, was the hours Eddie put into his work. Macqueen made a point of enjoying his down time. Eddie made a point of not having any.

'It was common knowledge that when he was with the Brumbies he would work a full day before going home for dinner at 7.30 p.m., then return to the office and work until 11 p.m., then be back in the office at six in the morning. This went on day after day, week after week.'

It didn't take long for the Brumbies to realize that things had changed when Eddie took over – just forty minutes to be precise. Eddie took the team to Japan for a pre-season trip in order for them to get to know each other before the start of the 1998 competition. At half-time in their first match he let them know his thoughts in no uncertain terms.

Recalled George Gregan, who had watched the match from the grandstand, 'Eddie really blew his top over the way we were playing and when he finally finished I watched to see how the boys reacted. They weren't happy.'

After the game Eddie was approached by team captain Brett Robinson, who, according to Gregan, told him, 'I can understand your frustrations, Eddie, but maybe they need more specific stuff at half-time.'

Gregan says Eddie took the advice on board, but it wouldn't be the last time that he and Brett Robinson had a difference of opinion.

The season started badly with a 32-7 loss to the Waratahs and didn't greatly improve. In Eddie's first year in charge, the Brumbies won just three matches and finished tenth, ahead of only the South African Bulls and Cats. There was speculation in the media that Eddie wouldn't see out a second season if things didn't improve. They did. In 1999 the Brumbies won five of their eleven matches and finished just one spot out of the play-offs. More importantly, fringe players were starting to respond to Eddie's confrontational style. They may not have enjoyed the way he spoke to them, but it brought results.

Hooker Adam Freier, who would play twenty-five Tests for the Wallabies, was nineteen years old when he signed a $6000 contract with the Brumbies in 1999 as back-up to Test hooker Jeremy Paul.

He would stay for just two seasons before going on to great success with the Waratahs and Melbourne Rebels, but counts the time spent with Eddie as the most influential on his career – and his life.

'He was tough on a lot of us. He'd call me into his office and sit me down and say, "Mate, I really don't think you want to be a professional rugby player, mate . . ." I'd tell him, "No, Eddie, I really want to, of course I do, I really do," and he'd say, "You obviously don't, mate. You don't even want to be here. Why should I even let you train? You're only in the way out there. You'll probably get in the way and hurt someone." I'd leave his office in a state of rage, ready to run through a brick wall. I'd be straight to the gym, lifting weights, throwing a thousand balls. I was like him, a little hooker from Randwick. He told me because I was small I had to be fitter and stronger than anyone else, and that's what I became. I never would have played for Australia if it wasn't for him. He taught me a lot about football but he made me the person I am today, which I think is more important. I owe him a lot.'

The players always knew when they were about to cop the full force of an Eddie Jones blast. One eyebrow would rise and he would focus his gaze on them like a laser beam. They came up with a term for it, 'stink-eye', but not everyone experienced it. Eddie was selective in the way he treated people. George Smith, for instance, the open-side flanker who Eddie considered the best player he ever coached, rarely heard anything but praise. Others, who Eddie believed needed a prod to reach their potential, would be driven mercilessly. One more than others: Troy Jaques.

Jaques had played for Australian Schoolboys and Australian Under-21s when he joined the Brumbies as a foundation player. He made his way into the top squad for the third-round match of the 1997 season, but when Eddie held his first training session of 1998, he couldn't believe what he was seeing.

'He had no idea of where to be or what to do.'

Eddie rode him day and night. Freier jokes, 'I still wake up hearing Eddie screaming his name across the training paddock, "Jaques, Jaques, what are you doing . . . ?"' George Gregan recalled Jaques finally reaching breaking point and shouting back, 'Mate, treat me like a man. Talk to me like a man.' The personal attention continued, Jaques put in the hard work, refined his game, and in 2000 played two Tests for the Wallabies. Eddie would later use Jaques as an example of hard work and commitment overcoming all else.

The 2000 season was a turning point for Eddie at the Brumbies. For the previous two seasons he had built on the foundations laid by Rod Macqueen and added his own innovations. One was to videotape training sessions to better analyse players' performance. Another was to prepare dossiers before upcoming games, not just on opposition players, but the referees.

Gregan recalled: 'Before each game he'd give us a two- or three-page dossier on the referee which described their strengths and weaknesses, how many penalties they'd give in a game and when and where they'd be most stringent.' He even assessed the physical fitness of referees, telling his players which refs would be tardy getting to the breakdown, allowing them to lie longer on tackled opponents and slow down play.

Coming into the new season, Eddie believed it was time to take the team to the next level. At the wedding of Brumbies Test back-rower Owen Finegan he told Gregan, 'Mate, we're going to change the way rugby is being played. There is a way our game is going to be played, and we're going to be the first ones to play it.'

The grand plan started badly with a 15-18 loss to the Auckland Blues, but a 51-10 win at home over the Sharks was the start of a five-match winning streak, including the Brumbies' first-ever win in South Africa,

29-15 over the Stormers in Cape Town. With Gregan passing the ball 150 times, the performance against the Stormers was the embodiment of Eddie's blueprint for the future of rugby: played with greater width and variety, speed and aggression at the breakdown and fast recycling of the ball to negate the spoiling tactics of sides that attempted to play the game in tight. With controlling body SANZAR keen to present an open, exciting spectacle to Pay TV subscribers, it was a style of play that referees were instructed to support.

On a high from the win, the players celebrated that night and again the next day, travelling out to the beach area of Camps Bay for lunch and a few beers. Most left in the early afternoon, but some stayed behind for more drinks before catching a cab back to the hotel late in the evening. In the early hours Eddie was advised by team manager Phil Thomson that the players had been detained at a police station after an incident with the cab driver.

When the news reached Australia it started a media storm, with reports the players had been on a drunken rampage, severely damaged the cab and that police reinforcements had been called to subdue them. The Brumbies' version was that they had become concerned that they were being overcharged for the ride and had insisted the driver take them to a police station. Once there they had tried to remove the fare meter – a small device plugged into the cigarette lighter – to provide evidence. No charges were laid, but Brumbies management found that three players had breached team protocol by drinking excessively two days in a row and issued fines of between $500 and $1500 and two-match suspended suspensions to Joe Roff, Rod Kafer and Peter Ryan.

The Australian Rugby Union felt that the punishment was too lenient and that players should have been sent home or at the very least suspended from upcoming matches. Relations between the Brumbies and the sport's ruling body became strained, with Australian Rugby CEO John O'Neil concerned about the club's attitude.

'I found their soft disciplinary approach almost as disturbing as the actual incident. The Brumbies were keen to keep the ARU at arm's length when these problems occurred. Their opinion was, "We'll look after this – it's got nothing to do with you blokes."'

The question over where the ARU's jurisdiction over the players began and where it ended was one that O'Neill and Eddie would disagree over at Wallaby level in years to come.

The off-field drama could have derailed the Brumbies' season almost before it started, but Eddie used it to their advantage, creating a siege mentality that brought the team closer together. When they arrived back in Australia to be confronted by reporters, there were tense scenes between team supporters, officials and the media. Former journalist Peter Jenkins, then of the *Australian* newspaper, says that a member of the Brumbies management team said, 'I'd love to put one on your chin.'

'The taxi affair was a massive indictment on the player-led culture of the Brumbies at the time. They ran the show. When a handful of players, including high-profile Wallabies, trashed a cab, ripped out the meter, and then had to pay damages for the vehicle's repair to avoid further police action during a tour to South Africa, there was only one disciplinary option for a coach and manager to take. Send the boorish brats home on the next plane out of Johannesburg. Eddie and Phil Thomson failed to do so. The players stayed on for the following game and flew back to Australia with the rest of the squad. They were later sanctioned, if you call suspended bans and low-level fines a genuine penalty. But it was too little too late. At a time when they should have been decisive, the Brumbies management wilted. The players and others within the Brumbies organization then turned on the media, supposedly for going too hard on them. It got to the point where George Smith, as a kid on debut in a Test against France later that year, refused to speak to me in the dressing room post-match because of the stance I'd taken against the Brumbies over the taxi debacle some months before. I didn't know it at the time, but on the same night as that infamous taxi incident in Cape Town, George Smith had been involved in a punch-up with a team-mate in the hotel car park. It was detailed in his biography. In the midst of all this and for years later at the Brumbies and Wallabies, Eddie was a players' man. Behind the scenes he loved to ignite the us-against-them mentality. The "them" were usually the ARU establishment or the media. He was not the first coach to employ such tactics, and won't be the last, but he certainly did it better than most. Still, I found Eddie an engaging character and good company. We discussed plenty of issues and players off the record over the years, and I'm not about to break those confidences. He was a driven coach, obsessed with detail, and was consumed by the game in a way I've rarely seen before or since. But on the Cape Town incident he should have taken out the big stick and didn't.'

The Brumbies went through the minor rounds of the competition losing only one more game, to arch-rivals the Waratahs, finishing top of the table and meeting the Canterbury Crusaders at Canberra's Bruce Stadium in the grand final. The New Zealanders won by a point, 20-19, but Eddie's prediction of ten months earlier was coming to fruition. At full-time Crusaders fly-half Andrew Mehrtens told Gregan, 'Well done for the way you've gone this year. You've changed the way the game is played.'

John O'Neill, watching from the grandstand, recalls that the manner of the loss would have lasting ramifications for Eddie and the way he handled his players in the future. O'Neill, who had two stints at the ARU as well as helping engineer the shake-up of Football

Federation Australia, culminating in the team qualifying for the 2006 FIFA World Cup under Guus Hiddink, is reserved in his opinion of Eddie's coaching prowess.

'As a general comment, Eddie was clearly a very good coach, but during his very successful periods he had very good cattle.

'When he took over at the Brumbies their seasons in 1998 and 1999 were not that good, but in 2000 and 2001 he had a superb group of very special players. I'm not dismissing Eddie but in my long career in two sports I have found that there is always a coincidence that great coaches always have great players.

'At the Brumbies Eddie had George Gregan, Stephen Larkham, Joe Roff, George Smith, Rod Kafer, David Giffen, Justin Harrison . . . he virtually had a team of Wallabies.

'The reason they lost in 2000 was that the players took matters into their own hands. They wanted to win the Brumbies way instead of playing grand final rugby. They tried to run it from everywhere. The Crusaders wore them down, and they lost. They were doing what the players wanted, and I think that taught Eddie a lesson. He was always seen as a players' coach, but they were badly scarred over that loss. I remember walking into the dressing room after the game, and there was a lot of emotion. They were the better side but they weren't smart. In 2001 they got it technically right. They played grand final rugby and won.'

In 2001 the Brumbies lost three times, but went one better in the game that really mattered, the grand final against the Sharks. Eddie's analysis had informed the players that the Sharks were the fastest-starting team in the competition. If the Brumbies could hold them in the first ten minutes of each half, they should have their measure. With the score locked 6-6 at half-time, the Brumbies came out full of confidence and ran away with the match 36-6.

It was a storybook ending in what would prove to be Eddie's last Super 12 game in charge of the Brumbies. The players and their supporters celebrated long and hard, but Eddie still had two appointments to fulfil before the season was over: against the British and Irish Lions.

The Graham Henry-coached Lions squad that toured Australia in 2001 included the core of the England side that would return to vie for the Rugby World Cup two years later, including captain Martin Johnson, scrum-half Matt Dawson, winger Jason Robinson and fly-half Jonny Wilkinson. They would come to know Eddie Jones very well over that period, just as he would learn everything there was to know about them, but before 19 June 2001 he was very much an unknown quantity.

Early in the season, as the best-performing Australian Super Rugby coach, Eddie had been appointed coach of the Australia A team to take on the Lions in their fourth game on tour. The Lions were also scheduled to play the Brumbies between the first and second Tests. To Graham Henry and the Lions' management they might have just been two more tour matches. To Eddie Jones, they were a priceless opportunity to show the Australian Rugby Union his credentials against the most famous touring side in the game.

Leading into the Australia A game, the Lions had won their first three matches in style, beating sacrificial lambs Western Australia 116-10, and Queensland President's XV 83-6. Queensland Reds had been expected to put up more of a fight but they too were pushed aside, 42-8. With Australia A thrown together just before the match and many of the side never having played together, there was no reason to think they would fare any better. No reason except Eddie Jones.

Australia A fullback Richard Graham says there was no sign of the obsessed Brumbies coach with his dossiers and sideline temper tantrums when Eddie led the team for its first training session.

'He only had us for a week so he had no time to go into it too deeply. It was all about "What do we need to do to win this game, and what don't we need?" He brought us together as a group, built relationships and gave us confidence that we could actually beat the Lions. We were a pretty mixed group in terms of age and experience. There were some like me who were old enough to remember the Lions tour in 1989. I'd been in my last year of school back then so I'd watched every Test and I understood the enormity of a Lions tour and what a big deal it was to play against them. There were others who were younger who didn't understand that, so Eddie encouraged us to share that feeling. I worked on Eddie's coaching staff at Saracens, so I saw the ridiculous hours and heard the sprays, all that stuff, but during that week there was none of that. It was the first time I had met him, and he was intense but relaxed at the same time. It was all about him having a really clear plan and delivering it to the group, and he did it perfectly.

'There were some aspirational players in that group who saw playing the Lions as a stepping stone, and others who saw it as a highlight of their career. Eddie brought us all together. It was a great week.'

With a great ending for the Australians. Graham Henry chose a strong side, with Welsh fly-half Neil Jenkins the only non-Englishman in a backline containing Matt Perry, Ben Cohen, Will Greenwood, Mike Catt, Jason Robinson and Austin Healey. Future England captain Lawrence Dallaglio led the pack.

Any thoughts the visitors might have had that the trip to Gosford, just over an hour's drive north of Sydney, would be a diverting visit to the coast were soon dispelled. Mike Catt limped off with a calf injury that put the rest of his tour in jeopardy, young Australian lock Tom Bowman dominated possession at the lineout, and the Lions went to the break 6-15 down. In the second half, after Australia A winger Scott

Staniforth scored the first try of the match, Henry hooked Jenkins, moved Healey to fly-half and brought Matt Dawson on at scrum-half. The changes energized the Lions. League convert Jason Robinson scored a typically electrifying try that Dawson converted, but it was too little too late. Eddie's side held on to record an historic 28-25 win.

Two weeks later the Lions would have a second encounter with Eddie Jones when they took on a Brumbies outfit missing its nine Test players. After taking a 19-3 lead midway through the second half and heading the Lions 28-23 as the game entered injury time, the Brumbies only had to hold on to give Eddie a 2-0 record over the tourists, but in the tenth minute of extra-time Austin Healey finished off twelve phases of play to score under the posts. Dawson kicked the conversion, and the Lions sneaked home 30-28.

The two Englishmen may have combined to spoil what would have been a perfect on-field end to Eddie's year, but off-field he was still very much a winner in the boardroom. Four days after the ACT–Lions match, in a move than had shocked Australian rugby, Rod Macqueen announced he planned to step down after the Test series. To say John O'Neill was surprised is an understatement.

'I had gone through a long negotiation with Rod, who agreed to stay until the end of 2001, then lo and behold he had a change of heart. We had just won the second Test in Melbourne, and in the dressing room after the game Rod told me, "I can't go on."

'Eddie had just coached the Brumbies to win the Super 12 and he'd coached Australia A to beat the Lions. We were caught on the hop with Rod's sudden change of heart, so Eddie was really seen as the only candidate.

'Brett Robinson had been appointed as the ARU's Head of High Performance. He'd been captain under Eddie of the side that was beaten in the 2000 Super 12 final. Brett was a big fan of Eddie but knew of his idiosyncrasies. He told us Eddie would be a good coach, but it wouldn't be easy dealing with him. He was right.'

Eddie was once again anointed Rod Macqueen's successor, this time earning him the Wallaby blazer he had been denied as a player. The rugby world was about to hear a lot more from Eddie Jones, and so was the media.

5

FIGHTING HARADA

Just days after the end of the 2001 season *Sydney Morning Herald* chief rugby writer Greg Growden received a strange phone call from Eddie Jones. A month earlier the Brumbies had become the first Australian team to win the Super 12 competition, and Eddie fronted a media conference after the match at which he had made special mention of the team 'proving the Sydney media wrong'.

By 'Sydney media' Eddie meant Growden and Peter Jenkins, by then with the *Daily Telegraph*, whose coverage twelve months earlier of what became known as the 'Cape Town Taxi Scandal' is still a sore point with many ex-Brumbies players and officials.

Eddie left a message on Growden's phone saying he wanted to speak with him. When Growden returned the call, the conversation was brief.

'I just want to ask you one question. Were your employers pleased with the job you did this season?'

'As a matter of fact they were, Eddie. They just gave me a pay rise.'

'Fair enough. See you next year.'

While the reasoning behind the call puzzled Growden at the time, in retrospect it seems obvious: typically, in preparation for taking over as Wallaby coach, Eddie was leaving no stone unturned. Dealing with the press, assessing what the major media organizations expected from their journalists, and how to use that knowledge to his best advantage would have been just as important to Eddie as making sure he had the right number of tackling bags or water bottles for upcoming campaigns. The *SMH,* with its strong readership of high-income professionals, was seen as the preferred newspaper of record for Australia's most influential rugby community. Eddie was never one to kowtow to the media, but he has always followed the adage 'know your enemy'.

Eddie has an analogy he uses when describing facing the media.

'When you have a press conference it's like those old Wild West movies where the new cowboy comes into town, and they're all standing with their guns ready as he walks into the bar. That's what it's like walking into a media conference. They're waiting to shoot you.'

That being the case, there are plenty of journalists around the world who have been beaten to the draw. They don't come much quicker than Fast Eddie.

Media conferences with sporting coaches take many forms. In some cases, such as with former Manchester United manager Sir Alex Ferguson, the relationship is prickly at best. Brisbane Broncos and England rugby league coach Wayne Bennett has been known to 'play the straight bat' in the extreme, giving answers that amount to little more than 'yep', 'nope' and 'maybe'. Former Chelsea and current Manchester United boss José Mourinho plays along with reporters, his jokes, facial expressions and mangled English often turning weekly pre-match conferences into comedy shows.

Eddie's dealings with the media have elements of all of the above. He can be angry, charming, belligerent, caustic and humorous, but according to Growden, one thing he could never be accused of is being boring.

It was during the 2003 Rugby World Cup, when Eddie's media conferences were more like sparring sessions, that Growden christened him with a nickname that Australian journalists still use: Fighting Harada.

As a sports-mad youngster, Growden, like every other Australian kid of the period, followed the career of Aboriginal boxer Lionel Rose, who became a national hero by defeating Japan's world bantamweight champion Masahiko 'Fighting' Harada in February 1968. Two years later Harada was back in the Australian media spotlight when he made an unsuccessful bid to take the world featherweight title from another Aussie champion, Johnny Famechon.

After a particularly combative performance at a Sydney press conference during the 2003 tournament Growden turned to respected *New Zealand Herald* rugby correspondent Wynne Gray and said, 'This bloke's like Fighting Harada.'

'Wynne said, "Who?" I told him. He loved it. It stuck.'

It was apt, and not just for the facial resemblance the two shared. Like Harada, Eddie was small, quick and always on the front foot. Reporters learned they needed to be on their toes if they wanted to avoid the infamous Jones counter-punch.

'He didn't suffer fools,' says Jenkins, 'and he was the one who decided who was a fool. Someone might ask a valid question, but if Eddie didn't like it, he'd rip them apart.'

The media identity who saw more of Eddie in action than anyone else was veteran Queensland television cameraman Anthony George. Better known by his nicknames 'AJ' or 'Kong', George had travelled the world covering Wallaby tours for television networks for years when he came up with a brilliant idea. With Rod Macqueen and then Eddie basing the Wallabies at training camps in regional areas and the cost of sending film crews to far-flung locations becoming exorbitant, towards the end of the 2001 season George approached Australian Rugby Union communications director Strath Gordon with a proposition. Under his plan he would become a full-time contractor to the ARU, living and travelling with the Wallabies and filming daily news feeds that he would professionally edit, package and make available for free download to all media outlets. Gordon took the idea to ARU CEO John O'Neill, who signed off on it immediately. The major networks, seeing the cost savings, were delighted. Journalists, not so much. Rather than spending time at Camp Wallaby – during Macqueen's time at Caloundra on the Queensland Sunshine Coast and under Eddie at Coffs Harbour on the north coast of NSW – picking up any breaking news or scandal, they were stuck in the office waiting to receive the ARU's daily version of events. Instead of TV reporters asking their own questions, coaches and players were served up Dorothy Dixers by Wallabies' media manager Djuro Sen, using a microphone bearing the ARU corporate logo. The official name of the team led by AJ was the 'ARU Media Unit'. Journalists preferred the term 'Ministry of Information'.

All of which made the opportunities the reporters had to confront Eddie face to face at media conferences all the more sought after and, on occasions, volatile.

AJ, who viewed every media conference Eddie gave between 2002 and 2005 through the lens of his camera, says he could always tell when things were about to get exciting.

'When the right eyebrow went up you knew he was about to get on the front foot. The thing with Eddie was that he knew the importance of the media better than anyone. He understood his role in getting the message about rugby out to the public, and the way to do that was through the media. He'd say things that he knew would bring attention to the game. Even when there was nothing happening, he'd come up with something for the press to run with. He was like a boxing promoter in a rugby coach's body.

'At the same time he liked to go toe to toe with the media. He liked to be tested. Some journalists have to be hand fed, and Eddie didn't like that. He liked the ones who fronted up, the ones who said, "I disagree." What frustrated him was people who would come along and ask questions who didn't know anything about the game.'

The key, says Growden, was to do your homework.

'Eddie never gave you an easy ride, but if you worked on your research and asked a good question he'd give you a good answer. He was never one of those coaches that a reporter could ring and say, "What's happening?" but if you said, "Eddie, I've noticed at training that you've got so and so working on his left foot kicking, does that mean such and such?" he'd really go into it. He'd tell you what was happening and why. On tour the players used to have Mondays off, so Eddie used to front up on his own. We used to call it the Monday Sermon. He'd sit there and just go on about anything that was on his mind – about problems with the administration, changes to laws he'd like to see. It was gold. It had nothing to do with the upcoming game, because he wasn't ready to talk about that yet, but it was always great stuff. You'd always get a page lead out of it. He'd say he didn't like dealing with the press, but I think he loved it. He liked the intellectual jousting.'

Before the England–Italy match in 2017, a television reporter asked Eddie if there had ever been a time in the lead-up when he had considered a much-mooted backline reshuffle. He answered with a half-smile: 'If I read the newspapers there would have been but I don't read the newspapers.'

If that is the case, there has been a major change in Eddie's modus operandi, says Growden.

'He was a media tart. He read every word that was written about him and the team, and he knew who wrote it. During the 2003 World Cup he would start every day at the Wallabies training camp in Coffs Harbour sitting on the exercise bike with all the papers in front of him, reading them while he pedalled away. I reckon he was a frustrated journalist.'

In 2007 Eddie got the chance to experience life on the other side of the keyboard when he was offered a regular column in the Queensland *Courier-Mail* newspaper. For the next eight years it was a job he took very seriously. Rugby writer Jim Tucker was given the task of guiding Eddie through the editorial process each week.

The role of the newspaper column 'ghost writer' can on occasions be one of glorified copy-taker, recording the columnist's thoughts during a quick phone call and reproducing them in a readable form. Other times the involvement of the big-name contributor under whose by-line the column appears is even less. Many are the anecdotes shared by sports writers about highly paid athletes who would give only one instruction at the start of their collaboration: 'Just give me a ring each week to let me know what I've written about, will you?'

Tucker says his experience with Eddie could not have been further removed from that.

'Every week he would send it in from wherever he was in the world. At first it was written longhand and faxed. Sometimes the only reason I would contact him was because I couldn't make out a word or two of his handwriting. In the later years he'd type it and send it by email. I remember there were times when he might have taken the Japanese players away to some remote training camp in the mountains. I wouldn't hear from him for a few days, and then the message would come through that he'd come down the mountains and was back in radio range, and the column would come through.

'It was always good stuff. I might have to clean it up a little bit, move the lead up to the top if it was buried or turn bullet-points into paragraphs, but considering he wasn't a trained journalist it was very clean. The copy itself was great. It was obviously for a local market, and he had such knowledge of the inner workings of Australian rugby. He knew all the intrigues and where the skeletons were hidden and he was always ready to have a go. He also had that experience in South Africa and Japan. I think Eddie has consumed more information about rugby than anyone. Even when he was living in Japan he was watching all the Super Rugby and European matches. He knew just about every player in the game. The Wallabies might call up a player who no one knew anything about, and Eddie would write about him in the column, talking about his background and what he'd bring to the team. And that's when he wasn't even living in Australia. I agree he was a frustrated journalist. If he wasn't a coach he would have made a very good rugby writer.'

The column, which only ended when Eddie took on the job as England coach, gave him another outlet to display his passion and insight into the game, but the true Eddie Jones experience has always been a live act, once seen, never forgotten.

The atmosphere at an Eddie Jones media conference is confrontational. Questions are often belted back at the reporter like tennis balls over a net. Other times reporters can be shut down with one of Eddie's favourite lines: 'I'm not telling you, mate.' He likes to engage journalists, almost daring them to debate with him, answering a question with a question, in effect asking them, 'If you're so smart, what would you do if you were in my position?'

One of the best examples was during Eddie's most famous media conference meltdown, after Japan's 2012 loss to the French Barbarians. While much of the attention afterwards was about the tongue-lashing he gave his captain Toshiaki Hirose, the way he turned the journalists' questions back at them was classic Eddie.

Asked whether poor selections had been a key factor in Japan's 21-40 loss, Eddie snapped, 'I made the mistake but I'm trying to pick the best young players in Japan. I expect them to give more in return. I'll take responsibility for it. I'll resign now if you like. Do you want me to resign now? I'm happy to. I take responsibility for the defeat and the performance, so it's my bad coaching. It's my fault. So who would you select? If I pick six New Zealanders in there we win the game. Do you want me to do that? So before, when [former All Black] Kirwan was coach everyone complained about the number of foreigners. Now we want to develop Japanese players, and you're complaining about it. Which way do you want it?'

Another reporter asked what message Eddie would give his players at their next training session.

'Well, do their job. Rugby is a simple game. If you're at the breakdown you've got to clean out. If you're a tight-head prop you've got to scrum. There's no special message. As I said, if you think I'm responsible for the loss, I'll resign tonight, because I'm not putting up with performances like that. I mean it. Find a Japanese coach to coach the side. Is that what you want?'

Not all Eddie Jones counter-attacks are as explicit. He is a great exponent of sarcasm in his dealings with the media, as a reporter found when he asked if England were lucky to have had two contentious decisions from referee Ben O'Keeffe and the Television Match Official go their way in the 2017 win over Australia at Twickenham.

'Well why do we have referees? Why do we have TMOs? I don't understand the question. How were we lucky? They do ten replays of the video and they make a decision. This is the best referee in the world today. We have the best TMOs in the world and you say we were lucky because the decisions went our way. Sorry, sorry, sorry. We were lucky. I'm sorry mate, we were lucky.'

Another signature move is to win over the pack by isolating and humiliating one of their own. This tactic was on show in May 2017 when Eddie spoke at Oxford University's historic Oxford Union Q&A, an open forum addressed over the years by such luminaries as Winston Churchill, the Dalai Lama and Mother Theresa. In a room full of serious-minded young students, Eddie encountered a reserved audience until one slightly built young man asked a question.

'Obviously there are some exceptions, but I wonder if you think the importance of skill in the modern game is a little bit less, and it's more about mentality, physique and being able to run into a brick wall week in week out?'

Eddie teased: 'Well *you* definitely need to do some training.'

For a split second there was stunned silence in the room, then gasps of surprise and a loud burst of laughter, followed by applause. As the young man stood red-faced and embarrassed, Eddie pushed on.

'Look, some guys choose to spend more time at the bar and some spend more time at the gym. Maybe you need to spend more time at the gym.'

He then turned on the charm.

'Bet you're a good player, though.'

If the young man thought he was off the hook when Eddie moved on to the next question, he was sadly mistaken. Over the next half hour, at every opportunity, Eddie got a laugh at the expense of his helpless prey. Asked about the culture of rugby, Eddie again brought the lad into the spotlight, this time implementing another of his favourite tactics – the 'name and shame'; asking the name of his victim in order to personalize his attack.

'If you play rugby you can go anywhere in the world, and a rugby club will look after you. That's the reality of it. You go into the club and say, "I play rugby," and it doesn't matter what shape you are, what size you are . . . even the little bloke over there who needs to train, he walks into a club and they still say we'll give him a game, we'll look after him.'

When the laughter died down he asked, 'What's your name, mate?'

'Mark,' the young man answered.

'Mark, I'm going to get you a gym membership. There's a good gym here. Pure Gym. We used it when we were here with the England side.'

The ordeal still wasn't over for Mark, but at least he wasn't alone, with another student feeling the bite of Eddie's caustic wit when he raised the issue of player behaviour.

'Eddie,' he asked. 'So much in the media we see players hitting the headlines for all the wrong reasons . . . late nights and drugs and stuff like that. As a coach, how do you manage that, and what are the reasons for it?'

Eddie shot back, 'I don't know what newspapers you're reading, mate. Stop reading *The Sun* and *Daily Mirror* and start reading *The Times* and the *Guardian*, mate. I thought you blokes were supposed to be educated.

'Our players hardly drink. You'll always get one or two who are silly. Look around this room. If you have a reunion in twenty years' time, there's going to be someone here who's over-indulged in drugs, someone who's over-indulged in alcohol, so just look around and see who it's going to be. Mark, you get to the gym, mate. You'll be all right.'

The last question of the day came from a female rugby player, who asked for advice.

'Keep at it. Just love it, love the game. Go to the gym with Mark sometimes.'

Eddie's last words before the moderator brought the session to an end were: 'Mark, I love you, mate. Don't worry.'

Engagement, sarcasm, isolation, name and shame . . . all have been used to maximum effect by Eddie over the years, but rarely all in the one media conference, as they were the week before England's Six Nations clash against Ireland in 2016.

As Peter Jenkins noted, Eddie is quick to swoop on what he considers a poor question. Most people with an understanding of rugby – or any contact sport for that matter – would probably agree that the questions Eddie was asked about his views on 'targeting' a key opposition player that day fell into that category.

The confrontation came in the press conference following England's 40-9 win over Italy. The previous day Ireland had gone down 10-9 to France, with Irish supporters angered over the rough treatment meted out to their star fly-half Jonathan Sexton, a player with a history of head injuries.

Eddie was asked, 'Are France targeting him? Would a team of yours ever target a fly-half like that?'

'I don't know about France, mate. You'd have to ask the French coach.'

'Would you ever . . .'

'Go and ask the French coach, mate.'

'Would you ever target him?'

'We target players all the time. That's part of rugby isn't it?'

'Absolutely.'

Another reporter picked up on the theme.

'Is it legitimate to target a fly-half in particular?'

'I didn't know ten had any particular requirements.'

'Well, he's the playmaker on the field.'

By now the right eyebrow was well and truly up, and the left was about to join it.

'Is there some sort of special law, is there? Let me know.'

'I didn't say there was. I just asked if it was legitimate to target a fly-half.'

'Well there's fifteen players out there. What, are we supposed to not run at one player? Hang on, hang on, he's got a red dot on his head, we don't run at him . . .'

'Have you made special dispensation for a player because of his playmaker role?'

'I don't understand the question, mate. Obviously it's a different rugby here. There's fifteen players on the field. If you've got a weak defender, you run at him. Why wouldn't you?'

'Do you think Johnny Sexton is a weak defender?'

'I'm not commenting on Johnny.'

It was there that the debate appeared to end, with another journalist asking a question on a different matter, but Eddie couldn't let it rest. Inspired by the hulking 208 cm (6 feet 10 inch) physique of 1993 British Lions lock Martin Bayfield sitting amongst the media in his role as a commentator for BT Sport, he went back for another crack, this time picking out slightly built reporter Nick Heath sitting in the front row and employing some 'name and shame' to get the crowd on side.

'Can I just get back to the Sexton question? I just think that's a really silly question. Rugby's a game of fifteen players on the field. When we're attacking we attack weak defenders. We're looking for weak defenders. Why would we run at the strongest defenders? So, if Martin's there and . . . sorry, what's your name?'

'Nick.'

'Nick. So if Martin's there . . . and Nick's there, we're not going to run at Martin are we?'

As the room erupted in laughter, the diminutive Heath did his best to fight back.

'You never saw me play.'

'Maybe, maybe,' said Eddie, picking out another target. 'Well, maybe we'll run at this bloke here. We're not going to run at their strongest defenders. We'll always run at their weak defenders. Now I'm not saying Sexton is a weak defender. Maybe France did, but we're going to be targeting players in the Ireland side because we want to win, and you win a game of rugby by attacking their weak points, and to say that's unfair is just ridiculous and you shouldn't be asking those questions.'

The reporter who had asked the original question returned serve.

'I don't think anyone said it was unfair.'

'No, the question was whether it was legitimate or not. It's not a great question to ask at all.'

'I think it's a reasonable question.'

'I think it's stupid. We'll agree to disagree.'

The 'agree to disagree' concept is a cornerstone of Eddie's dealings with the media, says Growden.

'There was no bullshit about him. You knew where you stood. If there was a problem you'd sort it out and move on. I always thought he was a pro. There were some volatile times, but at the end, when he was sacked by the Wallabies I wrote him a letter thanking him and wishing him good luck. It had been fun.'

Certainly Eddie for the most part seemed to enjoy his interaction with the media. Light-hearted banter was always a feature of his relationship with journalists. There was the time during the 2003 Rugby World Cup when a reporter asked him the significance of the beaded bracelet he wore on his left wrist.

'It was a gift from a friend in Japan,' he said. 'It's supposed to bring luck.'

'Is it working?'

'Ask me after the tournament.'

After England's win over Italy in the 2016 Six Nations he attempted to defuse the tense 'Johnny Sexton media conference' by asking the assembled journalists if his favourite football side had won earlier in the afternoon.

'Did Arsenal win? They did? Well it's been a good day, then.'

Or at least it was until he read the next day's reports about the media conference. There was little interest in the merits of the 'to target the fly-half or not to target the fly-half' interchange, let alone Eddie's interest in the fortunes of Arsenal. All the headlines were about Eddie's early comments that had sparked the Johnny Sexton debate in the first place.

Questioned about the make-up of the Ireland team that England would be facing the following weekend, he had answered, 'Sexton is an interesting one. They've talked about him having a whiplash injury, which is not a great thing to talk about, I'm sure his mother and father would be worried about that. Hopefully, the lad's all right to play on Saturday.

'I'd just be worried about his welfare if he's had whiplash injuries. That's quite a distinct way to talk about the injury. You don't like to see that with any player.

'If you're saying a guy has got whiplash then he's had a severe trauma. Maybe they used the wrong term, but if you've had severe trauma then you've got to worry about the welfare of the player.'

The media jumped on the comments, with some expressing outrage that Eddie had mentioned Sexton's parents, others accusing him of 'scaremongering' in an attempt to put Ireland management, and Sexton himself, in two minds. Eddie was forced to clarify his comments, saying, 'The only thing I've suggested is that if they say he's had whiplash injuries, then I'd be worried about him. That's all I'm suggesting.

'We've got medical staff here, the best medical staff in England, and we'll make the best decision for the player. I'm sure Ireland have done the same.'

Sexton entered the debate, saying of Eddie, 'Maybe he is just trying to jump on the bandwagon about head injuries. I have been branded. It can be pretty frustrating when people are diagnosing you that have absolutely no idea what is going on behind the scenes, frustrating when you are being labelled with being concussed when you're not. If I said over and over again that a member of the media had dementia, I'd be sued for slander. It is not ideal.'

Pressed in an interview, Eddie admitted he would apologize to Sexton when he felt the time was right, but at the press conference after the Ireland game, won 21-10 by England, he was not in a conciliatory mood. Asked by a reporter to give his view of a refereeing decision during the match he fired back, 'Why should I, mate?'

'Well, that's how press conferences work. We ask your opinion, and you give it.'

'Well, you can give your opinion, mate. The referee has adjudicated on it. If I say something about the referee, then the headline tomorrow is "Jones Complains About Referee", so I'm not going to give an opinion, mate.'

Eddie was then asked if he had watched the performance of England's next opponent, Wales, in their game against France the previous night.

'I definitely did.'

'What did you make of it?'

'I'm not going to tell you, mate.'

Eddie then announced that he was putting a media ban on himself, to which a journalist can be heard muttering, 'Oh Jesus . . .'

'I don't want to say anything that offends the media or offends people's parents, so from now until Friday, before the Wales game,

I'm not talking to the media, so you won't have to worry about all that scaremongering and all that sort of stuff.'

A reporter asked, 'Is that just gamesmanship?'

'Well, mate, if I don't say anything, you come away from the press conference saying it's boring. If I say something, I'm scaremongering. So I can't win. So the easiest thing is I don't come to press conferences.'

The final question was whether Eddie regretted his comments about Sexton.

'I don't regret anything, mate, I don't regret anything. Why would I regret it?'

For the English media it was a first look at Eddie in full flight. Up until then, with the England team five matches into a record-equalling seventeen-Test winning streak, love had been in the air. The Sexton incident had been a learning experience on both sides of the microphone. Eddie had seen how quickly, and sharply, the British press could bite. They, in turn, saw how much he relished the fight. It was one he had come prepared for. Asked by an Australian reporter just days after taking on the England job how he would deal with the notoriously judgemental British journalists, he was emphatic.

'I'll just treat them with respect and let them do their job. Back when I took on the job at the Brumbies I went and spent some time with one of the top rugby league coaches. He told me that when it comes to the media, you're never as good as they say you are and you're never as bad as they say you are.

'I've tried to stick to that policy ever since.'

6

BOSS WALLABY

The Wallaby team that Eddie inherited from Rod Macqueen was a side in flux. There was a feeling amongst some within ARU ranks that Macqueen had got out at exactly the right time. His team of champions was ageing. Some of his World Cup side, like centre Tim Horan and open-side flanker David Wilson, had already moved on, and others were to follow at the end of the season. Plus, he had been preaching the same sermon – albeit with phenomenal success – for four years, and the message was losing its impact. In that time the Wallabies had played forty-three Tests, won thirty-four, drawn one – against England at Twickenham in 1997 – and lost just eight, for a winning percentage of 81.4 per cent. It was a stunning record that simply couldn't be maintained. Macqueen was tired, and his core players were tired. It was time to put a new band together under a new conductor. Eddie attacked the assignment with typical gusto.

First step on the road that led to the 2003 Rugby World Cup final was the 2001 Tri-Nations series between Australia, New Zealand and South Africa. It didn't start well, with Eddie's first Test as Australian coach a 15-20 loss to the Springboks in Pretoria just two weeks after the Lions series. A fortnight later the Wallabies turned things around with a 23-15 win over the All Blacks in Dunedin, followed by a 14-14 draw with the Springboks in Perth. The Tri-Nations and retention of the Bledisloe Cup hinged on the return match against the All Blacks in

Sydney. Adding to the occasion was the fact that Wallaby captain, and arguably Australia's greatest-ever player, John Eales, had announced it would be his last game. The Wallabies did the right thing by their captain, and their new coach, winning 29-26.

To win the Tri-Nations and retain the Bledisloe after such a short time in charge was a huge achievement, diminished in the minds of some critics who felt that Eddie had simply taken over Rod Macqueen's side and pointed them towards the field. Those closer to the team knew differently. As one ARU insider of the time said, 'I'm not sure Rod could have got them up for the Tri-Nations after the Lions series. He was at the end of the road.'

With Eales gone, the captaincy for the Wallabies' end-of-season tour to Europe and beyond was handed to Eddie's skipper at the Brumbies, George Gregan. It was on that tour that Eddie began to pull together what he saw as the core players for the 2003 World Cup campaign. One who would play a major role was Queensland inside back Elton Flatley.

A schoolboy prodigy who made his Reds debut in 1996 aged eighteen, Flatley was brought into the Wallaby squad by Rod Macqueen the following year, but it was not until Eddie took over at the end of 2001 that he became a first-choice Test player.

'I was a fringe player with Rod, but when Eddie came in everything changed. Eddie didn't have the same team on paper that Rod did. Heaps of senior players like Tim Horan and John Eales had retired, so Eddie had to develop new players and make a new team. It was a totally different set-up. Rod had his specialist coaches and he sort of took a supervisory role. Eddie was more hands-on. There was only one boss when Eddie was there, and if you weren't on board, you weren't on board. I probably wouldn't want to be one of his assistant coaches, but it was a highly professional environment.

'Technically he's the best coach I ever had. He knows the game and he'd pick out things you needed to work on, like passing left to right or right to left. He's good at explaining things. With me he said, "You've got to be a world-class goal-kicker. Let's work out how you can get there," and he and the specialist coaches put together a programme.

'We all know how tough Eddie can be. He set high standards, but I enjoyed that. He was great for me. I've got a very high opinion of him. I played my best footy under Eddie.'

The spring tour was a mixed bag. Australia started strongly with a 92-10 win over Spain in Madrid but then lost 21-15 to England at Twickenham in a result that would prove a painful portent for Eddie and his players. The Australians scored two tries to nil but were sunk by the boot of Jonny Wilkinson, the England fly-half kicking five penalties and two drop-goals for all the home side's points. A one-point loss to France at Marseilles and a 21-13 win over Wales in Cardiff capped off a disappointing tour for the reigning Tri-Nations, Bledisloe and world champions.

The next year brought even more cause for concern. With the World Cup just over twelve months away, the Wallabies dropped to second in the Tri-Nations, and on the spring tour they were beaten by Ireland for the first time in twenty-three years. A week later Jonny Wilkinson was again their undoing, kicking six penalties and two conversions as Australia went down to England 31-32 despite scoring three tries to two. The bright spot was retaining the Bledisloe Cup thanks to a penalty goal after the siren by Matt Burke, securing a 16-14 win in Sydney.

Even that wasn't enough to win unanimous support for Eddie at ARU headquarters, as his working relationship with his employers was becoming increasingly strained. Former Australian Rugby CEO John O'Neill believes the retirement of senior Wallaby players John

Eales, Tim Horan and David Wilson – all Queenslanders – led to a distinct change of culture in the side.

'My personal observation was that Rod Macqueen's team had a very good culture and that culture was predominantly Queensland-driven. The Queenslanders were the heart and soul of that side. They came from a more conservative environment, where it was all about serving in the trenches beside your mate. They brought that culture to the Wallabies. The Brumbies culture that Eddie and George brought to the table was very different.

'When I was working with Rod Macqueen and John Eales you could have thrown a blanket over us, we were that close. There were no differences of opinion, and if there were they'd be sorted out behind closed doors. From 2001 onwards, after Eddie took over, it was a case of "us and them". It was far less compatible. Eddie didn't see himself as part of the ARU. He saw himself as the Wallabies' coach, the players' coach.'

One point on which Eddie and O'Neill did find common ground was a desire to strengthen the Wallaby ranks by luring some big-name rugby league players.

O'Neill's interest in making a raid on rugby league was very much 'big picture'. Following the Super League War of 1995, when the game was torn apart by competing media interests and players and clubs had gone to the highest bidder, many rugby league supporters had become disillusioned with what had previously been considered a working-class game. With the Wallabies enjoying an unprecedented period of success culminating in the 1999 World Cup win, O'Neill felt the time was right to win over any 'swinging voters' from rugby league. His view was: bring over some big-name players, and the fans, corporate sponsors, advertisers and TV deals will follow. Eddie's view was more narrow-minded. He just wanted to win footy games.

Eddie had a lifelong affection for rugby league, having played it as a youngster. Like most sports fans in NSW and Queensland, he watched it on television and, as a rugby coach, continued to learn from it.

'It's the most simple game in the world. They've taken every bit of contest out of the game. Thirty years ago they had a contest at the scrum. Twenty years ago they had a contest at the play-the-ball, and you used to be able to contest the ball carrier. Now you can't even do that, so because it has become such a simple game they've had to become good at other skills. Their ability to run lines and put options at the line is better than anything we do at rugby, so I'm continuing looking at that and continually meeting with rugby league sides to learn about that. They are so far ahead of us in those areas it's ridiculous. The gap is huge, and I'm always looking to bridge that gap. It's a good game, a great game. I love it.'

If Eddie's aim in bringing across league players was to improve his team's attacking prowess, and O'Neill's was to fire a marketing broadside across the bows of his code's number one rival, Brisbane Broncos winger Wendell Sailor could not have been a more perfect target. Big, brash and a magnificent athlete, Sailor was a walking, talking, publicity magnet. A Test player against Great Britain at twenty, by 2001 he had sixteen rugby league Test caps and had played in fourteen State of Origin matches for Queensland and four winning grand final sides with the Broncos. But as much for his powerful running and exceptional pace for a man of 191 cm (6 feet 3 inches) and 106 kg (16 stone 10 pound), 'Big Dell' was known for his charisma, confidence and penchant for jewellery. His Broncos coach Wayne Bennett told the story of being with Sailor when he stepped into a store to buy a pair of diamond ear studs for his wife Tara. After holding them to his own ears while looking into a mirror, Sailor liked them so much he bought them for himself, much to the bemusement of the old-school Bennett. When English rugby league giant Wigan made an abortive £500,000 bid for Sailor's services in 1998, Super League chief executive Colin Myler described him as 'the Ronaldo of rugby league'.

The successful negotiations to bring Sailor to rugby union were handled by the then head of the ARU's High Performance Unit, Jeff Miller, but Sailor recalls that it was actually Eddie Jones who made the first move.

'Eddie was the instigator of me moving across. After the 1999 Rugby World Cup we had a meeting in Brisbane, and he wanted to get me to the Brumbies. He said playing on the end of the Brumbies backline would further my career and I could play for the Wallabies. He sold me on it right then and there.'

With the media and fans salivating over the prospect of Sailor and the All Blacks' mighty Jonah Lomu coming face to face on a rugby pitch, the 'will he or won't he?' saga of Sailor's contract negotiations was back-page news for weeks in early 2001. After an on-again-off-again process that saw talks break down several times, Sailor finally rejected a late bid from the Brumbies and signed with the Queensland Reds from the start of the 2002 season. The contract, following the late sweetener of matching cars for him and his wife and an extra $75,000 in salary, was worth $625,000 a season. In the next few months the ARU would also succeed in signing fellow rugby league internationals Lote Tuqiri and Mat Rogers but there was no question which of the three outside backs was the biggest catch. When Sailor arrived for his first training at the Reds' home ground, Ballymore, he walked past the turnstiles and told his new team-mates, 'Dell sells. Watch these babies spin.' And spin they did. It was estimated that admission fees from the extra crowd that came through the gates for Sailor's Queensland debut – a trial game in which he dropped the first ball that came his way – covered the Reds' portion of his season's salary.

He was everything O'Neill had hoped, if not what he was accustomed to. The first time the ARU boss actually met his star signing was at a luncheon function in Brisbane the day before Sailor played in a pre-season international rugby sevens tournament.

Wearing a tight body shirt, best to show off his impressive chest and biceps, and bedecked in his diamond studs, gold chains and numerous rings, Sailor walked up to his employer, stuck out a hand and said, 'G'day, Johnny.' Somewhat stunned, O'Neill answered, 'Hello Wendell. I haven't seen anyone wearing so much jewellery since Isaac Hayes.' Sailor looked confused. 'Who's Isaac Hayes?' he asked.

Not everyone was as happy to see the three league converts make the switch to union. In his *World Cup Diary*, published in 2004, Wallaby fly-half Steve Larkham noted there was some initial unrest amongst the ranks.

'I would be less than honest if I said that senior players were overjoyed at the prospect of big-name league recruits joining the Wallabies. On the contrary, there was discontent, maybe even some resentment. For one thing it rankled with senior players that the league recruits were reportedly on bigger contracts than they were. Somehow it just didn't seem fair that rugby players who had spent most of their lives in the game and worked their way up the ranks should be leap-frogged money-wise by league players who had just arrived on the scene and had yet to prove themselves in rugby. One or two rugby players who were hoping to make the Test side as wingers had special reservations about the influx of wingers from league. Again, some players felt that after doing the hard yards over many years to get to the top they were about to be pipped at the post by recruits who had contributed nothing to rugby.'

Eddie had no such reservations. He brought Sailor into the Wallabies for the first home Test of the season, against France. It was the start of a close, if at times tumultuous, relationship between the two.

'I always got along really well with Eddie. I used to sit next to him on the bus. He'd sledge me, and I'd sledge him. He was pretty funny. He could give it, but he couldn't always take it. We used to have these court sessions, and everyone would have a song that would play when they were charged with something in the court. One day when Eddie got up they played "Kung Fu Fighting". I can't remember who was in charge of the music, but Eddie wasn't impressed. He gave him the stink-eye.

'Eddie and Wayne Bennett were the two best coaches I've ever had. The best thing about him is that he knows your strengths and works to those. He knew my kicking game was never going to be anything special. My strength was always going to be running the ball and backing myself. He told me I shouldn't be floating in and out of the game. He said, "Look at Jonah. Every time he touches the ball something happens. That's what I want from you."'

And if he didn't get it, he would let Sailor know it.

'If I'd had a quiet game, had two runs and two tackles, he'd say, "You wouldn't be too sore would you?" He knew that a bit of tough love worked well with me. He pumped up my tyres from time to time but he could deflate them too. One time against Ireland we lost 18-9 at Lansdowne Road. I'd been reading the press and thought we were going to win pretty easily. I've always admired the lairy-type players. I used to watch Campo [David Campese] in his long-sleeved jersey and this day was cold so I've decided to wear the long-sleeved jersey and gloves. I've had three carries and dropped the ball once and when I've walked in after the game Eddie's said, "If you ever wear a long-sleeved jersey again you'll never play for the Wallabies again."'

There were also some off-field issues, but according to Elton Flatley, Eddie was more forgiving of some players than of others.

'If he thought you were training hard and doing your bit for the team, he'd like you and he'd stick up for you. I know I got into a bit of trouble, and he had my back. From a player's point of view some others might have a different opinion. He was hard on a lot of them – he was hard on me too, but it brought out the best in me. It would be unfair to name players. There wasn't anything personal about it, but he would rip into guys. Over time you get better at managing players and if you asked him now there might be some things he would do differently, but he had high expectations and he expected you to meet them. He loved the league boys. He loved the way they trained.'

He also saw them as a ready source of information, says Sailor.

'Sometimes he'd talk to me about the Broncos. He wanted to know about how we did things, how we approached big games. He'd ask me how Wayne got the best out of his players. I told him some people need love and some people need a bit of a kick. We had some great players at the Broncos, like Darren Lockyer and Glen Lazarus and Shane Webcke, but I'm different to Locky, and Locky is different to Lazo, and Lazo is different to Webby. Eddie could get stuck into me if I'd done something wrong, and it was the right thing for me, but if he'd spoken to Locky like that he wouldn't react the same way. Locky would just shut down. I told Eddie that, and I think he took it on board.'

Eddie wasn't the only one learning from the league converts, says Elton Flatley.

'When I started playing it was the first year of professional rugby, but it wasn't professional like it is now. It has evolved over time, and Eddie lifted the bar. That's why Eddie had such big affection for the league boys. They brought plenty to the side. Firstly there was the public exposure, but then there was the work ethic they brought to training from their league background. Now the rugby training is probably similar to rugby league, but back then they were a long way in front, and Eddie wanted them to show us how to get to that level.'

Sailor agrees.

'I know some people might think the biggest thing we brought to the Wallabies was a drinking culture, but if you ask a lot of those players themselves they'll tell you we brought a new training ethic. We helped Eddie take the training standard to the next level.'

Things might have been coming together on the training paddock but in the corridors of power at the ARU's North Sydney bunker they were falling apart. In 2002 Eddie's former captain at the Brumbies, Brett Robinson, had replaced Jeff Miller as high performance manager. Eddie was now expected to take orders from someone to whom he had once given orders. It was a reversal of roles that never worked, says John O'Neill.

'His captain was essentially now his boss, and that didn't sit well with Eddie. On one occasion, with my support, Robbo called Eddie into his office and took him to task over something, and a massive blue broke out. They were shouting at each other, and finally Eddie stormed out and slammed the door so hard that the lock broke. Robbo came to see me and said, "This is unmanageable," so I called Eddie into my office and told him in no uncertain terms that he either complied with our management structure or started looking for a new job. He backed down, but it was never an easy relationship.'

One of the biggest blow-ups between the ARU and the team – and by extension Eddie – was over bonus payments for the 2003 World Cup. In 1999 John O'Neill had dealt directly with senior Wallabies John Eales and Tim Horan on behalf of the players over the same issue.

'They came in, we discussed it, and it was all agreed in half an hour. As it happened they won the World Cup, and we made the decision to double the bonus in the dressing room after the game.'

The 2003 negotiations were anything but simple, with the players represented by Rugby Union Players' Association boss Tony Dempsey. With the players required to sign a participation agreement with the International Rugby Board to become eligible to take part in the World Cup, Dempsey used this as leverage for them to receive a larger part of the profits the ARU was expected to reap from hosting the event.

'RUPA took us to court in what was an unsavoury piece of litigation,' O'Neill recalls. 'By having the players hold off signing the IRB agreement Dempsey was effectively holding us to ransom over the bonus payment. For me personally the most distressing part was that a key part of RUPA's case was an affidavit from George Gregan in which he quoted from an address I had made to the players and which I expected to be kept between me and them. For any member of the team to breach that confidence would be upsetting enough, let alone the Wallaby captain. In the end the case was dropped, and we reached agreement over the bonus by going around RUPA, but it was a very unpleasant and difficult period.'

The imbroglio ended when Robinson and ARU lawyer Peter Friend flew in secret to Cape Town, where the Wallabies were playing a Tri-Nations Test against the Springboks. The night before the game the pair met with Eddie and told him they wished to speak to the players at their hotel the morning before they flew home. Robinson later told O'Neill that Eddie was his 'usual disagreeable and belligerent self', but he agreed to organize the meeting. Robinson gave each player a copy of the ARU's offer, which amounted to a $10,000 one-off payment for use of their image or likeness during the tournament, $2,500 extra in match payments (taking the total per game to $12,500) and a $20,000 bonus for making the final, rising to $80,000 for winning. He also advised that the same offer had been put to all 120 professional rugby players in the country, the clear message being that if they didn't sign, the ARU would find players who would. The players signed, but O'Neill said the affair would leave a bad taste in further dealings with Eddie.

'I found out later that behind the scenes Eddie had not been helpful to us. His advice to the players was, "Hang tough, stare them down, and you'll get more." That was indicative of Eddie's different style. He sees himself as being born on the other side of the tracks. He is anti-establishment, and I think he liked to use his influence over players to stick it up the ARU. Alan Jones did the same thing. A lot of those motivational-style coaches do. They tell the players, "I'm your only friend. Those blokes in the suits aren't your friend." It's old-fashioned siege mentality.'

O'Neill says when Eddie moved the team into 'Camp Wallaby', the training facility at Coffs Harbour, in preparation for Tests and the World Cup, he and Robinson were never made welcome.

'When Robbo and I would go to the camp we were treated like outsiders. We'd go to dinner, and Eddie would sit at a different table. After dinner he wouldn't have a drink with us, he'd go off with his own little coterie, the inner sanctum like Glen Ella and AJ, the cameraman who made Eddie laugh. The rest of us were persona non grata.'

It was all part of Eddie's plan to make Camp Wallaby the players' fortress; their own little world away from the distractions and rules of everyday society. In a move that did not sit well with the ARU, except during the World Cup, he also opened it up to the players' families. O'Neill called it "a creche".

The concept of Camp Wallaby was one that Eddie would refine and improve upon for his preparation of Japan at their camp outside the city of Miyazaki before the 2015 Rugby World Cup and will no doubt take to an even higher level when he bases England in the same location before the 2019 tournament. In comparison to the Japanese, the Wallabies had it easy.

Unless players wanted to go for an early walk or swim, the day's activities at Camp Wallaby began with team breakfast at 7 a.m. Divided into three groups of tight forwards, loose forwards/inside backs and outside backs, they then had a ninety-minute gym session followed by lunch and a team meeting attended by all players, coaches and medical staff. Around 3 p.m. they would start a ninety-minute full training session, followed by individual skills training, such as hookers practising lineout throws, kickers going through their drills and wingers practising catching high kicks. Dinner would be served at 6.30 p.m., followed by physiotherapy if required. Thursday was the players' day off – a luxury the Brave Blossoms could only dream of.

It was this routine that took the team into the crucial 2003 season and at first it appeared to be working. The Wallabies won their opening Test of the year 45-16 over Ireland in Perth on 7 June and a week later downed Wales 30-10 in Sydney. Then the wheels fell off. First there was a 14-25 loss to England in Melbourne, with Ben Cohen, Will Greenwood and Mike Tindall scoring tries and Jonny Wilkinson kicking two penalties and two conversions to a Wendell Sailor try and three Joe Roff penalties. It was then the turn of the Springboks, who triumphed 26-22 in the Tri-Nations opener at Cape Town. But it was the Wallabies' third Test loss in a row that turned the media and all but their most forgiving supporters against them. On 26 July at Sydney's Stadium Australia, the ground that would host the Rugby World Cup final in four months' time, the All Blacks thrashed the Wallabies 50-21 in front of a stunned crowd of over 82,000. It didn't help that Sailor copped ten minutes in the sin-bin for tackling Kiwi fullback Mils Muliaina in the air, but Eddie was more concerned about the stat showing the Wallabies had gone down seven tries to three despite having 60 per cent of possession. He stormed around the dressing room after the match, swearing and shouting, 'Sixty per cent of possession. How could we lose like that with sixty per cent of possession?' If the Wallabies had thought their preparation had been tough up until then, he told them, it was about to get tougher. 'I don't want to hear any complaints,' he bellowed. 'I want you on time, every session, ready to give 100 per cent. If anyone gives me anything less, you're out.'

By the time the Australians ran out for their return match against the Springboks in Brisbane a week later he had calmed down, but not for long. After the Wallabies won 29-9 John O'Neill received a call from a staff member telling him he'd better get down to the Australian dressing room, and fast.

'When I got down there, Eddie was going crazy. All coaches are prone to be wound up at the end of a game, but this was something else. Our hooker, Brendan Cannon, was claiming that South Africa's Bakkies Botha had bitten and eye-gouged him. Eddie wanted to go to the press conference and hand out photos of the attack marks to the media. He was getting AJ the cameraman to take pictures. I was trying to calm him down. I was saying, "Eddie, you can't do that. It will cause an international incident; you have to let the judiciary handle it," but he wouldn't listen. Finally I told him I was going to have to lock him in the room unless he calmed down. He promised he would. Then he went straight out and showed everyone the pictures. They were on the back pages of all the papers the next day. South Africa complained, and all hell broke loose. Dealing with Eddie was a laugh a minute, let me tell you.'

Eddie told the media that the Springboks were 'a disgrace for international rugby'.

'We're absolutely filthy about what they did. We need to expose them. They really need to have a good look at themselves, because that sort of rubbish should not go on.'

Sitting beside him, George Gregan accused his opposition captain Corne Krige of spitting on Wallaby back-rower Phil Waugh. Krige later admitted spitting but said it was to clear blood from his mouth. Some blood had accidentally hit Waugh, and he apologized immediately. He threatened to take legal action against Eddie for repeating the accusation, but nothing further was heard.

The biting allegation could not be proved against Botha. Instead he received an eight-week suspension for 'deliberately attacking the face of an opponent'. Springbok prop Robbie Kempson was suspended four weeks for a late, high hit on Toutai Kefu that saw the Wallaby number eight stretchered off and hospitalized for the night with 'spinal concussion'. Both South African players missed just one Test and were available for the opening round of the World Cup.

The Australians ended their on-field preparation for the World Cup with a 17-21 loss to New Zealand at Eden Park. To rugby followers it was just further evidence that the Kiwis were in a class of their own. To Eddie it was an encouraging sign. The All Blacks were anything but invincible. His analysis of the 50-21 blitzing in Sydney three weeks earlier had showed that New Zealand scored five tries from Australian mistakes – three lineout turnovers and two botched kick-offs. Add in a try scored when Sailor was in the sin-bin and that accounted for six of the Kiwis' seven tries. Cut down on the errors, Eddie told his team before the return match, and we can beat them. But for a disallowed Stephen Larkham try, when referee Jonathan Kaplan ruled All Black flanker Richie McCaw stopped him short of the line, the Australians would have done just that. Instead, the New Zealanders were jubilant to have won back the Bledisloe Cup for the first time in five years.

Eddie was almost as pleased himself. He left Auckland knowing that his team could beat this New Zealand side. All they had to do was follow his plan to the letter.

When Eddie announced his twenty-nine-man squad for the World Cup on Thursday, 4 September, he rang each member personally to break the news and offer congratulations. He then called the eleven players from the original group of forty who had missed out.

Before they embarked on the 2003 Rugby World Cup, though, Eddie had one last trick up his sleeve, and it might just have been the best of his career. He took them to one of the hottest, most isolated and spiritual parts of the country, an area that Australians call 'The Top End'. Some sections of the media labelled it a publicity stunt, but Eddie knew better. Gregan dubbed it 'the greatest bonding session you could ever imagine'.

The squad flew 4000 kilometres from Sydney to Darwin, capital city of the Northern Territory. They arrived at the end of the dry season, during which average monthly rainfall is just 5 mm (0.2 inch). Average high temperature in September is 33°C (90.7°F) and average humidity 30 per cent. In the words of Wendell Sailor, 'it was hot as'.

The team had four sessions under fitness trainer Jason Webber in Darwin, the last without doubt the toughest they had undertaken all year. It started with skills and defence work followed by a forty-minute fitness session that included a game of 'Hammer', a form of touch football played at top speed without breaks. This was followed by a series of short sprints between halfway and 10-metre lines, hitting the ground and jumping up at the end and start of each run. The session ended with six 50-metre sprints. It was a gruelling routine that the players had become accustomed to in the friendly conditions of Coffs Harbour and Sydney. In the draining heat and humidity of Darwin they found it excruciating. The medical staff kept a close check, weighing the players each morning to check for undue weight loss and monitoring vital signs to avoid dehydration. Several became ill and threw up during training but pushed on. The training sessions under the most extreme conditions the players had ever encountered showed them just what their bodies were capable of enduring, but it was the final night of the camp that was, in the words of George Gregan, 'Eddie's masterstroke'.

The afternoon after Webber's horror session, the players headed to a remote stretch of wilderness near Mount Borradaile in northwest Arnhem Land, adjacent to Kakadu National Park. Considered sacred ground by the traditional owners, it was only through contacts of backs coach Glen Ella that they were allowed access.

On arrival they were paired off and assigned two-man tents, then shown some of the natural wonders of the area by members of the local indigenous community. Some fished for barramundi in a nearby billabong, others took a boat trip as crocodiles eyed them from the river bank. Gregan was part of a group that was taken to view Aboriginal rock paintings said to be between 30,000 and 40,000 years old.

That night they sat around a campfire and were entertained with traditional dances. The players were informed that one of the dancers had never performed in front of 'outsiders' before. That he had chosen to dance for them was considered a special mark of respect for the team. The dancers painted Gregan's face and gave him two ceremonial sticks for luck. The dancers then left the Wallabies by the fire. One by one the players and management got up and spoke from the heart about what it meant to them to be representing their country in the World Cup. Later, the traditional owners returned, painted the faces of the rest of the players and presented them with an ochre painting of a wallaby on a piece of ironbark. The team carried it with them throughout the tournament.

The next day, when the Wallabies headed back to Coffs Harbour to prepare for their opening match against Argentina, they felt closer, stronger and more confident than they ever had before.

As Wendell Sailor puts it, 'Mentally Eddie took us places we'd never been. We worked so hard but we also got in touch with our culture. We learned what Australia is all about.'

7

THE CLIVE AND EDDIE SHOW

When Clive Woodward arrived in Perth for the start of the 2003 World Cup he might as well have had a target on his back.

With the tournament being held in Australia, the local media was looking for a villain, and Woodward fitted the bill to perfection. Not only that, he knew his role and was prepared to play it to the full.

Woodward and Australia had a long history. In his twenty-one-Test career the Leicester centre played just once against the Wallabies – in England's 15-11 win at Twickenham in 1982, best remembered for the half-time appearance of streaker Erica Roe – but it was nothing that happened on the field that cemented the public's perception of him as the archetypal haughty Englishman looking down his nose at the colonials (or as Australians would put it, 'a stuck-up Pom'). It was what he said and did off it.

In 1986, two years after the end of his Test career, Woodward accepted a job transfer to Sydney with his employers Rank Xerox and joined the Manly rugby club. Delighted to have an England international boosting their ranks, the Manly board pulled out all stops to make Woodward and his bride-to-be Jayne comfortable. Charged with finding the couple somewhere suitable to live, they called on local real estate agent and club stalwart Bernie Bergelin.

Bergelin, who died in 2011 at the age of sixty-five after battling melanoma, was Manly rugby royalty. A front-rower, he played 214 games for the club, including a record 122 as captain. But as much as being a robust and talented player, Bergelin was a true rugby character who enjoyed a beer and a song and had no time for airs and graces.

During the 2003 World Cup when local reporters were calling former Manly team-mates of Woodward in the hope of digging up spice on the England coach, they were told, 'Get on to Bernie. He's got a story you won't believe.'

Sure enough, Bergelin's anecdote earned widespread coverage in newspapers around the country. The way he told it, the club had asked him to find Woodward something special; a home that delivered all the many spectacular features that one of the city's most popular beachside suburbs had to offer. After an intensive search Bergelin found just the place, a modern apartment on the headland between Manly Surf Club and the exclusive beach known as Fairy Bower. The club took a twelve-month lease, and Woodward moved in. Four days later he was at Bergelin's office.

'He told me he had to move out because the sound of the waves was keeping him awake. I thought he was joking. I had people ringing me every day trying to find a place with half the views that unit had. These days it would be worth millions, and he didn't want to live there because of the sound of the waves. Unbelievable.'

Woodward was talked into giving the unit a second chance and eventually grew used to the sound of the sea below his balcony. He and Jayne enjoyed a four-year stay in Manly, but the story of 'the Pom being kept awake by the waves' became part of club legend and was grist for the anti-England World Cup mill.

For as long as he could remember Woodward had dreamed of being involved in a World Cup – but not the rugby variety. As a child his major passion in life was football, and his sporting heroes the England players who had beaten West Germany in the World Cup final at Wembley in 1966. The euphoria he felt as a ten-year-old when England won their first and only major trophy would drive and inspire him for the rest of his life, he explained in his 2004 autobiography *Winning!*.

'When the final whistle went England had won 4-2, but it was more than that. That team achieved something that was so perfect, so powerful, that it inspired a nation. It certainly grabbed me. I was hooked. My entire sporting life since then has been a quest to understand and achieve that same ultimate level, that same incredible feeling of success, although it was some time before I realized it.'

Woodward was a promising junior football player, dedicated to practice and improvement, at the expense of his studies. It was a situation that did not please his father, Squadron Leader Ronald Woodward, a Royal Air Force pilot instructor. On the day that a scout from Everton Football Club had attended one of thirteen-year-old Clive's matches to assess his potential, Squadron Leader Woodward informed his son that at the beginning of the next term he would be attending HMS *Conway*, a naval boarding school in Wales. Woodward was devastated, not because he would be leaving his family and their home on an air base in North Yorkshire, but because HMS *Conway* was not a football school. Its major sport was rugby.

Woodward ran away from HMS *Conway* three times in the first few months before he accepted the inevitable and, reluctantly at first, began adapting to the strange fifteen-a-side code. In his first season, playing halfback, he was captain of his age group A team. In 1973 – his final year at HMS *Conway* – by now playing fly-half, he was chosen to trial for the Wales schoolboy team, only missing selection because he was deemed English. A year later Woodward, at eighteen, was playing in the top team for Harlequins and representing England Under-19.

His next move was to take him along a very similar road to that travelled by another son of a military man – Eddie Jones. Putting aside plans to study law, Woodward chose instead to attend Loughborough University. The university had recently absorbed Loughborough College and its physical education teaching course and was offering a three-year bachelor degree of sports science. Woodward was accepted as part of the 1975 intake.

The chance to study the latest advances in sports science and gain a teaching degree at the same time was of major interest to Woodward, but just as attractive was the opportunity to play rugby under Loughborough's inspirational and innovative coach Jim Greenwood. A Scotsman, Greenwood's philosophy on rugby could not have been more at odds with the safety-first, kick-and-chase, run-it-as-a-last-resort mindset of the England national set-up in which Woodward had found himself. Greenwood espoused the virtues of what he called 'Total Rugby' – what Eddie and the boys from Matraville High would come to know as 'Randwick Rugby'. Woodward soaked it all up like a sponge.

After graduation from Loughborough Woodward joined Leicester rugby club and began work at Rank Xerox. In 1980 he was selected on the bench for England's first match of the Five Nations championship, against Ireland. Midway through the second half he got his chance when centre Tony Bond was stretchered off with a leg injury. Woodward played the rest of the tournament, which saw England win their first Grand Slam for twenty-three years. At the end of the season he heard his name read out in the British Lions side to tour South

Africa. It was the start of a very respectable but not totally fulfilling international career for Woodward, who grew increasingly frustrated at the stodgy attitudes of England's coaches and administrators. He became known as a player who could either win a Test match, as in his man-of-the-match performance in the final match of the 1980 Grand Slam, against Scotland, or lose one, as he did by giving away a penalty against Wales in the opening game the following year.

'At times in my international career I could be effective, but then in the very next game I would be disastrously vacant and haphazard. I so wanted to play a more exciting game of rugby that I was desperate to get the ball to make something happen. Unfortunately, the England coaches, all of whom worked as volunteers on a part-time basis, couldn't provide a competitive enough environment to keep me interested. The England set-up was more about maintaining the status quo than anything else. The England players fell right into the routine, playing safe, no-risk rugby so they could keep their spots in the selectors' minds.

'There was no motivation to change anything. Tickets for the international matches at Twickenham were sold out for every game, seemingly regardless of whether England won or lost. The organization was well funded, the RFU being the only sporting body to own its home stadium outright. There was no need to change. This was a different era for rugby union. There was no World Cup to be won, no global rankings.'

When Woodward returned to the UK after his four years in Sydney – two seasons playing with Manly while working with Xerox and two years establishing the Australian arm of an international finance and leasing operation – he thought his rugby days were behind him. Now married to Jayne and with two children, he wanted to concentrate on family and earning a living. Buying a home twenty minutes out of

Henley, the town best known for its annual rowing regatta, in April 1990, he started his own office equipment leasing company. By chance, an old team-mate from Loughborough was coaching the local second-division rugby side and asked Woodward if he might come along and have a word to the players one night at training. Bitten again by the rugby bug, by the next season Woodward was head coach. Over the next four years Woodward completely turned the club around from a semi-social outfit to League contenders, and then winners. He brought in new levels of professionalism, improved basic skills, served tea in the dressing room instead of alcohol and even engaged an aerobics instructor for weekly fitness sessions. Most of all, he preached the gospel of Jim Greenwood, banned kicking and encouraged his players to run the ball and have fun. In four seasons Henley were promoted three times, making it to the National Leagues in 1994.

The following year Woodward took over at London Irish, a club with a long, proud history that had just been relegated to the second division and was without a coach following the resignation of former All Black hooker Hika Reid. Within two seasons, based on the same formula of innovation and enjoyment that he successfully instigated at Henley, Woodward orchestrated the club's return to the top division. Even so, a month into the next season, having upset influential members and committee-men with his forward-thinking ideas and abrasive personality, he was out. A call soon came from Bath, and he accepted a role as assistant to club coach Andy Robinson, with whom he had worked part-time at England Under-21s while still with London Irish over the previous two seasons. That too was short-lived. In September 1997, Woodward was appointed England's first-ever full-time professional coach.

At his initial meeting with his new squad Woodward laid it all on the line and mentioned the unmentionable: that his ultimate objective was to coach the first England team to win the World Cup.

'My aim is to develop a team capable of winning the World Cup in 1999,' he declared. 'To do this we have to transform the way we play. It will be high-risk by definition, and we may have to take some time to convince critics who have got used to the subdued style that's been the hallmark of England rugby for decades. There is a reason the Southern Hemisphere sides have dominated world rugby up until now. When I played for England we would be told at almost every coaching session what the All Blacks or Wallabies or Springboks were doing and that we had to copy it. We were comfortable following others and nobody ever seemed to think we should aspire to be better than the Southern Hemisphere teams. From now on our sole aim will be not to copy them, but to practise a game and a style of play that can beat them convincingly every time. We'll play, coach and manage rugby in a way that is so different to theirs that they will be copying us for a change. Until we achieve that, nothing else matters.'

The Woodward era began with promise. In his first Test in charge England drew 15-15 with Rod Macqueen's Wallabies at Twickenham. Then followed an 8-25 loss to the All Blacks at Old Trafford and another loss, 11-29 to the Springboks at Twickenham. The final result of the year at the same venue raised the confidence of the England players and supporters: a 26-26 draw with the All Blacks.

The 1998 season started with a loss to France before England went through the rest of the Five Nations undefeated, including a 60-26 win over Wales, but it would be a result on the subsequent tour of Australia, New Zealand and South Africa that would be a black mark on Woodward's record and kick-start his rocky relationship with Wallaby supporters and administrators.

While Woodward would never back away from the criticism he copped in Australia over the years – and in fact use it to his advantage at times – on this occasion he was not to blame. When rugby turned professional after the 1995 World Cup, the RFU chose not to sign its players to contracts. Unlike its counterparts in Australia, New Zealand and South Africa, the English ruling body left it to the clubs to contract the players and would then 'borrow' their services when required. With the clubs paying large amounts to their players, and needing them to attract paying customers through the gates in order to stay in the black, they were at times understandably reluctant to release their big names for what they saw as meaningless Test matches and trips. The 1998 tour fell into that category, and Woodward saw his selected touring party decimated by the day as clubs declared their players exhausted, injured or simply not available.

The Australian Rugby Union was counting on a competitive Test match in Brisbane to lure a large crowd and fill its coffers leading into the 1999 World Cup season. When Woodward arrived in town with a team of no-names – twenty of the thirty-two-man squad having never played for England before – Australian officials and fans were appalled. ARU vice president Dick McGruther likened it to the infamous First World War military landing at the Dardenelles, in which Australian troops became cannon fodder due to the incompetence of British commanders.

'This is the greatest English sell-out since Gallipoli, but we'll welcome them to their fatal landing here. While we wish the English well, unfortunately for them Australians relish the opportunity to witness a Pommy thrashing, and we invite them all to come out and enjoy it.'

The English media responded by labelling McGruther 'the biggest Dick since Turpin'.

McGruther's distasteful outburst added some much-needed spice to the build-up, but unfortunately the inexperienced England players couldn't live up to it on the field and were thrashed 76-0.

ARU CEO John O'Neill said after the match, 'This is not what international rugby is about. It wasn't a contest. Those poor players, as determined and proud as they were, are not Test players.'

O'Neill was correct in what he said at the time, but his remarks would come back to bite him. Playing fly-half for England in that eleven-try embarrassment was a nineteen-year-old by the name of Jonny Wilkinson.

Wilkinson, who would have an enormous influence on the lives of both Woodward and Eddie, was one of very few people in the game as obsessed with winning as they were. At eight years of age, after watching New Zealand beat France in the final of the first-ever Rugby World Cup in 1987, he wrote down a list of ambitions: to play rugby for England, to be the kicker, to win the World Cup and to be the best player in the world. He then devoted his life to achieving them.

In the 2015 documentary *Building Jerusalem*, which traces England's journey to the 2003 World Cup, Wilkinson gave an insight into the childhood personality traits that drove him throughout his career.

'If I wasn't playing I'd be in my back garden kicking a ball against a wall. Left foot, right foot, left pass, right pass, could I make them as good as each other; competing against myself. In a game if I made a hit and got smashed to the floor it would only spur me on to go harder. I don't remember ever thinking that I had to escape the pain on the field. That part came very naturally. I struggled more with the mental anguish behind it; that pressure riding on the result, that lack of control. Losing or not getting things right came with a sense of gloom. Things would happen on the rugby field, and I would think about them for months, things that no one remembers but me. It was like, "No one remembers that moment on the field, no one cares. Why are you still upset about it?" The perfectionist angle was in everything. I had a major fall-out with my parents over how upset

I was getting nineteen out of twenty on a spelling test. I misspelt the word "gauge". I still remember it now.'

The humiliating loss against Australia in Brisbane had a profound effect on Wilkinson. He broke down on the phone to his father back home in Farnham, Surrey.

'There were floods of tears. I was saying, "I'm a waste of space. It's all a lie." He took it for a while and then he said, "All right, what are you going to do about it?"'

What Wilkinson did was go back to his club in Newcastle and, with the help of trainer Steve Black, totally rebuild himself from promising boy wonder into the ultimate professional. As Black said, 'He works at it twenty-three hours a day. I'm not sure what he does with the other hour.'

At the same time Woodward was orchestrating a similar transformation on the England team, as scrum-half Matt Dawson recalled.

'It all went totally extreme; best fitness and nutrition and gimmicks. If you were a half-decent salesman and you had something that was going to improve your ability to play rugby and you got in front of Clive, Clive would buy it.'

The best example of this was ProZone, a video program that allowed analysts to view the entire field at once and freeze-frame and enlarge to decipher opposition defensive patterns and attacking moves. It was used by Premier League football clubs. Woodward convinced the RFU to invest a large sum in having it adapted to rugby and made available to him and his staff from the start of the 2000 season. Woodward also adopted the suggestion of a business colleague and had the players change into clean jerseys at half-time in order to reinforce the mental concept that they were starting afresh in the second half. It worked and is now standard practice with most international sides. He took the team on a training camp with the Royal Marines and employed the services of South African vision expert Dr Sherylle Calder. Sceptical at first, the players soon came to appreciate the improvement Dr Calder's techniques made to their hand–eye coordination. She is now part of Eddie's staff with the England team.

There was no doubt Woodward was making progress, but it was by no means all smooth sailing. His close ally Lawrence Dallaglio was stripped of the captaincy after being tricked into admitting to drug use in a *News of the World* sting, and the players went on a twenty-four-hour strike over bonus payments and image rights.

Even so, Woodward embarked on the 1999 World Cup being held in England, Wales and France with cautious optimism. The English opened the tournament with a strong 67-7 win over Italy before their crunch match against the All Blacks. Woodward concedes he made a critical mistake in playing Wilkinson at fly-half against the Kiwis ahead of the more experienced Paul Grayson. New Zealand won 30-16. 'I believe that result cost us the World Cup,' Woodward said.

'Instead of England, the All Blacks were on the fast track to the knock-out stages while we were lumbered with an extra game before the quarter-final and a trip to Paris to meet the waiting South Africans.'

England won their next two matches against Tonga and Fiji, but at a cost, with a number of key players suffering serious injuries. With only three days' preparation and Woodward again making a mistake with Wilkinson – this time leaving him out of the side altogether in order to bring Grayson in at number ten – South Africa proved too strong, fly-half Jannie de Beer kicking five second-half drop-goals in the Springboks' 44-21 win.

Woodward and his players returned home to face a barrage of criticism while the two teams that had ended England's World Cup hopes had their own dreams shattered. Australia beat South Africa and the French upset New Zealand to book places in the final in Cardiff, Rod Macqueen's Wallabies prevailing 35-12.

For Woodward it was decision time. The English media had jumped on a pre-tournament comment in which he said, 'All coaches will be judged on their results at the World Cup.' Based on that criterion, commentators said, he had no future in the job. England had failed, so he should either resign or be sacked by the RFU. Following weeks of speculation the RFU decided to offer an extension to his contract, which expired at the end of the 2000 season, and after much soul-searching he agreed to stay.

At his first meeting with the players after the World Cup, held at their new training centre at Pennyhill Park in Bagshot, Surrey, half an hour's drive southwest of Twickenham, he outlined a four-year plan.

'In Australia in 2003 I want us to arrive as favourites, ranked number one in the world, with a full squad of players who are in peak physical condition and have had the best preparation of any team in the tournament. That will be our focus from now on.'

As anyone involved in elite sport knows only too well, talk is cheap. Woodward may have told his players where he intended the England team to be by the time they arrived in Australia, and the players might have been true believers, but the rest of the rugby world took a little more convincing. They had heard it all before and, despite England making it to the 1991 final, the World Cup remained a Southern Hemisphere monopoly won twice by Australia and once each by New Zealand and South Africa. As Woodward started his preparations there was little reason to think the status quo would change in 2003, especially with the tournament being played on the Wallabies' home turf. But as preparations gained momentum there were those in Australia who started to take notice of what was happening on the other side of the world. A year out from the opening ceremony the ARU held functions in the cities where the matches would be played. After the Brisbane event guests were enjoying a drink at the bar and discussing the chances of the three favourites, Australia, New Zealand and South Africa. No other team seemed worthy of mention. Tim Horan, the former Wallaby centre who had been player of the tournament at the previous World Cup, had just returned to his home town after a playing stint with Saracens.

'I wouldn't rule out England,' he said. 'They're a lot stronger than you think.'

No one laughed, but they weren't overly concerned either. Not yet anyway.

By the time Woodward and his men arrived at Perth airport in October 2003 to begin their World Cup campaign no one in the Southern Hemisphere had to be told that England were the team to beat. Starting the 2002–03 season with three wins at Twickenham over the All Blacks 31-28, Wallabies 32-31 and South Africa 53-3 – the biggest losing margin in Springbok history – they then won the Six Nations Grand Slam. They followed their unbeaten home season with an equally successful short tour of New Zealand and Australia, beating the All Blacks 15-13 in Wellington and the Wallabies 25-14 under the closed roof at Melbourne's Telstra Dome.

England were now number one in the world, just like Woodward had predicted, but the Melbourne Test was notable for something else: the escalation of the media war between Clive Woodward and Eddie Jones.

The first signs of the growing animosity between the two coaches had broken out on the eve of the 2001 Australia–England match at Twickenham – the first time they had faced each other as national coaches. New Zealand-born rugby league convert Henry Paul was eligible for England selection due to his English grandfather. Woodward had brought Paul straight into his twenty-six-man squad after just eighty minutes of rugby union experience with new club Gloucester. Eddie took aim and fired.

'Our guys have to earn a Wallaby jumper,' he said. 'England obviously have a different selection policy.'

Given that Australia had recently signed their own rugby league recruits, Woodward hit straight back.

'Does Eddie have the balls to utilize his own cross-code players Mat Rogers and Wendell Sailor with immediate effect?'

As it turned out, neither coach gambled on playing their former league stars in the match, won 21-15 by England, but the battle lines were set for what would be a tetchy relationship between the two.

The next time they met was twelve months later on Australia's 2002 spring tour of Europe. The week before the Wallaby Test England had narrowly beaten the All Blacks, but Woodward was upset that South African referee Jonathan Kaplan had ignored what he believed was illegal obstruction in two of the All Blacks' tries. Worried that New Zealand referee Paul Honiss would take a lenient 'Southern Hemisphere' view of similar tactics by the Wallabies – or as he called it 'the old Eddie Jones trick of having decoy runners in front of the ball carrier' – he took the unprecedented move of calling a media conference to air his concerns. It was there, for the first time, that Woodward unveiled the ProZone system that he had been using for two years, showing the journalists video footage and freeze-frame graphics of the two tries scored by Jonah Lomu in England's win.

'In the Zurich Premiership our guys are pinged for running these lines. On Saturday, the opposition were not. Either such ploys are outlawed or we've got to do the same thing ourselves. It's like football having no offside in the Premier League and then deciding to have it in the World Cup. The Wallabies will do exactly the same thing on Saturday. I don't want to be in a position when I whinge after we've lost. That's why I'm airing it all now.'

Woodward added, 'There's not a ref that I've shown these video clips to that hasn't said that the tries shouldn't have been allowed,' but declined to identify who those referees were.

When Eddie was asked before the Test if he had managed to speak to referee Paul Honiss about how he intended to officiate the match, he said he had not.

'No,' he said. 'Apparently he's still looking at Clive's videos.'

Given the preliminary sparring, it was inevitable that the main event would not be far away, and it began in earnest when England arrived in Melbourne in June 2003.

In the lead-up to the game Eddie likened Woodward's side to an English Premier League football team, kicking the ball forward and then hoping to score via the boot. He also called on Scottish referee David McHugh to pay close attention to the tackle area, hinting that England were masters at slowing down the play. There was much discussion on whether the retractable roof should be left open or closed. Eddie preferred open to the elements, but Woodward, saying he trusted the abilities of his ball-players, wanted it closed to ensure they would not be affected by weather. The Australian media construed this not as a desire to promote an open, high-pace game, but instead to provide benign conditions for England's kicking machine, Jonny Wilkinson.

In the three matches England had played against New Zealand and Australia in the previous twelve months – two wins against the All

Blacks and one against the Wallabies – they had scored seventy-three points, of which thirty-nine came from Wilkinson with one try, thirteen penalties, four goals and two dropped goals. In the Wellington match a week before the Melbourne game he had scored all of England's fifteen points with four penalties and a drop-goal, and his six-penalty-goal haul in the one-point win over the Wallabies at Twickenham in November was still fresh in the minds of the Australian media and public. To them, the implication was obvious: England were a one-trick pony. With a massive and experienced – but unimaginative – pack, they would simply lumber around the field with one aim in mind: get close enough to the posts for Wilkinson to kick points. Throughout the week leading up to the Melbourne Test the local press onslaught was relentless, labelling the England pack 'Dad's Army' and calling Woodward's perceived tactics negative and boring.

After England won the match 25-14, with Wilkinson contributing ten points from two penalties and two goals, the media was ready to pounce, but so was Woodward. Setting the scene for what was to come during the World Cup, he was straight on the front foot from the first question about the quality of the England win.

'I must be missing something here,' he said. 'I thought sport was all about winning. Everything seems to have changed in Australia; certainly it seems to have with respect to rugby union since I lived here. I thought you Aussies were all about winning, and not about marks out of ten for performance. Eddie Jones and the Wallabies have been trying to wind us up all week about what an old, tired, slow and boring team we are. Well that's all bullshit. For this match you guys all asked us both whether we want to play with the roof open or closed. I wanted the roof shut so that the game could be played in perfect conditions, giving the best chance of a great running game. Eddie Jones wanted it open to introduce the uncertainty of weather conditions – and you call us boring?'

Woodward was full of praise for the performance of David McHugh, 'considering the amount of hassle and pressure he's been under all week', and critical of Eddie for trying to influence the referee.

'I don't believe in coaches putting pressure on referees that's obviously totally premeditated. I don't think it's my job or anyone else's to put pressure on the referee through the media. It's not good for the sport, it's not good for the game but if he keeps doing it, I'm very pleased we've won four out of four against him. We'll wait until October for the next media campaign orchestrated by him. We're used to it by now and we thrive on it.'

So much so that Woodward claimed Eddie's comments about his team's 'kick-and-hope' tactics had provided the main motivation for their win – England's first-ever on Australian soil.

'I was very confident we could win this game – especially with all the ballyhoo in the press all week. It didn't need any team talk from me. Fortunately Eddie did our team talk for us. It was a highly motivated team and we were very confident we could win.'

Eddie, as so often the case throughout his career, expressed surprise that anything he said could have caused offence.

'When he wins, Clive tends to be very exuberant in his comments,' he told the *Daily Telegraph*. 'Last week we promoted the game. I hardly see that as being a bad role model. We spoke about the match, we spoke about England and we spoke about the need for the laws to be reinforced. I thought our commentary was very fair and complimentary of England. So if they want to use that for a team talk, well, I just can't understand it.'

The next day the *Australian* likened Woodward to Douglas Jardine, the England cricket captain who was architect of the notorious Bodyline tactic in the Ashes series of 1932–33. Designed to neutralize Australia's champion batsman Don Bradman with dangerous short-pitched bowling, it earned Jardine the title 'the most unpopular Englishman ever to visit these shores'. Woodward was delighted.

'If I'd known how much of a stir it would cause, I would have done it sooner.'

8

ALL OR NOTHING

The 2003 Rugby World Cup began on 10 October, with the Wallabies taking on Argentina at Sydney's Telstra Stadium. Australia won 24-8, with Wendell Sailor scoring the first try of the tournament, but it was hardly a convincing performance from the reigning champions in front of a crowd of 81,000. Two nights later, on the other side of the country, it was England's turn. Woodward and his men had arrived in the Australian football stronghold of Perth ten days before their first match, a 'soft' opener against Georgia. They won 84-6, but at a cost, with injuries to Richard Hill and Matt Dawson. The English then had six days to prepare for their second – and arguably most important – match of the tournament, against South Africa, but before they could get on the field Woodward had another fight on his hands – and he fired the first shot.

After Australia's win over Argentina, Woodward told reporters that the Wallabies' second try to Joe Roff should not have been allowed because Matt Burke had obstructed a defender. Much as he might have wanted to hit straight back, Eddie stayed on the sidelines – for a short while at least – letting 1999 World Cup-winning Wallaby captain John Eales mount the first wave of counter-attack. Dismissing Woodward's criticism of the Australian backs in a newspaper interview, Eales claimed that it was in fact the England forwards who were breaking the rules.

'England's mauling amounts to obstruction because Neil Back is being shepherded at the back of it without always being attached. It is the forward equivalent of a decoy play in the backline. The referee should give a penalty if he feels that Back is not bound to the maul. As long as he is bound there is no problem, but that is not always the case.'

Eales' comments were immediately jumped on by England's major rivals, with Springbok coach Rudi Straeuli calling on referee Peter Marshall to pay close attention to England's maul play in their upcoming match and France's forwards coach Jacques Brunel taking the opportunity to focus on the English lineout.

'They only pretend to contest the ball. They put their arms around the opponent's jumper while he is coming down to stop him from releasing. At the same time another of their players goes through and round the lineout with his arms in the air as if to say, "Sorry, ref, mistake," but he is actually slowing down their opposition's support players and should be blown up.'

Of course, Eddie couldn't keep out of the fray.

'There is validity in what Eales is saying. If you have a situation where there is no contest for possession it has to be looked at very carefully by referees. If the maul is refereed to the letter of the law, then what England are doing is illegal because the players with the ball must be connected to the defending team. This has nothing to do with any supposed war of words with Clive Woodward. The critique is not coming from our side. I am just giving a commentary.'

Woodward had learned a hard lesson early in the tournament. Anything he said critical of the Wallabies would come back at him, two, three, four times harder. From then on he did his best to bite his tongue and concentrate on his own team, not Eddie's. Besides, he had more important things to worry about than paper-talk. England were about to play the game that could make or break their entire World Cup campaign.

England had spanked the Springboks by a record score at Twickenham the previous season, but not too many pundits were taking much notice of that. It was a tour match, and coaches often experimented with their teams in the lead-up to the World Cup, they said. In Australian parlance, this next game would be 'fair dinkum' and would undoubtedly decide which of the two teams would finish at the top of Pool C and avoid playing the All Blacks in the quarter-finals. For rugby followers and the media it would also give the strongest hint of how Woodward intended to play the tournament. What the men in white showed in their one-try-to-nil 25-6 win might have thrilled Woodward and England supporters, but it was also the subject of the most memorable headline of the World Cup.

Recently appointed sports editor of the *Australian* newspaper was Neil Breen, a young, enthusiastic Queenslander who had been brought to Sydney with the brief of brightening up the staid national broadsheet. A former first-grade rugby player, he saw the World Cup as a perfect opportunity to win over new readers and redefine his newspaper's reputation at the same time. On the night of the England–Springboks game he was having dinner at an inner-city restaurant with his wife and some friends.

'There was a pub next door showing the game from Perth. I kept getting up from the table and running in there to see the score, and every time I did, Jonny Wilkinson was kicking a goal. They won, but they only scored one try, and I didn't see that. All I saw was Wilkinson kicking points. I thought, "That's how they're going to do it. They're going to play ten-man rugby, draw the penalty, and Wilkinson is going to kick goals." The next day I went into work and got a picture of Jonny Wilkinson lining up a goal. I drew it into the page and had about ten goes at coming up with a headline.

'The Sydney *Daily Telegraph* and the *Herald Sun* in Melbourne always had these big, sexy back-page headlines, so that's what we were up against.

'My chief sports sub, Darren Hadland, has come in and asked me what we were going with on the back, and I showed him the picture and I said, "Jonny is all they've got. They're going to get into range, draw the penalty, and Jonny will kick it. They're going to win the World Cup, but it's going to be boring."'

'We went back and forth trying to come up with the line. It was Jonny this, Jonny that . . . "Can't You Do Anything Else?" Finally I've written down "He's All You've Got". I've said to Darren, "I've got it. I win." Ten minutes later he comes back with "Is That All You've Got?"

'I said, "That's it!" We went with it, and all hell broke loose. The next morning they had me on *The Today Show*, and I was interviewed on the BBC and on BSkyB in England. It took on a life of its own. When they won, the *Daily Mirror* in England had a front-page picture of Martin Johnson holding up the trophy with a tear-out of our back page with an arrow pointing to the cup and the headline "Yes, That's All We've Got".

'Woodward, Johnson, they all mentioned it in their biographies. Clive was still talking about it during the 2015 World Cup. It wasn't supposed to be nasty. It was just our way of saying, you're the favourites, you think you're going to win and you might, but we're not going to make it easy for you.'

The headline might have hit a raw nerve with Woodward, but in truth he was not concerned. Why should he be? His team had just beaten their main rival at pool level. If anyone had cause for concern, it was Eddie.

The media coverage of the Wallabies' form had been negative from the first match. The team might be winning, racking up huge scores against Cup minnows Romania and Namibia, but they never looked totally in synch. There was also criticism of Eddie's selections, especially in the backline. Australia had gone into the tournament with three highly regarded fullbacks: Matt Burke, who scored twenty-five points in the 1999 World Cup final win over France; Queensland's exciting Chris Latham, and the Brumbies' versatile Joe Roff, who had played on the wing in the 1999 final. All were reliable, proven Test performers, but Eddie preferred to give the number fifteen jersey to rugby league convert Mat Rogers, a talented utility player without the experience, or dependable kicking game, of the others. He also seemed unsure of what to do with another former league international, winger Lote Tuqiri, using him only once in the pool matches – as a flanker off the bench against Romania – before doing a total turn-around and starting him on the left wing for the knock-out stage. It all added up to an impression of a coach making it up on the fly, and the disjointed displays of the team did nothing to instil confidence that Australia would come anywhere close to defending the trophy.

Some of the press coverage was brutal, especially when Ireland came within a missed drop-goal of beating the Wallabies in the final pool match. The 17-16 win saw Australia taking on Scotland in a quarter-final at Suncorp Stadium in Brisbane on 8 November, with England facing Wales at the same venue the next day.

Once again the Wallabies won without looking overly impressive. The general feeling amongst media and fans was that the uninspiring 33-16 win had achieved little more than prolong the inevitable, with their next match a semi-final against the seemingly invincible All Blacks in Sydney.

But if Australia seemed out of sorts against Scotland, so did England against Wales. In fact, with Wales ahead 10-3 soon after half-time and playing by far the most enterprising rugby, it appeared that England could well be on the next plane home. Instead, despite being outscored three tries to one, England prevailed 28-17 and progressed to the semi-final against France, thanks once more to the boot of Wilkinson, who contributed twenty-three points through six penalties, a goal and a drop-goal. Australia headed back to Team Wallaby at Coffs Harbour to prepare for the All Blacks, while Woodward led his troops to a base where he felt right at home: Manly.

Woodward had requested that the team – and their families who had joined them a week earlier – stay at the plush Manly Pacific Hotel, where he and Jayne had been put up when they first moved to Sydney. The beachside suburb was an environment that he knew well, and where he could gather his thoughts after the scare against Wales and a heated post-match clash with French journalists, who were critical of England's performance against Wales and especially the form of Wilkinson.

'There was one from *L'Equipe* newspaper in particular who really went to town on it,' Woodward said. 'He kept asking questions that underlined what he saw as England's inability to perform when it mattered. It wasn't so much the questions as much as his tone. He picked on Jonny Wilkinson several times as highly underperforming.'

Woodward reacted with a sarcastic counter-attack that could have come straight out the Eddie Jones media play-book.

'Absolutely,' he said, agreeing with the journalist in fake praise of France. 'They are the standout team and must be favourite to win. If you want to bet against England beating France, fine. Go ahead.'

It is unknown if the French reporter took Woodward's advice and had a few francs on 'Les Bleus', but a lot of other people did. Not only had England struggled in the quarter-final, they had also appeared rattled in the final pool match against Samoa, where they trailed at half-time and a coaching mix-up saw sixteen players on the field for thirty-two seconds, resulting in a £10,000 fine. Meanwhile the French had breezed through all their pool matches and easily accounted for Ireland 43-21 in the quarters. On that basis, and the less than convincing form of the Wallabies, many were predicting a repeat of 1987 with a France–New Zealand final.

When Eddie brought the Wallabies down to Sydney early in the week before the All Blacks clash he faced his own trial by media. Press coverage of the Australians throughout the tournament had swung between withering and dismissive: Eddie's selections were wrong; Gregan was a shadow of his former self, the team played like strangers who had met for the first time in the dressing room before kick-off – and it wasn't just journalists who were saying it. Former Wallabies were also vocal in their dissatisfaction at the way things were going.

At a media conference on the Thursday before the game, after Eddie had announced his team, an Australian reporter asked straight out, 'Eddie, do you really believe you can win the World Cup with this side?'

'With this side?' he answered. 'Yes, I do.'

There weren't too many in the room who believed him. As Eddie himself had said a few minutes earlier, 'A lot of people didn't think we'd even get this far.'

The media then jumped on that remark too, but he was right. Even the Wallabies' most loyal supporters looked at the All Black clash with hope rather than confidence. The last time the two teams had met at Telstra Stadium New Zealand had inflicted an embarrassing 50-21 thrashing, and nothing Australia had shown in the World Cup so far hinted that the result would be reversed in the semi-final.

Those inside the Wallabies inner circle knew differently. After Eddie's initial anger following the one-sided loss in July he had gone through the tapes and come to the conclusion that the All Blacks were beatable. Australia had managed to secure the majority of possession in that match but had handed it back to the Kiwis through unforced errors. They had given the All Blacks the opportunity to counter-attack, and their dangerous back three of fullback Mils Muliaina and wingers Joe Rokocoko and Doug Howlett had taken full advantage, Rokocoko scoring three tries and Howlett one. The Aussies had also played without confidence, as if cowed by the New Zealanders' reputation even before the kick-off. Eddie and his assistant coaches had worked on all those areas in the lead-up to the return match in Auckland three weeks later, and the Wallabies came within a disallowed try of squaring the series and retaining the Bledisloe Cup. The seed had been sown. Eddie put a circle in his diary around the date 15 November 2003. All going to plan, that was the night on which he would pull off the greatest victory of his career: the night his Wallabies would beat the mighty All Blacks.

Eddie wasn't concerned about the criticism of the team's earlier matches, or even about their form. The Wallabies' World Cup campaign would later be compared to a 'Melbourne Cup preparation', in which trainers bring their horses along slowly in order to peak precisely on the day of Australia's greatest race. Nothing was left to chance. The players might have been preparing for a game against

Namibia or Romania, but they were being drilled at training about the best way to starve Rokocoko of possession, or how to take advantage of what they believed was a weakness in the Kiwi lineout. Most of all though, they worked on attitude.

At a staff meeting at Coffs Harbour in the week before the game Eddie asked if everything that could be done was being done.

'Has anyone got any suggestions?' he asked.

Anthony 'AJ' George, head of the media unit, spoke up.

'I'd like to get Vossy in,' he said.

Michael Voss was one of the most respected Australian Football players of all time. The captain of the Brisbane Lions team that a month earlier had won its third consecutive AFL grand final, he was a commanding figure on and off the field whom AJ had got to know well when working as a cameraman for Channel 7 in Brisbane.

'Do it,' said Eddie.

Voss addressed the team at Coffs Harbour a few days before they headed to Sydney. He told them not to listen to the criticism they had been receiving through the media.

'I'm not fat, but if someone kept telling me I was, week after week, I'd start believing it.'

He then provided them with the perfect first-hand scenario for the task they were about to face. At that time the Brisbane Lions were recognized as arguably the greatest AFL team of the modern era, but it wasn't always the case. They entered their first grand final in 2001 as outsiders against reigning premiers Essendon who, like the All Blacks, many believed were unbeatable. In his biography George Gregan recalled Voss' talk making a firm impression on all the Wallabies.

'The Essendon side, he told us, always charged out really hard, as if they were trying to blow teams away, All Blacks-like, to establish the mood of the match and set up an early unassailable advantage. Brisbane's response was to make sure they were as fit and well-prepared as they could be, and to work really hard early, on the basis that if they could match them, then they would forge clear at the end. The key was for everyone to do their job from the opening bounce. The idea was not to win the game then, but not lose it. When they followed through with this they suddenly discovered that this great Essendon team was human after all. The Lions trailed at three-quarter time but overwhelmed their much-vaunted opponent in the final term to win by twenty-six points. Michael underlined the fact that, in the end, they didn't have to do anything extraordinary to win the premiership. No one had to do anything more than fulfil their role within the team. The key was doing your job as well as you possibly could all the time. To hear what is essentially a simple message put so eloquently by someone who had been so successful is empowering. There is a lot to be said for surrounding yourself with winners.'

As the game approached the confidence of Eddie and his coaching staff grew. On the night that the team arrived in Sydney, the Ella brothers were honoured with a testimonial dinner at the Four Seasons Hotel. Eddie and his attack coach Glen Ella broke camp to attend. Gary Ella, who was coaching at Leicester, flew back from England especially for the function. He says he couldn't believe the demeanour of Eddie and Glen.

'They were super relaxed and confident. I was pretty surprised. They were playing the All Blacks in a couple of nights' time and they were just so certain that they were going to win. They didn't have any doubts about it.'

It was the same with the players. Elton Flatley recalls an unusual sensation coming over him as he ran onto the field with his team-mates on the night.

'I remember running out and thinking, "I don't think we can lose this." It was a weird feeling, especially since they'd smacked us on the same field a few months before, but everything we'd done in camp had been planned so that we'd peak in the last week or two of the tournament, and I felt like that's what was happening. I don't think I'd ever felt like that before in a Test match, but this time it just felt like everything was going to go the way we'd planned.'

One thing that wasn't planned was the Australians' response to the haka. The question of how to counter the All Blacks' traditional war challenge is one that has vexed their opponents for over a century. Should they stand close and eyeball the Kiwis, or stand back and appear nonchalant? Some teams have threatened to boycott it and remain in the sheds until it is over, others to turn their backs. No matter which option they chose, history would show it was rarely successful but on the night of 15 November 2003, the haka was finally overshadowed – and it had nothing to do with the players.

As soon as the haka had ended the Australian supporters amongst the sell-out crowd of 82,957 launched into a rousing, full-throated rendition of *Waltzing Matilda*. Seldom has an Australian sporting crowd voiced such passion. Rarely has an Australian rugby team started a match with such daring and precision.

For Eddie Jones, sitting up in the coach's box, it was like seeing a dream come to life.

In 2007 Eddie told a reporter about his early days playing alongside the Ellas and marvelling at the skill and joyful audacity with which they played the game.

'That's always been my dream,' he said. 'To go back to those days and to see the game played the way they played it.'

Asked if he had ever managed to achieve it, he answered, 'Just once.

'The first ninety seconds of the 2003 World Cup semi-final against New Zealand. It was perfect. We won that game right then. We moved the ball 40 metres and they were thinking, "What's happening?" If we'd dropped one pass then we probably would have lost the game, but we didn't. It wasn't classical rugby but it was courageous and inventive and it was rugby the way we wanted to play it.'

Those ninety seconds began with Carlos Spencer's kick-off taken by Lote Tuqiri, who powered forward a few metres down the left touchline before pushing the ball back to Elton Flatley at the back of the ruck. Flatley passed to Stephen Larkham, standing well behind his 22-metre line. The obvious move was for Larkham to kick for touch, but there was nothing obvious about the Australians' play. Larkham spun the ball out to scrum-half George Gregan standing in midfield, who sent a perfect cut-out pass that missed number eight David Lyons and hit flanker George Smith, who advanced just over the Australian 22. At the breakdown Gregan passed back to Larkham, who was again in the perfect position to kick for touch, but again he rejected the logical and went for the unexpected, running cross-field and sending a long pass to fullback Mat Rogers who took two defenders with him for a couple of metres before being pulled to ground. Gregan came in and handed off to Tuqiri on the short side. When Tuqiri was pulled to ground, Gregan cleared to Larkham, who passed to Flatley. If there was one sequence of play that summed up the Wallabies' performance, this was it. Flatley threw a long pass behind decoy runner Lyons that was picked up low at full stretch by lock Nathan Sharpe. It was the type of high-risk play that would be a fifty-fifty proposition at training, let alone in the pressure-cooker of a World Cup semi-final against the All Blacks, but it worked with surgical precision. Sharpe took the spinning ball cleanly with two black-gloved hands as if he was a fleet-footed fly-half, rather than a 2-metre-tall, 115-kilo forward. As Sharpe was pulled down, Wendell Sailor charged in and advanced the play another metre. From the ensuing ruck Gregan's infield pass went astray, but tight-head prop Ben Darwin ran onto the bouncing ball and charged into the Kiwi defence. Gregan then passed to Larkham, who feinted to kick but instead passed inside to centre Stirling Mortlock, who was brought down by Ali Williams and Richie McCaw. Referee Chris White blew his whistle and penalized McCaw for hands in the ruck as the crowd – and the All Blacks – took a breath, stunned by what they had just witnessed.

In that minute and a half the ball had gone through Australian hands twenty times over nine phases. Other than Gregan's pass, which was picked up on the bounce by Darwin, not once had it gone to ground as it went from one side of the field to the other four times. Due to typically solid Kiwi defence the Wallabies had not made a great deal of ground, but they had achieved something ultimately more important. They had shown intent and execution. They had sowed the seeds of doubt in the All Blacks' minds. It was, as Eddie Jones said, perfect.

The New Zealanders would not get their hands on the ball until six and a half minutes into the game, when Mils Muliaina fielded a Mat Rogers clearing kick. Even so, they had the first two chances to score with Joe Rokocoko and Muliaina denied by the former league players Sailor and Tuqiri. The All Blacks had a third opportunity as the clock approached the nine-minute mark. From a Kiwi lineout win 10 metres out from the Australian line McCaw set up the ruck, and scrum-half Justin Marshall fed Spencer, who threw a long pass out to his centre, Aaron Mauger. If the pass had hit its target Mauger had Rokocoko outside him with the line beckoning. Instead it was

Wallaby centre Stirling Mortlock who took the intercept at full tilt and ran 90 metres to score under the posts. With Flatley converting, the score was only 7-0, but in truth the All Blacks were shot. For the fourth time since winning the first World Cup in 1987 the pressure of being favourites, and the enormous expectations of the New Zealand public, proved too great.

Australia went in at half-time 13-7 and Eddie, as Stephen Larkham recalled in his *World Cup Diary*, was calm and matter-of-fact.

'During the break Eddie didn't seem overly excited about our lead. It was as businesslike as always. He ran through the main points in the game plan: keep the ball in hand as much as possible, work to get to the breakdowns, come up in defence quickly.

'The game was well into the second half before I really felt we had it won. Until then, things had been pretty tense. About halfway through the second half, after we began making some big hits in defence – big enough to drive the All Blacks backwards – it became apparent that they had nothing left to offer. They were trying one-out runners off the ruck and other poor attacking options, which signalled that their attack had gone to pieces. I saw their heads go down, and I knew then that we were on top. We had the momentum to go on and win.'

It was at the seventy-two-minute mark, when replacement New Zealand scrum-half Byron Kelleher gave away a penalty for hands in the ruck that George Gregan declared the last rites on yet another failed All Black campaign.

'Four more years, boys,' he taunted the shattered men in black. 'Four more years.'

The sound of the full-time hooter signalling a 22-10 win to Australia sparked a scene of emotion the likes of which Stephen Larkham thought he would never see.

'Immediately after the final whistle, a television camera picked up Eddie Jones and Glen Ella hugging one another with joy. I saw this on a replay a day or two later and could hardly believe it. Anyone who knows anything about Eddie and Glen would also know that this public display of happiness and affection was very uncharacteristic for both men. They normally keep their emotions to themselves. They are definitely not hugging types. Their hug showed, I think, how much our win meant to them.'

Eddie will always be remembered for orchestrating the greatest upset in Rugby World Cup history when Japan beat South Africa in 2015, but the Wallabies' 2003 semi-final win over New Zealand was his finest hour. It was also the ultimate slap in the face to the critics who had either doubted his ability or were upset by his controlling personality. Or, in the case of certain ARU officials, both.

But it had come at a terrible cost. Early in the second half a scrum wheeled and collapsed. As he pitched forward head-first into the ground and the All Black forwards applied pressure, Australian front-rower Ben Darwin felt what he described as 'like a firecracker going off and being punched in the face'. Knowing he was in serious trouble, Darwin called out, 'Neck, neck!' and his opposite number, Kiwi loose-head Kees Meeuws, immediately stopped pushing. For two minutes Darwin lay on the ground without any feeling from the neck down.

'It was terrifying, but the medical staff did a great job of getting me into the right position, and then I felt pins and needles in my arms and legs, which was a great relief. I asked if they could make sure my wife knew I was okay, as that was hugely important to me. In the ambulance on the way to hospital the staff put the game on the radio so I could hear what was going on. It was great to see the boys finish the match off.'

The next day Darwin paid tribute to Meeuws, who said he had only done what he hoped any front-rower would have done in the same situation.

'I'd hope that if I ever got into that predicament and I called out "neck", someone wouldn't think it was a chance to carry on and try to cause some permanent damage. It's hard enough out there without having idiots trying to kill people.'

Eddie watched the next night's semi-final knowing he would have to face the winner without the services of the front-rower he had brought to the Brumbies as a twenty-two-year-old in 1998 and then pushed and driven to become one of the most respected tight-heads in the game. Darwin was cleared of permanent injury, but his career was over.

It soon became apparent that Australia's opponent in the final would be England. The game against France was as good as over hours before kick-off when the heavens opened and the rain began bucketing down. The French, who said later they had prepared only for a hard, fast surface, were never in the contest and, with the English forwards controlling possession and territory, lost 7-24 in a game once again dominated by Wilkinson's boot. The French scored the only try of the match, and Wilkinson scored all England's points through five penalties and three drop-goals. Woodward, typically, would not accept that the inclement weather was advantageous to his team, telling the media: 'I've been to France on holidays. It rains there too.' Had it been dry, he said, England would have won by more.

The room was packed with Australian reporters hoping to kick-start the pre-final war of words over England's tactics, but Woodward refused to be drawn into a slanging match.

'I've taken two Valium so I won't say anything I regret.'

The media weren't so restrained. For the next seven days the onslaught was overwhelming. The World Cup final might have been between two rugby teams but the uninitiated could have been forgiven for thinking it was actually all about two men, Clive Woodward and Eddie Jones. Hardly a story was published or broadcast that did not mention the rivalry – if not deepseated animosity – between the pair. And while the two coaches themselves were careful not to say anything that could be construed as derogatory about each other, some articles published in the days leading up to the match appeared to have the fingerprints of one or other all over them.

Woodward had made his feelings clear about Eddie putting pressure on the referee in the past, and Eddie was uncharacteristically quiet in that regard. Which is not to say that questions over England's interpretation of the law weren't aired in the press. Just not by Eddie. The day before the game it was Eddie's former coach and mentor Bob Dwyer who took up the cudgels on his behalf.

In an interview with News Corp's Jim Tucker, Dwyer claimed the England back row of Richard Hill, Neil Back and Lawrence Dallaglio were 'masters of every trick at the breakdown' and should be penalized in the final by referee Andre Watson.

'Often, when English ball carriers are tackled they don't play to the laws of the game. The tactic they've grown into is a great strategy but a blatant abuse of the law. It's not borderline at all. When an English player is tackled one or two team-mates will arrive, most often from the side, to lie across the front of that tackled player to seal it off. The guys coming from the side should be penalized. The law is also very clear that both teams should be allowed a shot at the ball after the tackle yet with those bodies there as shields, there's no split second where a George Smith or Richie McCaw can reach in, over the top, for the ball. If the English disagree with what I'm saying, I can spend two hours showing them proof of play at the breakdown where their players are coming in from the side.'

Other Australian journalists weren't concerned about anything so technical. Veteran *Daily Telegraph* columnist Mike Gibson devoted a full page to the fact that England were boring, and not just the rugby team. The entire nation.

'So, England play boring rugby. You're kidding. What else is new? The Pope is a Catholic? Hitler was a bad guy? Kylie has a cute rear end?

'Come on.

'Didn't we know it would boil down to this?

'If England made the World Cup final, surely we realized they would do so by roofing the ball down the other end, so Jonny Wilkinson could pot them over.

'Did anyone seriously believe that the English rugby team came here to win friends and entertain people?

'No. They came here to win the World Cup, and bore the pants off those who paid for the dubious privilege of watching them.

'It's only halfway through the week, but already I've had it up to here with rugby fans complaining that England are boring.

'News Flash. England have always been boring.

'Down through the years, English sporting teams have turned boring into a fine art.In a country that produces bores like we produce blue heelers, England's sporting super-bore was Geoff Boycott.

'When Boycott took the crease, cricket fans used to designate a member of the crowd to wake them when he finally got out.

'Anyone who doubts the English are boring has only to check what they've watched on television over the years.

'*Coronation Street*, the sorry saga of a bunch of miserable Poms living in the dullest backwater on Earth, is the most successful programme in British television history.

'So fascinated were the Brits with *Coronation Street*, they moved it south to London, and called it *EastEnders*.

'And you thought they were going to play entertaining rugby?

'Hey, we're talking about a nation where the most popular actor is that tedious twit, Hugh Grant. Where their idea of a summer holiday is taking a bucket and spade to Brighton or Blackpool.

'We're talking about a nation of people whose idea of risk-taking is to buy a ticket in the Pools. Whose idea of excitement is to join a queue . . .'

Incredibly the newspaper also published instructions on how to make a Jonny Wilkinson voodoo doll and noted: 'England are staying at the Manly Pacific, 55 North Steyne, and the hotel's fire alarms are easily accessible.' The tongue-in-cheek campaign attracted a flood of letters of complaint, and a retaliatory column in *The Times*, which described the Australian press as exhibiting 'the classic symptoms of the spotty adolescent: surly, complaining, resentful' while 'tearing daily into the England rugby side with a ferocity that in other circumstances might have infringed the Race Relations Act'.

Woodward told reporters that he had been kept awake by someone chanting 'boring, boring' on the Thursday night before the game.

'It wasn't my wife in bed. It came from the street.'

An Australian journalist wrote, 'We weren't sure if it was supposed to be a joke. We'd never heard one from him before so there was no point of reference.'

Woodward certainly didn't see team security as a laughing matter. With talk that the Wallabies had snared a vital lineout win from the 2001 British and Irish Lions because they had pre-knowledge of the Lions' calls, Woodward was a stickler for secrecy. His staff had brought electronic anti-bugging equipment with them from England to sweep hotel meeting rooms and dressing sheds, and he ordered black plastic sheeting to be erected around their training ground Brookvale Oval to prevent 'spies' filming or taping sessions.

Eddie didn't need any espionage to determine England's game plan. The public and media may have labelled it 'boring', but the Wallaby coaching staff knew it was effective. So effective, in fact, that Eddie did his best to taunt Woodward into changing it. At his final media conference before the game Eddie 'dared' England to play expansive rugby as part of both teams' responsibility to promote the game to a huge TV audience.

'Our part of the responsibility is to play naturally and with freedom. Our natural game is to attack. We'll keep our part of the bargain. I assure you of that. If you can get England and the referee to do the same, we should have a great spectacle. It could be the world's greatest game of rugby.'

Woodward's response: 'If we want to play boring rugby we'll really play boring rugby. Australians have seen nothing yet if we want to play really boring.'

In the weeks leading up to the final there was plenty of discussion about which was the form team of the tournament. At times New Zealand and England appeared the sides to beat, then France achieved favouritism. Australia's win over the All Blacks brought the Wallabies belatedly into the frame, but from day one there was never any debate over who had the best support. England's white-shirted, 'Swing Low'-singing army of fans swept all before them. As they poured into the former Olympic Stadium at Homebush for the final, along with the team's number one fan Prince Harry, they set the scene for what would either be England's greatest sporting triumph since the 1966 World Cup, or another so-close-but-yet-so-far disappointment.

Throughout the week, poring over the long-range weather forecasts, Eddie had urged his team not to be concerned if the match was played in heavy conditions. They wouldn't be derailed like the French the week before, he said. They would play their natural game. Even so, the players felt that Eddie was beginning to show signs of nerves. After their first session of the week he berated them for being sloppy, even though they felt they had trained well. The next morning, after reviewing the tapes, he conceded he had been wrong. They had trained well after all. It was uncharacteristic behaviour, but as the weekend approached he appeared to regain his composure.

Woodward made one change to his starting team after watching Australia's win over the All Blacks, replacing Mike Catt in the centre with stronger defender Mike Tindall to counter the hard-running Stirling Mortlock. Eddie brought in twenty-six-year-old Alastair Baxter in just his seventh Test to replace Ben Darwin, but the injured tight-head still had a major role to play, as Stephen Larkham recalled.

'At 6.30 p.m., when we got to the jersey presentation, we were pleased to find that the captain's jersey was being presented by Ben Darwin, who had been out of hospital for only a few days and was still wearing a neck brace. It was a very emotional occasion. Ben told us that we should consider ourselves lucky to be able to run onto the field and play rugby. In the spinal unit at the hospital where he had spent much of the past week, he had seen some tragic cases of spinal injuries; one guy next to him couldn't move his arms and legs. We were all quite moved by this, and when George Gregan got up to thank him he actually choked up with tears. So here we were, not much more than an hour before the World Cup final, all standing around fighting to hold back tears. I think that one reason was seeing Ben in the brace and knowing that he might not play again. I also think that the tears that were shed, or almost shed, were a release of the emotions building up inside us for the past five months. Finally we boarded the bus for the stadium. As we drove, the windscreen wipers worked hard to sweep the rain away. Beating England in conditions like these, we knew, would not be easy.'

Just like against New Zealand in the semi-final, the game could not have started much better for the Wallabies. Throughout the week Eddie had told Larkham to be ready to kick for Lote Tuqiri, who had an 18 cm height advantage over his opposite winger, Jason Robinson. The opportunity came after just six minutes. Larkham kicked for the corner, Tuqiri won the leap, and Australia were up 5-0. England replied with three penalties from Wilkinson to lead 9-5. With ten minutes remaining in the first half England missed a certain try when lock Ben Kay spilled the ball with the line open. Robinson ensured the pain was only temporary when he scooted over in the left corner right on half-time. Wilkinson missed the conversion to leave the score 14-5 at the break.

England had gone into the match looking to target rookie front-rower Baxter in the scrums and to put pressure on the kicking game of Mat Rogers. At first it appeared the scrum would be the Wallabies' downfall, with England loose-head Trevor Woodman giving Baxter a fearful workout, but in the second half the young Australian found his feet, and referee Andre Watson began penalizing the England front row for collapsing. Unable to gain momentum from the set piece, England's attack lost its potency, and despite Larkham being on and off the field four times after copping a head-gash in a mistimed tackle on Ben Cohen, the Wallabies hung on and slowly chipped away at the deficit. Two Elton Flatley penalties brought Australia to within three points as the clock ticked down. The Wallabies threw everything they had at England. Jonny Wilkinson, speaking in the documentary *Building Jerusalem*, recalled, 'By the end of the game it was just do anything to hold on.' Halfback Matt Dawson took those sentiments literally.

'I was just throwing myself in. It was, "I know they're going to run over me, but I'm going to make myself a speed-bump."'

England captain Martin Johnson recalled seeing the scoreboard and feeling frustrated.

'I remember looking at the clock and thinking, "Wow, there's four minutes to go, and we haven't played well. We haven't scored a point in the second half, but we're going to win." I felt a bit flat, like, "Is this what the World Cup is all about?"'

Johnson was writing the final chapter prematurely. With a minute left Watson awarded the Wallabies a penalty, 22 metres out, 10 in from touch. Before Gregan had time to consider the options Flatley had his headgear off and was walking towards him.

'It was there to be kicked, and I had to kick it. I'd missed a couple earlier so I felt like I owed it to the team. George handed me the ball and said, "Knock it over, Flatty," and that's what happened.'

The scoreboard had barely registered 14-14 before Andre Watson blew his whistle, and the teams prepared for twenty minutes of extra-time. They went into their huddles in contrasting states of mind.

Said Johnson: 'We'd suddenly gone from "We should be world champions right now, getting pats on the back and well done," to "We could be in a bit of trouble."'

Gregan: 'The team was feeling really buoyant. Having come from 14-5 down to 14-14, if we could get our noses in front, it would be really, really hard for them.'

In his book *Watching the World Cup*, former *Sydney Morning Herald* rugby columnist Spiro Zavos recounted a conversation he had with Woodward in 2005, during which he asked him what he had told his players during the short break before the start of extra-time.

'His answer surprised me. "This was the first time in my life I'd ever been involved in extra-time in a rugby match," he replied. "I walked across to the players and saw that Martin Johnson was already telling them what needed to be done. So I went and grabbed Jonny Wilkinson. "Just make sure every time you get the ball you belt it down their end of the field," I told him. "We have to play it down their end of the field." I was aware how banal the instructions were. These were the obvious tactics. "Is that it, is it?" he snapped at me. "Is that it, is it?" I told him it was. He broke away from me and the rest of the team and started going through his goal-kicking drills again. That was the only time Jonny was ever rude to me. But he was right to do what he did. He wanted to get back into the zone of concentration he'd been in during the game. You know, minutes later he kicked a penalty to give us the lead from exactly the same spot where he'd been practising.'

Woodward's instruction to Wilkinson might have been 'banal', but he also made an ultimately brilliant substitution. With referee Watson penalizing the England scrum three times in the second half, Woodward took off tight-head prop Phil Vickery and replaced him with Jason Leonard. Unlike Vickery, who had tried to outmuscle his opposite Bill Young in every contest, Leonard simply concentrated on staying upright and not incurring Watson's wrath. It worked. England did not concede another scrum penalty in the match.

Wilkinson's goal from close to halfway, at the first-minute mark of extra-time, was cancelled out by yet another pressure kick from Flatley with just one minute and ten seconds left. Then came the sequence of play that would make Jonny Wilkinson a legend, bring Clive Woodward a knighthood and haunt Eddie Jones forever.

Wilkinson kicked off to George Smith, who was tackled just outside the Australian 22-metre line. From the ruck Gregan passed back to Mat Rogers for the clearing kick. Rogers, whose kicking had been identified as a possible weak link in England planning meetings, had kicked well during the match, but the pass from Gregan was a little low, giving England replacement back-rower Lewis Moody – the freshest player on the field – the split-second needed to charge through and apply pressure. Rogers, rushed, managed a gain of just 10 metres. With Australia expecting a throw to England's 'money man' Martin Johnson, the ball went instead to Moody at the back. Scrum-half Matt Dawson fed Wilkinson, who passed to another replacement, centre Mike Catt, on the angle. Catt was flattened by Larkham and Flatley, who were then both trapped under a pile of bodies.

Larkham, knowing Wilkinson was well within drop-goal range, could see Wallaby lock Justin Harrison standing at first defender at the side of the ruck and screamed at him: 'Field goal, field goal! Get the field goal!'

As Dawson put his hands on the ball, Harrison leaped towards Wilkinson, but Dawson didn't pass, instead darting through the slight gap that Harrison had left and snatching a priceless 15 metres.

Again Wilkinson was perfectly positioned, and again England delayed giving him the ball. This time it was the captain Martin Johnson, showing all the experience gained in eighty-four Tests, who took the ball unexpectedly as he ran a decoy line and charged back into the ruck, putting the Australian defenders on the back foot as Dawson passed to Wilkinson.

As if preordained, sixteen years after he had written his life ambitions: to play for England, to be the kicker, to win the World Cup, Jonny Wilkinson slotted the drop-goal through the posts.

'We knew they were setting for that drop-goal, but there wasn't anything we could do,' recalled Gregan. 'Often in the latter stages of that final I kept reminding the boys that "execution down the stretch" was the key. On that final play, the Englishmen executed perfectly.'

For the England fans, players, staff and, especially, Woodward and Wilkinson, the sound of Watson's full-time whistle brought a mixture of euphoria, shock, excitement and relief. For Eddie and his players the feeling was more one of 'if only'.

'They were English conditions, but it was always going to be hard to beat them,' says Elton Flatley.

'They had a great forward pack. One of the best I ever played against. There's no question they were a world-class team, and worthy world champions. It was just one of those nights that you always look back on when your career is over. You think about those little one-percenters that didn't go our way on the night, but that's sport, I guess. I still think back on it as one of the best games I played in. The atmosphere, what was on the line . . . it was something amazing to be part of. It probably wasn't the best game to watch, but the closeness made it exciting. Looking back, there might be a few things that you'd like to change, but overall it was a great campaign, and a great time for rugby in Australia.'

Probably understandably, given the hard time he had endured over the previous seven days, Woodward was not in a conciliatory mood when he faced the local media for the last time.

Asked if beating Australia in the final made winning the World Cup even sweeter, he answered, 'Yes. We wanted to beat them badly. It's what sport is about – winning – and if the conditions were better, we'd have won more easily. How can I put it politely without upsetting anybody? The little campaign this week has been clearly led by the Australian media and made no difference to the team. We went out and tried to win a game of rugby. We have won five in a row against Australia now. Australia have scored eight tries, we have scored seven. We played a far more expansive game than Australia tonight, and that's a fact as I see it. We play a certain way sometimes and get on and win a Test match and go home.'

In the losing dressing room Eddie was subdued, but still as defiant as ever.

'England are the best team in the world,' he conceded. 'By one minute.'

As for his now much-vaunted 'Melbourne Cup preparation': 'You struggle for 100 minutes and get beaten in the ninety-ninth minute. I guess that qualifies as a photo finish. We lost some battles to win the war. In the end we lost the war but we used the first four weeks as preparation. We did the hard physical work, which held us in good stead tonight. Fitness wasn't a problem. As far as strategy and tactics were concerned, we had our strategy in place a long time before the World Cup, and tactics were something we were continually developing.

'It wasn't a case of holding something in reserve, more that we just did enough to win. We used what we needed to use to win each particular game. If we sat down, the forty-four of us, now and asked, "Have we done everything we could?" I think we could look each other in the eye and truthfully say we have. We made some mistakes, there have been doubts and uncertainty, but even though we came up short I really think we've given it everything we had.'

The last game of the World Cup had been played, but Eddie still had one official duty. The next morning he contacted all the players and insisted that they meet at the pub owned by Bill Young's family, twenty minutes' drive from Telstra Stadium, for a final lunch and drink together. Wendell Sailor said he didn't want to go at first, but was soon glad he did.

'I was a bit depressed, to be honest. I'd never lost a final before, but Eddie and George made sure we were all there. We had lunch and some drinks, and then some of us headed to the Cargo Bar in the city. We'd been going for a while by then and when we arrived some of the England players were there with Prince Harry. At first we just sort of nodded and said "g'day", but after a while we all came together. At one stage Bill Young went to the bar and came back with a tray of shots and passed them around. He tried to give one to Prince Harry, but his minders said no. Bill said, "No way. It's one in all in," so Prince Harry said okay and downed the shot with us. Good bloke. Good day, good night. I think we went through until closing and headed home.'

And with that, the 2003 Rugby World Cup was over, but never forgotten. In 2017, speaking at the Oxford University Union Q&A, Eddie was asked, 'Back in 2003, after the World Cup final, did you ever think that one day you could be coaching the other side?' Eddie gave his little half-smile and raised an eyebrow.

'The only thing I know is that if Jonny Wilkinson didn't kick that field goal I'd be Sir Eddie Jones now, and Clive Woodward would still be working.'

9

DOWN AND OUT

The last of the crowd hadn't finished filing out of the stadium from the 2003 final before Eddie started discussing his plans for the 2007 Rugby World Cup.

'I'd say 70–80 per cent of our squad will be strongly in contention for the next World Cup, so there are some real positives for the future,' he said, urging Wallaby captain George Gregan to continue playing through to the next tournament, 'if he has the enthusiasm to keep improving as a player'.

Gregan would lead the Wallabies in their next Cup campaign, but Eddie wouldn't be there alongside him. Unbeknownst to Eddie, ARU boss John O'Neill would be speaking to potential replacements for his role within days of the World Cup final. As it happened, though, O'Neill would be the one to go first, pushed out on 11 December 2003 when the ARU board voted against renewing his contract. Eddie would stay, but his days were numbered. As the saying goes, he had one foot in the grave, and the other on a banana peel.

O'Neill's replacement as CEO was Gary Flowers, a successful solicitor and Harvard MBA graduate with a strong club rugby pedigree. A stalwart and lower-grade player at Manly, Flowers had been a selector for Alan Jones when the club won the 1983 premiership.

Flowers says his relationship with Eddie was 'never that bad until the end'.

'I didn't come in with any preconceived ideas. I think we got along pretty well to start with. We disagreed on a few things, but we'd move on.'

Two of those disagreements involved moves to sign rugby league players – one of the biggest names in the game in playmaker Andrew Johns, and one of the most notorious, in troublemaker Willie Mason.

'When I arrived in the job there was a furore about Andrew Johns. Before I got there the board had decided not to pursue Johns, and the NSW Waratahs decided they would go outside the system and do it themselves. There was a lot of criticism of the ARU from Waratahs coach Bob Dwyer. I found out that Bob was on our payroll. I told Eddie, "Hang on, this is a bit rich. We're paying Bob as a consultant and he's bagging the hell out of us." I believe that consulting role ended soon afterwards.

'Eddie was in love with league players. I'm not saying that was wrong, and we looked at any number of them, but I drew the line at Willie Mason. Eddie thought he was the answer to his prayers at number six. I said, "Eddie, mate, don't even go there. It's not going to happen." They weren't huge issues at that stage, and I don't remember us ever having any slanging matches. Everything started fine. We would have regular interactions one-on-one with no problems. It was different with his interaction with Brett Robinson. Eddie never wanted to report to the high performance manager, he wanted to report to the CEO. He'd always try to sidestep Robbo and make a bee-line to me, but I think that's probably pretty normal with coaches. It's a very tough job; they're under enormous pressure, and if the team is not winning that pressure just builds and builds.'

The 2004 season started well for the Wallabies with a 2-0 series win over Scotland before the-now-Sir Clive Woodward brought England to Australia in June for a one-off Test. The English were suffering what many believed was a post-World Cup hangover, having lost to Ireland and France in the Six Nations and going down twice to the All Blacks on the first leg of their tour. Even so, he was in a good mood when he arrived in Brisbane. 'Has Success Changed Clive Woodward?' asked one headline. The local media certainly thought so. The jovial, relaxed peer who met the press at the team hotel was a far cry from the tight-lipped sergeant-major type who had snapped his way around Australia seven months earlier. When he made light of talk that rugby league star Andrew Johns might cross codes and sign with the Waratahs and quipped, 'That's great. He's got English grandparents, we'll take him,' one reporter told Woodward it was the first joke the Australian press had ever heard from him. He took mock offence.

'Not at all,' he said. 'You obviously weren't down in Sydney for the World Cup. I cracked lots of jokes at Manly. I worked on them, wrote them down; rehearsed them. It's just that no one laughed.'

Asked how he took the news of his knighthood, he answered, 'I'm not sure how I took it actually. I just got a letter. I opened it, read it. Thought, "This is a great honour, and I accept." The only difference it has made to my life is that I had to have my business cards reprinted. See, there's another joke. That's three.'

He did stop the comedy routine long enough to get in one dig at Eddie, though. Claiming that his team was close to exhaustion after a long Six Nations campaign and two-Test series in New Zealand, he said, 'Probably Eddie Jones has never had a better chance of beating England. He hasn't succeeded yet.'

Predictably, Eddie hit straight back.

'No one was complaining in June last year when they came out and beat New Zealand and Australia. There weren't any signs of tiredness then. Why are they tired now? I suppose when you've won three of seven Tests this year you want to take a bit of pressure off yourself.'

It was yet another points win to Eddie in the verbal sparring between the two – one of many according to former chief rugby writer for *The Independent* Chris Hewett.

'Clive always thought he was a clever manipulator of the media but he never won a battle over Eddie. I remember that time in 2001 when Clive was worried about the Wallabies' blocking tactics and he gave us that video presentation. We all went straight down the road to the Australians' hotel, which was a mile down the road. We put it all to Eddie, and he said, "I'm glad Clive is so in tune with the laws. Have you seen what England is doing in the lineout?" He took us through it all and turned it all on its head. We went in talking about Australia's decoy runners and went out talking about England's lineout. He was so quick. Clive never had a chance against him.'

That might have been the case off the field, but it was the Wallaby players who had the last word at Brisbane's Suncorp Stadium a few nights later, when they beat England 51-15. Without Martin Johnson, Neil Back, Phil Vickery and, crucially, Jonny Wilkinson due to retirement or injury, the English were no match for the Australians, who ran in six tries to two. It was a crushing victory for the Wallabies, but small comfort for the World Cup loss. As George Gregan said, 'You can never change what happened in the past, but this is a good start.'

It would be the last time that Eddie and Woodward would face each other as opposing coaches, with Sir Clive resigning in September after falling out with RFU management. He coached the British and Irish Lions on an unsuccessful tour of New Zealand in 2005, then worked with Southampton Football Club and as director of sport for the British Olympic Association in the lead-up to the 2012 Games. In recent years he has been a high-profile rugby commentator and columnist. Since Eddie was appointed England coach at the end of 2015 the two have put their differences behind them and even claimed that their antagonism as opposing coaches was all 'a bit of fun'. Not too many who were around at the time are buying it.

'Don't you believe it,' says Australian journalist Greg Growden. 'They hated each other.'

Australia's massive win over England augured well for a successful season, but it was a mixed bag. The Wallabies beat a Pacific Island selection 29-14 but couldn't maintain the winning run against the All Blacks, going down 7-16 in Wellington. They then beat the Springboks 30-26 in Perth and upset New Zealand 23-18 in Sydney. A win over South Africa in Durban would give Australia the Tri-Nations title, but despite leading 7-3 at half-time they went down 19-23 after the Boks scored two converted tries and two penalty goals immediately after the break.

'We made more mistakes in that twenty minutes than we have made in the last three games put together, and the reasons for that we don't know,' Eddie admitted ominously.

The spring tour was equally frustrating. Not so much for the on-field results, but for the cracks that were starting to emerge in the relationship between Eddie and the players. The Wallabies beat Scotland twice, 31-14 and 31-17, and finished on top of England, now coached by Andy Robinson, 21-19, but it was after the 14-27 loss to France in Paris that Eddie showed that the strain was starting to tell.

Halfback Fabien Galthie, who captained France in the 2003 World Cup, once famously explained the vagaries of the French national side by saying, 'Some days we fly like the birds. Other days we play like shit.' On 13 November 2004 at Stade de France, they flew like the birds. At the media conference after the game, Eddie took the unprecedented step of criticizing his two closest lieutenants, a move that stunned his captain George Gregan.

'After the loss Eddie was critical of some on-field decisions made by me and Stephen Larkham and claimed we ignored instructions. It was the first time Eddie had publicly questioned us through the media, and naturally I was disappointed – not with the criticism, but because he went public. The leadership group had always been solid on these things. Win or lose, we'd back each other up. Eddie told me later that he wanted to see more leadership through the group, and that had motivated him to speak up the way he had. Too many players, he felt, were sitting back and waiting for the senior players to take command, and he felt he needed to do something radical, such as use the press, to achieve his objective. I could see his point, but I didn't agree with his actions. It was a move born out of a sense of frustration I'm not sure Eddie ever lost for the rest of his time as Wallabies coach.'

Eddie's 2005 *annus horribilis* started positively enough with four straight wins at home over Samoa, Italy, France and South Africa. And then the wheels well and truly fell off, with the Wallabies lurching from one loss to another – seven in succession – in what was Australia's worst losing streak in 106 years of Test rugby.

Injuries decimated the side, with fifteen experienced Test players unavailable at one stage. Key backs Steve Larkham and Stirling Mortlock were ruled out for extended periods, and forwards David Lyons and Dan Vickerman underwent surgery that ended their seasons. Elton Flatley suffered blurred vision during the warm-up for the eighth Test of the season against South Africa in Perth and, after extensive neurological tests, never played again.

On top of that was Eddie's dogged determination to stick to a new style of play that he wanted to implement in preparation for the 2007 World Cup. With the intention of utilizing the entire width of the field, it revolved around the first receiver orchestrating three or four phases to move players into designated areas. Once in place, moves would be worked off the fly-half or centres, split on either side of the field. For the system to work, it required scrum-half Gregan to resist any natural inclination to chance his arm in attack in order to dutifully feed Larkham or, after his injury, replacement fly-halves Matt Giteau and Mat Rogers. To the media and public, not privy to Eddie's instructions, it was taken as evidence that Gregan had lost his spark and should have retired after the World Cup. The cries for Eddie to replace Gregan with livewire Waratahs' scrum-half Chris Whitaker became louder. As the losing streak worsened, Gregan asked Eddie to reconsider the new system and allow him to play his more natural game. Eddie refused, putting added pressure on their relationship. When Gregan did run the ball more in one game he was lauded by press and public but again accused of ignoring instructions by Eddie, according to assistant coach Andrew Blades.

'There was some paranoia creeping in. Eddie thought the players were trying to sabotage him. There was the time that he accused Steve Larkham and George Gregan of changing the game plan in France, and it happened another time with George as well. I'm not sure if he really meant what he said, it could have just been a pressure release, but it shows the stress he was under, and it was filtering down to everyone else.'

The closeness and discipline the side had prided itself on during the World Cup campaign was being eroded by the day. It came to a head on a two-match tour of South Africa. For future Test captain Stephen Moore, touring with Wallabies for the first time, the behaviour of some players came as an eye-opener.

'I'd have to say that it wasn't the most professional environment I've been in. Eddie had a lot of history with some of those players going right back to the Brumbies days, and maybe the whole thing was getting a bit tired. Some players were doing things they shouldn't have been doing.'

The discipline problems hit the headlines when back-up halfback Matt Henjak was sent home to Australia in disgrace after an incident in a Cape Town nightclub three nights before the second Test of the tour in Pretoria. It later emerged that Henjak, Wendell Sailor, Lote Tuqiri and front-rower Matt Dunning had all been at The Pulse night spot at around 4 a.m when Henjak and Tuqiri became involved in an argument with each other that turned physical. When a local patron commented on their behaviour, Henjak threw ice at him and was removed from the premises by security staff. While Henjak, who was not part of the Test squad, was sent packing, Sailor, his room-mate Tuqiri and Dunning were hit with cursory fines of $500 and allowed to play the match – although Sailor says the dressing-down he received from Eddie was cruel punishment in itself.

'We'd had a pact not to go out before the Test but after dinner we decided to have a couple. Matt and Lote had a bit of a wrestle, and the bouncers got involved, and me and Matt Dunning stepped in to try to calm things down. When we got back to the hotel I said to Lote, "If Eddie finds out, we're dead." Lote is always optimistic. He said, "We'll be right." The morning of the game it's in the paper, and Eddie's filthy at breakfast. I said to Lote, "Did you see Eddie's face?" Three hours before the game the phone rings in our room. Lote answers it and says, "It's Eddie, he wants to talk to you." He says, "Dell, were you out with the boys?" I've said, "Yeah." He says, "Come to my room." I've gone around there, and he's absolutely blasted me. He's said, "You'd better have a go today." Then we've got beaten, and he's ripped me another one in front of the boys in the dressing room.'

The matter of team discipline and in particular the behaviour of the three high-profile rugby league converts, was an ongoing issue for the ARU officials. Many believed that Eddie's unqualified support for his favoured players created an environment in which they felt they were above censure, as John O'Neill noted in his biography *It's Only a Game.*

'In South Africa in 2003 I observed Mat Rogers first-hand during a rowdy incident in a Johannesburg hotel. The team had been given the night off after a Test against the Springboks and at 11 a.m. the following morning I heard a ruckus in the corridor. Leaving my room to investigate, I found an inebriated Rogers on his knees and shouting through the crack beneath another door. He was pleading loudly with teammate Owen Finegan to return his mobile phone. Rogers looked up, saw me, and said, "Owen, we're in trouble here – guess who's arrived?" Finegan looked through the peep hole, opened the door and explained he took Rogers' phone during the night to stop him making so many calls while clearly under the influence. When the bus left almost two hours later, Rogers was still not sober. It was by no means a serious example of player misbehaviour, but it did leave me thinking why the cultural assimilation of Rogers and Sailor, a moth to the nightclub flame, never really happened. They should have been pulled into line at the first instance of straying from what we would view as acceptable behaviour for Test representatives. I know I could be viewed as a snob by making such a comment. In one breath I'm saying I wanted rugby union to be the people's game and in the next I am suggesting we have a superior attitude to rugby league when it comes to a binge drinking and partying culture. My point is this: rugby league has a different look – a brasher and sometimes abrasive look. Yet, Wayne Bennett was able to keep Wendell on the straight and narrow at the Broncos, so what was it that we did wrong? Perhaps we felt the Wallaby culture, or the one that existed just prior to their arrival, when players weren't saints but did tend to handle any rebellious elements through internal discipline, was strong enough to influence them.'

Sailor has a simpler explanation.

'I was more interested in being a rock star than wearing the gold jersey,' he says.

All three of Eddie's league players departed rugby union before their contracts expired, but it was Sailor who suffered the most ignominious fall from grace. Early in the 2006 season, after transferring from the Queensland Reds to NSW Waratahs, he was involved in another late-night incident in Cape Town after a Super Rugby match. Drunk in a nightclub, he pushed another patron to the ground and staggered outside to throw up in a pot-plant. Sent home in disgrace, four months later his rugby career was over after he tested positive for cocaine prior to the Waratahs' final match of the season.

Sailor remains bitter about the way he was treated by the ARU executives. From the day his two-year ban was announced and his contract terminated, he says he did not hear one word from the men who once proudly paraded him internationally as their most prized signing. 'I was upfront with them from day one,' he says. 'I never denied doing the wrong thing, never tried to make up any excuses. I said, "Yeah, I did it, I was an idiot," but not once did they call to see how my wife was doing or how my kids were coping. When I think of everything I did for them . . . I never said no to anything they wanted me to do. Charity stuff, hospital visits. I know that's all part of the job, but I was happy to do it.'

The exception was Eddie.

'He was rock solid. From the moment the word got out he was there for me. He'd be on the phone, saying, "Dell, you've made a mistake but you've got to stay strong for your family." For two years he never gave up on me. Even if I got into trouble now, he'd be the first person I'd call.'

By the time Sailor was drummed out of rugby in disgrace Eddie was no longer Wallaby coach, having not survived the disastrous 2005 spring tour.

Following two defeats in South Africa, the Wallabies had gone down to the All Blacks in Sydney, Springboks in Perth and New Zealand in Auckland for five straight losses before heading to Europe. The first Test on tour was a 16-26 loss to France in Marseilles, but it was the next week, against England, where things reached the point of no return.

'The scrum was pulverized,' says Gary Flowers. 'It was embarrassing.'

Much was made of the crippling injury toll that beset the Wallaby pack throughout the 2005 season, but against England Eddie was still able to field five of his starting eight from the World Cup final two years earlier, as well as 2003 bench player Matt Dunning. Even so, the Australian scrum was no match for the English, especially their 195 cm (6 feet 5 inch) 128 kg (20 stone) loose-head Andrew Sheridan. A competitive power-lifter, Sheridan dominated his opposing front-rower Al Baxter to the point where, after receiving two cautions from French referee Joel Jutge for collapsing, the Wallaby tight-head was sent off. With Baxter replaced by reserve hooker Tafuta Polota-Nau, the next scrum also collapsed, and Dunning was stretchered off with a neck injury. This led to the ultimate humiliation for a Test pack: the rest of the match, won 26-16 by England, being played with uncontested scrums like an Under-8s game.

Back home in Australia the calls for Eddie's head were deafening, and leading the charge was Alan Jones. Now Sydney's leading radio host, twenty-one years earlier Jones' Grand Slam Wallabies had destroyed the much-vaunted Welsh scrum with a push-over try at Cardiff Arms Park. With Eddie's side suffering similar ignominy at Twickenham, Jones was scathing in his condemnation. There was nothing new in that. In 2003, when the Wallabies were beaten 50-21 by the All Blacks in Sydney, Jones said on a regular TV spot, 'The Wallabies have problems, but they are not player problems, they are coaching problems. Sometimes what the coach says borders on the indecipherable. God only knows how the players work out what he means. Sometimes it's better to be not coached than badly coached. Australian rugby is full of talented players. Our talent is being betrayed. The real tragedy is that Eddie Jones, the unsuccessful coach, has the permeating influence right throughout Australian rugby.'

The onslaught quietened down somewhat with the Wallabies' success in the 2003 World Cup but began to build over the next two years, reaching a climax after the England loss.

'What on earth does this man do for the money he is paid?' Jones asked on his radio show. 'We have outstanding players. We are smack bang in the middle of a leadership that can't adjust to the modern demands, a leadership that can't coordinate the team to meet the challenge offered on the other side.'

While Eddie would later blame his demise on a vendetta against him by Jones, there is no doubt the views of the former coach-turned-broadcaster were very much in line with those of the majority of Australian rugby followers.

A lone voice of support for Eddie came from the most unlikely of directions – yet another Jones. Chief rugby writer for the *Sunday Times*, Stephen Jones is no great fan of Australia or Australian rugby, believing the public to be boorish and one-eyed and the style of play to be superficial. On the subject of Eddie Jones, however, he was prepared to make an exception. As calls for Eddie's dismissal

Matraville's 1977 first XV, featuring Eddie (circled in second row), Glen Ella (circled in front row) and Mark Ella, third from the left in the front row. The team captain holding the ball is future Wallaby Lloyd Walker.

Eddie, far left, with his team mates at Randwick including Mark Ella (fourth from left) and Lloyd Walker (far right).

© Brett Dooley/Randwick RFC

Eddie with future Wallabies coach Ewen McKenzie following a Randwick win.

© Brett Dooley/Randwick RFC

Above: Playing for NSW (#2) on the 1989 Lions tour of Australia.

Right: Eddie with International Grammar School colleagues Rita Fin and Peter Balding, on a mufti day in December 1987 when the staff came dressed as the students.

Eddie (wearing red jumper), sitting between Rita Fin and Reg St Leon in the International Grammar School staff photo, 1987.

ACT Brumbies captain and halfback George Gregan and coach Eddie field questions at a press conference in May 2000.

Eddie and John Eales in the Wallabies' dressing room following victory in the Bledisloe Cup, 2001.

Training drills for the Wallabies, August 2004.

A tense Eddie, coaching the Reds, looks on as his team loses to Western Force 38-3 in the Super 14 competition, March 2007.

Jake White, Eddie and Allister Coetzee celebrating South Africa's victory over England in the final of the IRB 2007 Rugby World Cup.

A Japanese fan shows his support for Eddie during the 2015 World Cup match between USA and Japan.

Early in his England tenure, Eddie leads his squad in a training session at Pennyhill Park.

Eddie celebrates with Danny Care following England's victory over the Wallabies in Melbourne, June 2016.

Eddie and his schoolfriend (then England skills coach) Glen Ella at Sydney's Coogee Beach during the England tour of Australia, 2016.

Eddie accepts the World Rugby Coach of the Year Award from Sir Clive Woodward in Monaco, November 2017.

Eddie with wife Hiroko chatting to fellow Australian, sporting legend Rod Laver and Andrea Eliscu in the royal box during Wimbledon 2017.

Irish fans send a message to Eddie following the Six Nations clash between England and Ireland at Twickenham on St Patrick's Day, 2018.

escalated, he wrote a column urging caution on the part of the ARU.

'You can always tell when Australia's results are bad. Former Wallaby coach Alan Jones will pop up with a view to his radio show ratings, castigating the incumbent. The only time he has ever shut up was when Bob Dwyer's great Wallabies won the World Cup in 1991. Jones was silent for the whole presentation ceremony. Now he's off again. He told a lunch last week that it is Eddie Jones, not the awful Australia props, who must be blamed for the remarkable collapse in tight play of a once-vaunted set of forwards. Alan Jones related that he had sent Al Baxter, the tight-head prop who was humiliated at Twickenham, a missive lauding his "very distinguished contribution to Australian rugby". Baxter has clearly been playing Test matches in private.

'Eddie Jones can lack grace and become tiresome with his winding-up of the opposition in the media the week before a Test match. He and many Australian observers regard these mock outbursts as the height of psychological warfare, whereas they usually tend to make school first-form tiffs seem elevated.

'After a slow start, caused by Jones's adherence to Australia's candyfloss rugby philosophy, I have grown to admire him. Tactically, he did a spectacular number on New Zealand in the 2003 World Cup semi-final, and even though he is not as expansive a coach as Dwyer, he continues to turn up class players behind the scrum. If Australian domestic rugby had thrown up two front-row pillars, Jones would be contemplating sainthood, not the sack.

'Australian rugby should be very careful about ditching Eddie Jones. He has been clever, cunning, controversial, voluble and entertaining in the style of play of his team. He is a professor of world rugby; any successor would still be sitting his O-levels. And it must never be forgotten that Jones toured this autumn without nine key players. He deserves another chance with his first XV.'

Australia bounced back to beat Ireland 30-14 in the next match, but it wasn't enough to save Eddie. On the eve of the Wallabies' final match of the year against Wales – the one that proved to be Eddie's last as national coach – Gary Flowers gave an interview to Australian journalist Peter Jenkins that revealed the writing was on the wall.

'In hindsight it probably wasn't the smartest move I made,' Flowers says. 'I was in Cardiff for the match and for the first time I showed my hand of how Eddie was travelling. It did cast some doubt over Eddie's ability to continue in the role. The funny thing was, when I started in the job, Eddie and I had a meeting and I joked that "If I ever have to trot out that old line about the coach has my full support, you'll know you're in trouble." That's pretty much what I did in Cardiff, so Eddie knew he was in trouble.'

Tipped off by the Jenkins interview, Eddie and his assistant coaches prepared for the Wales game believing their futures rested on the result. Win, and they would live to fight another day. Lose, and they were gone.

As was so often the case in the season, the Wallabies started well. Winger Lote Tuqiri and fullback Chris Latham were electrifying in attack, and Australia scored the first two tries of the match to lead 14-6 well into the second half. On the sideline Eddie and his staff were clinging to hope, but once again the scrum proved the weak link. With the Wallabies collapsing three times close to the Wales line, English referee Tony Spreadbury awarded a penalty try. Kicking coach Ben Perkins turned to Wallaby manager Phil Thomson and said, 'I think this could be last drinks.' He was right. Their confidence lifted, the Welsh went on to claim a 24-22 victory – their first over Australia since 1987. Six days later Eddie was sacked.

'I called him into my office and told him we were terminating his contract, as we were entitled to do,' says Gary Flowers. 'I can't remember us having any great slanging match or anything like that. I told him, he listened, and that was that.'

Over the next day Eddie gave numerous interviews, telling reporters, 'I'm extremely disappointed. My dream was to coach the team and win the next World Cup. That's been taken away. I still believe I'm the right person to coach Australia. The results have not been as they should have been, and I certainly take full responsibility for those results, but we've actually set the base for the World Cup for 2007. I'm still young, forty-five, even though I've lost some hair, so there's no reason why I won't coach the Wallabies again. That's my intention. I want to become a better coach and coach the Wallabies again. It's the greatest honour and privilege you can have.'

Eddie said he had no hard feeling towards Flowers or the ARU.

'I don't hold any malice against them or any ill feelings. They've made a decision they think is in the best interests of Australian rugby, and so be it.'

Who he did blame, however, was Alan Jones. Alluding to his sledging of Brian Smith over twenty years earlier, he said, 'Ever since I took on the job he's been trying to get me out. Alan and I had a disagreement when I was a player and he was a coach, but that's a long time ago.'

Alan Jones stands by his criticism of Eddie's coaching of the Wallabies but rejects claims that he had plotted his dismissal from the start.

'When he got the job, I congratulated him and indicated I would give him my support but I believe his obsession with the pick and drive has ruined the game, and Australia cannot regain pre-eminence in world rugby until we change the way we play. When it falls apart with Eddie Jones, it falls apart. And the results always bear witness to that.

I suspect that in recent years he's mellowed a little. He would need to. As to whether or not my commentary cost him his job as Australian coach I have profound doubts. The scoreboard and the players cost Eddie Jones his job. The argument that I'd been trying to get rid of him was a product of Eddie's imagination.'

Gary Flowers says the ongoing criticism by Alan Jones had no influence on his decision to terminate Eddie's contract.

'Alan was just another voice in a wall of disquiet about Eddie's performance. The results were poor, there's no way around that, but to be honest that wasn't the only factor. It was clear to me that he had to go. In some respects the results just made it easier.

'I always had the view about Eddie that he was really good at putting a programme together but I was not convinced that he was a head coach at that time. Since then he might have got there but by the end of that spring tour Eddie had lost the player group in my assessment. At that time the leadership group was critical to the success of the team and that leadership group had ceased to function. You could sense it in the dressing room. As he got under more pressure Eddie would train the bejesus out of them and harangue them after losses. You could sense he had lost them, and that was a major problem.

'Another issue that was always around was Eddie's management style. The one who did a great job holding things together was Eddie's team manager Phil Thomson. Phil was first class. He and Eddie had a level of mutual respect that allowed Phil to effectively manage Eddie, but that was pretty rare. I know Eddie's defence coach John Muggleton and attack coach Alan Gaffney were pretty upset when we let him go but he was really hard on his assistant coaches, and I mean really hard.'

10

THE HELP

Thirty-two-Test tight-head prop Andrew Blades thought the toughest job in rugby was packing down against the All Black front row. And then he became an assistant Wallaby coach to Eddie Jones.

A member of Rod Macqueen's 1999 World Cup-winning Wallaby side, in 2004 Blades was in England finishing up the second year of a three-year contract as team coach at Newcastle when the offer came to return to Australia and join Eddie's staff. Having enjoyed working as forwards coach with Eddie at the Brumbies in their Super 12 premiership-winning year of 2001, and thinking the experience at the Wallabies would be similar, he asked for a release from Newcastle head of rugby Rob Andrew and headed home.

It didn't take long for him to realize he had made a mistake.

'It certainly wasn't an enjoyable experience. I had such great memories of my time at the Brumbies. Eddie had a very good programme for developing players there. If you gave feedback to a player about something he should be doing better, it was then up to you to come up with a programme to help him do it, and I really liked that. Eddie had a great system in place. Maybe it was better suited to Super Rugby because you had that long pre-season, but Eddie would work out how he wanted the team to play and then put together a detailed plan to introduce the skills that enabled the players to play that way.

'He had a real process in place. Every player would have a personal plan. After every training session the assistant coaches would give Eddie a report on our players. It was like: "This guy did this well but he needs to improve this." Then we'd put together a list of extras that the player would have to do to improve in that area. Say I told Ben Darwin that he had to improve his tackling on his left shoulder, I'd have to give him six extra sessions over the next two weeks, and then we'd review it, and if it hadn't improved, it would be my fault.

'Nothing was left to chance, everything was documented. It was miles ahead of anything I'd ever seen. It was a very collaborative environment at the Brumbies. If you wanted to present something you might have a ding-dong discussion, but egos were parked at the door, and at the end of the day decisions were made and we moved on.

'Things were different at the Wallabies. Eddie was in a different mental state at that stage. I got the feeling he was under a lot of external pressure from the ARU. Even though we won six out of eight Tests when I was there, it just didn't feel like a cohesive group. It wasn't a happy place to work. I'd come straight from Newcastle, where Rob Andrew was so good to work with. Jonny Wilkinson was the captain, and we had some keen young players who would go on to play Tests, like Toby Flood, Tom Main, Jamie Moon and Mathew Tait. There was a really good feeling about the place. To go from that to what was happening at the Wallabies at the time, I found myself thinking, "What the hell am I doing here?"'

Stories of the demands Eddie places on his assistants are legion. One of the most oft repeated is of the time the Wallabies had come to the end of a long and arduous season with a win in their final Test. The assistant coaches were winding down with some well-deserved drinks when, around 2 a.m., their mobile phones started beeping.

It was a message from Eddie. He had been reviewing tapes of the season and was ready to begin the next year's campaign. All coaches were expected at a 6 a.m. planning meeting. He confirms the story.

'Yeah, that happened on the odd occasion. I made a few bad choices with assistant coaches. We didn't have a good relationship, and I think they're probably happy to keep those stories alive.'

Not all former members of Eddie's staff have painful memories of their time together. Former TV cameraman A. J. 'Kong' George, who headed the Wallaby Media Unit throughout Eddie's time in charge of the Australian team, remains a great supporter.

'I can't speak highly enough of him as a coach and a person. He is a knock-about bloke, like me, and we always got along. That didn't mean he wouldn't read the riot act to me. That was his thing, always wanting you to go to the next level. He'd say, "AJ, you can do better than that," and he was right. He made me a better operator. There's this impression of him always being "on", never relaxing, but that's not right. When we were in camp at Coffs Harbour some nights a few of us would pool our money, maybe throw in $20 each and go down to the Pier Hotel to have some bets on the greyhounds and a few laughs. Eddie was always great company. He could be tough in a work situation, but he cared about people too. When I was having problems with my marriage, long after he'd left the Wallabies and was living overseas, Eddie would ring me and say, "Are you okay? Do you want me to fly over?" People don't see that side of him, but I'll never forget it.'

Nor will he forget Eddie's tireless work ethic and attention to detail.

'He was demanding of his staff. Everything had to be 100 per cent perfect. When he was working it was a 24/7 job. He lived and breathed it and he expected everyone else to as well. My role wasn't quite as intense as that. I sat between him and the assistant coaches and the players, but he made me feel part of the management team. My main job was to provide footage to the media and film training sessions, but he wanted me to be multi-skilled and gave me jobs to do on match days. I was the tracksuit bitch; I sorted the drinks; if players had to be checked by the doctor or go to the head-bin, I was in charge of that. He put trust in me and would ask my opinion. He knew that I was filming training and he'd ask me if I'd noticed anything that he might have missed. I might tell him that I thought someone's shoulder wasn't 100 per cent or that someone was favouring a leg. He'd ask to see the footage. He was that thorough, nothing was too minor. I remember one time at Coffs Harbour it was a pretty quiet day, I'd finished shooting some training footage and I went up on the hill overlooking the ground to take a panoramic shot of the view to tack on the end of the package for the TV networks. Eddie saw it on the news and called me into his office to watch a replay. He pointed out that way off in the distance, in the corner of the shot, you could just make out these tiny figures of the forwards practising a three-man lineout. He said, "Kong, I didn't want that going out. Be more careful in future." He didn't miss a thing.'

The same can be said for current England forwards coach Steve Borthwick. The former England captain, whom Eddie first came in contact with when he coached him at Saracens, is said to be one of the few people alive who can match Eddie for work ethic and attention to detail.

As England front-rower Mako Vunipola said, 'Even the smallest things make a massive difference for Steve. He is all about getting the basics right first and the rest will come along with it. He picks up on anything. From my job as a lifter, you think you have a great lift, but he will pick up on where your feet are positioned.'

Eddie hired Borthwick to join his coaching staff with Japan prior to the 2011 World Cup and found a kindred spirit.

'Nobody in world rugby likes a laptop more than Steve,' he said.

After their success together with Japan, Borthwick was top of the list when Eddie put together his back-room staff for the England team. The only problem was, like Eddie, Borthwick had already taken another job before the offer came from the RFU. It took a reported £100,000 for the Stormers in Cape Town to release Eddie from his contract. Bristol, where Borthwick had already been working for a month as head coach, were initially not so accommodating.

One of the first things Eddie did when he took over as England coach was to call a mid-week meeting with deposed coach Stuart Lancaster's coaching staff of Andy Farrell, Mike Catt and Graham Rowntree. The following Monday, he sacked them, and the next day Borthwick submitted his resignation to Bristol, just hours before the RFU issued a statement announcing he had been appointed England forwards coach. Bristol immediately issued its own statement.

'We wish to make it clear that we have not agreed that Steve Borthwick can leave our employment. Steve Borthwick is subject to a recently signed long-term contract. Bristol Rugby did not give the RFU permission to speak with Steve Borthwick.'

Bristol owner Steve Lansdown was livid, threatening legal action and telling the BBC, 'The RFU think they can ride roughshod over everybody, but they are finding out they can't. I can't believe that the governing body has acted in such a way. It is totally unprofessional. I don't think the RFU have covered themselves in any form of glory whatsoever.'

Within a week the matter was settled, with the RFU reportedly paying close to £500,000 to buy out the remainder of Borthwick's eighteen-month contract. Eddie had got his man, but it was the start of what would be a fractious relationship with the English premiership clubs. Unlike in Australia, where the elite players are contracted to the ARU, in England they are employed by the often privately owned clubs. In August 2016 the RFU and the premiership clubs signed an eight-year £225 million agreement which included greater access to club players for national training camps. It took only four months for Eddie and the clubs to be at loggerheads after a camp held at Brighton between the end of the Six Nations and start of the end-of-year home internationals went wrong. As he had with Japan, Eddie brought in a judo expert to improve the players' tackling technique. During the session Wasps flanker Sam Jones suffered a broken leg, and Bath winger Anthony Watson fractured his jaw. Other players, including Saracens lock George Kruis, were unable to train ahead of the opening round of European club matches.

Saracens director of rugby Mark McCall labelled the timing of the camp as 'madness' and 'flabbergasting', and the premiership clubs issued a joint statement.

'In the interests of player welfare, Premiership Rugby believes that England should not be doing full training sessions straight after a Premiership weekend. This format was not anticipated, and we would not expect full training sessions to occur during the two remaining two-day England camps planned this season.'

Eddie paid little regard to what the clubs had to say, other than to use it as a way to build up yet another 'us against them' scenario. The resultant message to his players and staff was the same as it had always been: 'Circle the wagons, boys, it's you and me against the rest.'

Dr Sherylle Calder, another of Eddie's long-time assistants who first worked with him during the Springboks 2007 World Cup campaign, then at Suntory Sungoliath and currently England, says the English players and assistants have totally bought into what Eddie is selling.

'The players respect him. There is an unbelievable buzz in the team. He has a presence. When he walks in, everyone acknowledges it. Everyone wants to do well all the time. His training methods and how he inspires the rest of the coaching team are unbelievable.

'He's got this little edge he's looking for all the time and he uses whatever he can to do that.'

A South African who previously worked with the England team prior to the 2003 World Cup, Dr Calder is very much part of looking for that edge. Described as a 'vision awareness coach', her speciality is training athletes to use their eyesight more effectively, therefore improving reaction time. As well as training rugby and football players, she has been involved with fly fishing, ice hockey, sailing and even dog agility handlers. She has been contracted to work with the England team until after the World Cup, focusing initially on the squad's 'back-three' players – fullbacks and wingers.

'The concept is to get the eye to pick up the ball early and to judge early. We train players to such a level that when they get onto the field you often hear them say that they saw the ball big. Bryan Habana was famous for intercepts, but it is not just the ability to be physically quicker but seeing the play early and getting to the right place at the right time. It is about the ability to judge and respond in your peripheral. We are getting the players fitter for ten minutes a day, three or four times a week. The technology has progressed in leaps and bounds since the 2003 World Cup, and I have worked with Eddie a lot: I respect his thinking and a lot of things he says resonate with me.'

Former Wallaby kicking coach Ben Perkins is another who has fond memories of his time working with Eddie, although he concedes that it wasn't always smooth sailing.

'He has some really good qualities. He's made errors, but they are the same errors that any coach can make. He's got a dark side, but you name me a coach who doesn't. He's also got a side that is really good. It is up to Eddie to get the balance right.

'We had some clashes, but I basically like Eddie. There were times when he got mad with me, but he was right to. Our main issue was over the way the medicos and sports scientists were taking over. The fitness blokes, weight trainers, physios and doctors were running things. They'd say this bloke has done too many weights. He can only have five kicks or ten kicks. How could I work with that? It got so that I was having secret sessions with Chris Latham on his day off.

'There was one time I walked off training. The team was playing in Perth, and Eddie told me I wouldn't be going with them for the whole preparation. I told him I needed to be there to work with the kickers. If I wasn't there, how could I do my job? When he said I couldn't go to Perth I said, "Screw that," and walked off. Eddie was right to get mad, but at that time I was fighting for my job, I was trying to stay relevant.

'We had another big fight in Italy in 2002. We'd won, but there was criticism that Mat Rogers and Chris Latham hadn't kicked well. I came out in the press and said, "You can't blame them for not kicking well. They're not allowed to practise." Eddie wasn't impressed. He took it as a public criticism of the way he was running things.

'They were crazy times. The fitness blokes just came in and took over. The way some coaches treat the fitness blokes is they say, "Get these blokes fit enough so they can play 100 minutes," but you've got to balance that with their skills work.'

It is obviously an issue on which Eddie has had a change of heart in the ensuing years, with a reliance on physical dominance at the expense of creativity something he has actively sought to stamp out of the England team.

'The game of rugby is a balance between skill and physicality,' he said in 2017. 'I think in the Northern Hemisphere they've allowed the physical side to become too important. There is a brilliant young player – I won't mention his name – who has signed with one of the clubs. He's got all the skills, and his club has told him he has to put on an extra 7 kilos. That is just ridiculous. What they should be saying is, "get more skilful". The easy part is the physical. The hard part is the skill. It is hard to improve your catch-pass. To improve your decision-making is hard, and you've got to spend more time on those areas. The gym part is the easy part. It's easy to get fit, it's easy to get stronger.

'New Zealand has got a beautiful balance between athleticism and skill and that's why they're the best team in the world. We are trying to address that with our England players, and our players are much more diligent in their skill training, which is good.'

Perkins says one skill Eddie has had to work hard on is the way he speaks to people.

'A coach has to pick who he can be hard on and not crush and who he has to handle more carefully. Sometimes Eddie didn't always get it right. He can be brutal. Coaches have a euphemism for that. They say they are "challenging" people, but there are some people who can take that, and some who can't.'

Former ARU boss John O'Neill saw first-hand the expectations Eddie placed on his staff. 'Eddie was very tough on his assistant coaches, but selectively. I didn't see the same level of intensity around Glen Ella, for example.

'One memorable time Brett Robinson and I were at the camp in

Coffs Harbour, and Eddie wanted a particular piece of analysis done overnight and in his hands next morning. Link worked through the night and right on the dot of the start of training he handed it to Eddie. We saw him put it in his folder, and he didn't look at it all day.

'It's one thing to set high standards, but when you are demanding more analysis than you need, it's almost as if it's a security blanket.'

McKenzie, who would go on to coach the Wallabies in 2013–14, never complained about the heavy work load, and neither did his replacement, Andrew Blades.

'I wasn't worried about the hours. I was used to it from England, where we had fifty players and forty games a year. The hours were not an issue. For me it was more the poor communication. I don't know why Eddie changed from how he had been at the Brumbies. I guess there is a lot more pressure at Test level than at Super Rugby, and Eddie just wasn't communicating well. I couldn't see how it was going to work.'

While Blades had taken over from McKenzie after the World Cup, backs coach Glen Ella was replaced – somewhat ironically considering the reverse situation when Bob Dwyer had chosen Ella for his Test debut against Scotland – by former Queensland and Wallaby fullback Roger Gould.

Gould and Eddie clashed from the start, says Blades.

'Roger was a very popular, charismatic guy, and Eddie stamped on that. He wanted to put Roger in his place and establish who was boss. Roger wasn't going to put up with that.'

Says Gould: 'People might be impressed that someone works eighteen hours a day. I believe if you have to work around the clock to get something done you either don't have the right resources or you are not utilizing the resources you have got.

'Working as an assistant to Eddie, you were always having to defend your position. You would put everything on the table and have to convince him that you were right. When he put something on the table it was the exact opposite. He didn't have to convince you he was right, you'd have to convince him he was wrong. Trouble was, that never happened.

'He has bad managerial skills. I couldn't believe the way he talked to people in front of other people. I've managed enough people to know that there are some things you just can't do to people. You can't take away their dignity.'

Everyone who has worked with Eddie has witnessed what Richard Graham, his assistant coach at Saracens, describes as 'the infamous sprays'.

'When I worked underneath Eddie I saw it all up close when I was on the receiving end and when he gave it to others. As a coach he is very intense and he expects the people who work with him to be the same. He wants performance. It is all about quality of work and ultimately, if you put in the work, he will appreciate your effort, but when it comes to sprays I have seen him deliver some absolute pearlers.

'With most people, when they blow up about something, it all just comes out, but with Eddie it's almost like poetry. He can go for minutes without a pause. Sometimes at the end you feel like applauding. It's so good that you wouldn't be surprised if he had stood in front of the mirror and practised it.'

Blades says as the pressure mounted on Eddie during the Tri-Nations series against the All Blacks and Springboks in 2004, the attacks on players and assistant coaches intensified.

'Some things I would witness I'd just go, "Oh dear." Eventually I realized it was his way of feeling better about himself. I saw him destroy a few souls and then move on. It's all very well to say about Eddie that he gets things off his chest and then moves on, but what if the person he has been ripping into can't move on? In the end he was saying that certain people were purposely ignoring his game plans to sabotage him. There was some paranoia coming in.

'In that Tri-Nations we had beaten the All Blacks and South Africa at home and we just had to beat South Africa again in the last game in Durban to win the series. We were ahead with twenty minutes to go but we lost by four points. It was important that we win that game, and it still grates that we let that opportunity slip, but in the end it didn't really matter to me. I'd already made up my mind that I couldn't go on. I don't know why, but I woke up that week and thought, "Nuh." It was something I had always dreamed of doing, but there was a spring tour to the UK coming up, and I just couldn't get my head around that.

'I would never say that Eddie wasn't a good coach. He was bloody fantastic in a lot of ways. His systems were awesome, but at the end of the day I didn't feel we were functioning well. I wasn't enjoying it.'

When he got back to Sydney, Blades went and saw John O'Neill and Brett Robinson and told them of his decision.

'I never got to talk to Eddie about it because he'd gone straight on to Japan. It's a real shame, because we never got a chance to sit down over a beer and work it out. It's unresolved.'

One person Blades did get to speak to was his fellow assistant Roger Gould.

'I rang Roger to let him know I wasn't going on and he said, "Don't worry about me. I beat you to it. I've already resigned."'

Blades had been with the side for eight Tests. Gould lasted only two.

'I don't hold a grudge, but there was no point in staying,' Gould says. 'I had no feeling of self-worth in the contribution I was making. In a situation like that you might as well leave. It's a different world.'

The ARU tried to put a positive spin on things. A member of the media department rang Blades at his home and asked him not to speak to the press until they had issued a statement.

'You'll be getting a lot of calls on your mobile phone,' he was told.

'I won't be getting them,' he replied. 'I left the phone on my desk in the office. I'm never coming back.'

The statements sent out by the ARU claimed that Blades had decided to leave in order to pursue business opportunities. Gould's departure was put down to the amount of time the job was keeping him away from his family.

Former Wallaby back-rower and successful Sydney University coach Ross Reynolds was appointed as Blades' replacement for the 2004 spring tour.

'I was in the UK finishing up a role with Rotherham, and Eddie gave me a trial-run on the UK spring tour. My main focus was the lineout, and it went well in the four Tests, so we kept going.

'He wasn't the easiest person to work for, but I went in with my eyes open. I spoke to Roger Gould, and he told me what to expect.

'When it came to coming up with a game plan and implementing that plan, Eddie was as good as anyone I've ever seen, but working with him was very difficult, very demanding.

'We worked incredibly long hours. Sunday, Monday, Tuesday we'd work fourteen to sixteen hours a day. It didn't lighten up. We worked

165 days straight. You lost all context of weekends or public holidays. You worked backwards from the next Test. That was how you thought of days: as how many were left before the next game.'

But no matter how much time the assistant coaches were expected to put in, says Reynolds, Eddie would do even more.

'We certainly had some meetings at odd times. If Eddie decided that he wanted to get together at 6 a.m., we'd have to be there. The amount of video analysis we did was incredible, probably too much. We got analysis paralysis. After games we would be doing reviews and finishing up at 3 to 4 a.m. You'd send him an email and get an answer straight back.

'With the lineouts, the stuff we gave the players was amazing. Everything was worked out by centimetres. In the lineouts we'd give them video of the opponents' last four or five Tests, show them the patterns of what would happen for every throw. When the tight-head prop or the lock moved, they'd know where the ball was going to go. At training we'd get the dirty dirties [reserves] to play those roles. It probably wasn't anything that other coaches weren't doing, but Eddie was certainly good at picking other teams' weaknesses. He drilled it and drilled it into the players.'

Reynolds reinforces Eddie's reputation as 'a players' coach' but says that didn't mean he was ever soft on them.

'He'd do anything for the players. He was very supportive but he harangued rather than discussed.

'He's a difficult man manager. There was an enormous amount of stress. It's a very difficult job at the best of times. You are exposed every week to results, and Eddie forced things very hard. It was not always a group discussion. It was his way or the highway.'

Despite the long hours, high demands and stress, Reynolds lasted eighteen months as Eddie's assistant, their association ending only when Eddie was sacked as Wallaby coach at the end of the 2005 spring tour.

'We went at the same time. Because of his demise I was out. The tour finished, and everyone went their separate ways. It was a sad old end. When you're out, you're out.

'He could be a lot of fun when he had his social hat on. He was good to have a beer with but when the pressure grew he was not in a good place. He lost the change-room. He went against the players. Eddie had a group of elite players who had been with him, right through the Brumbies into the Wallabies. When things started to go awry and Eddie lost his cool, the inner sanctum didn't enjoy it. They thought they were above it. At one stage they had been winning 80 per cent of their games and then all of a sudden they weren't winning. People started turning on each other. It was a combination of a lot of things, but it became a pretty unpleasant environment.

'In the end it was an interesting experience. I was there for seventeen Tests, four in South Africa. I did two Tri-Nations series and two spring tours. I saw a lot of the world.

'Would I do it again? Probably not.'

11

RED FACES

For the first time since he walked into the office of Reg St Leon twenty years earlier, Eddie Jones was unemployed. But not for long. He may have been sacked by the Australian Rugby Union, but his record was still impressive. A Super Rugby title with the ACT Brumbies and fifty-seven Tests with the Wallabies for thirty-three wins, twenty-three losses and one draw – a winning percentage of 57.8 per cent. In his four seasons as national coach the team had won the 2001 Tri-Nations, successfully defended the Bledisloe Cup twice and been beaten in the last minute of extra-time in the 2003 World Cup. It all made for an attractive CV, and the offers weren't long in coming. The one he accepted was a three-year contract with the Queensland Reds.

News that the recently departed Wallaby coach was coming to Ballymore was met with delight by the majority of Reds supporters, and astonishment in the corridors of power at the ARU.

'I couldn't believe they signed him,' says Gary Flowers. 'We had two Queensland Rugby Union guys on our board. One of them was the QRU president. They'd been through it all with us. They'd seen all the reports, been in on all the discussions, and yet they signed him. I was gobsmacked.'

That might have been a common reaction at the ARU's North Sydney headquarters, but Queenslanders didn't really care what Flowers or anyone else from south of the state border thought, and they never had. If Eddie was a master of the siege mentality style of coaching he was going to the right place. No one did 'us versus them' better than Queenslanders, whose hatred of any sporting team wearing the blue of New South Wales was pathological. Just one rung below the NSW rugby union and rugby league teams on the Queensland sporting public's ladder of enmity were the Sydney-based Australian Rugby Union and Australian Rugby League – ostensibly administrative bodies with a charter to represent all stakeholders, but in Queenslanders' minds little more than a front for NSW interests.

That the ARU didn't think that Eddie should coach the Reds wouldn't have dissuaded Queenslanders from wanting to appoint him. In fact, it would have made him even more desirable. Not that a desire to 'stick it up the Sydney spivs' was a major factor in the QRU chasing Eddie – even if it may have contributed to his interest in the job. In truth, the Reds were in dire need of a spark of excitement and direction and saw Eddie as the ideal man to provide it.

Through the late 1970s and early 1980s, Queensland had been considered the best provincial rugby side in the world. Under the coaching of Bob Templeton and blessed with players such as Mark Loane, Tony Shaw, Paul McLean, Andrew Slack, Roger Gould and Michael Lynagh, they had gone through a long period of dominance over NSW, most notably winning 42-4 in 1976 and 48-10 in 1979. 'Tempo's' teams also had great success over touring international sides, beating Scotland in 1970, the British Lions the following year and All Blacks in 1980. When Templeton stepped down in 1989 after twenty-three seasons and 233 matches he was replaced by John Connolly, an astute former hooker who earned the nickname 'Knuckles' when working as a bouncer in the tough Northern Territory city of Darwin. Connolly led the Reds through a second golden period, notable for the emergence of brilliant young talents Tim Horan, Jason Little and John

Eales. The team won the Super 6 in 1992 and back-to back Super 10 competitions in 1994–95 and headed into the age of professionalism the next season showing every indication of remaining a major force in Southern Hemisphere rugby for decades to come.

By the time the QRU went after the signature of Eddie for the 2007 season and beyond, things had changed. In 2000 Connolly had been deposed and headed to success in Europe after the Reds finished seventh in the Super 12. Knuckles' twelve-year tenure had produced an exceptional record of 128 wins and four draws from 186 matches, including wins over France in 1990 and 1997, England and Wales in 1991 and Scotland in 1998, but QRU management, worried that the professional era was leaving them behind, felt he was too 'old school' and opted for change.

Connolly's replacement was former Queensland and Wallaby hooker Mark McBain. A builder by profession, McBain was hard-working and meticulous but, in media terms, hardly good copy. Under McBain the Reds had a good first year, finishing fourth in the 2001 Super 12 before being knocked out of the finals by Eddie's Brumbies on their way to the championship. The next season they won more matches, but finished fifth, missing the finals by one place. It was an adequate result, but in a market dominated by the Brisbane Broncos league team and the Brisbane Lions, who had just won the second of their three consecutive AFL titles, not enough to excite the masses.

McBain was dumped and replaced by one of Queensland rugby's favourite sons, Andrew Slack. Captain of Alan Jones' 1984 Grand Slam Wallabies, former centre 'Slacky' had never coached at any level, but his immense public popularity and media experience as local head of sport for the Nine TV network convinced the QRU that he was the ideal man to introduce an attractive style of play that would win matches, better utilize the skills of star recruit Wendell Sailor and have the crowds flocking. Once again, they were proved wrong. Likeable, sensitive and honest, Slack soon realized that professional rugby operated in a completely different world to the game he had played for enjoyment as an amateur. At the end of the first season of his three-year contract, in which the Reds finished in eighth position, he tendered his resignation.

The sudden departure of Slack left the Reds in a tight spot. The organization was in the process of recruitment and renegotiating existing contracts. Players and their managers were reluctant to commit for 2004 and beyond until they knew who would be coaching. With no time for a lengthy recruitment process, the Reds' CEO Jeff Miller stepped into the role. Miller, a former flanker who had been part of the 1991 World Cup-winning squad and a coaching assistant to Rod Macqueen when the Wallabies won in 1999, was a reluctant candidate for the job but he felt he had no option. Reds' CEO for just one year, his first big move had been to appoint Slack. He had got them into this mess, he thought, he'd get them out.

Unfortunately for Miller, the one-time Wallaby high-performance manager who had been on a career trajectory that could well have seen him one day succeed John O'Neill and Gary Flowers in the ARU top office, the on-field mess at the Reds went from bad to worse. In both 2004 and 2005 the team finished tenth. To add to the misery, at the start of the 2005 season, ruling body SANZAR announced that a new Australian franchise, the Western Force, would be included in the Super Rugby competition from 2006. The Force, based in the Australian Football stronghold of Perth, had no local players to fill their roster and had to plunder the rugby heartlands of Queensland, NSW and ACT to get them. The Reds were decimated, losing fourteen established and up-and-coming players, including their captain, Wallaby lock Nathan Sharpe.

The loss of Sharpe, coming on top of five years of poor results, was a blow that was as much symbolic as it was physical. In the days of Templeton and Connolly, Queensland rugby teams had built up an aura of mateship and solidarity that parochial fans had bought into in their thousands. As popular front-rower Chris 'Buddha' Handy said at Templeton's funeral in 1999, 'The first time I went to Queensland training I had fourteen new brothers.' For a player of Sharpe's stature to turn his back on the Queensland captaincy just thirty games short of having his name and photo added to the 100-cap board above the bar at Ballymore was unthinkable. The QRU needed to act, and it needed to act fast. It had to show that it would not take this attack on its players, and its values, lying down. It had to show it was still in the game. Enter Eddie Jones.

At the end of the 2005 season Jeff Miller was told that his contract would not be renewed when it ran out at the end of 2006. He asked to be paid out and released immediately but was refused. He would have to continue coaching the side through the 2006 season while the Reds interviewed candidates for his job. It was an almost impossible situation made untenable when the news broke in the media while Miller was in Argentina with the team on a pre-season tour. There was speculation that a good showing in the upcoming Super 15 might save his job, but two months later that was all academic. Eddie became available, and the Reds jumped.

As Queensland Rugby president Robin 'Buff' Thomson explained in the QRU 2005 annual report, 'had the Board not acted when it did, Eddie Jones would most certainly have been snapped up by overseas interests. The Board has made a hard decision but one that we believe to be correct in the interests of Queensland Rugby.'

In 2004, as Wallaby coach, Eddie was special guest at a Reds sponsors' and supporters' luncheon held before a Super 12 match at Ballymore.

Interviewed by the MC, he won over the crowd by declaring: 'Queensland has the best young talent in the country. They should win the Super Rugby title within five years.' Now he had a chance to make it happen but first he had another miracle to perform: a short-term rescue mission in the UK.

Like the Reds, the once-mighty Saracens were on the ropes. In 1998, spearheaded by Queenslander Michael Lynagh, France's Philippe Sella and the Springboks' 1995 World Cup-winning captain Francois Pienaar, the London club won the English premiership, defeating Wasps 48-18 in sparkling style at Twickenham. By the closing stages of the 2005–06 season that success was a fading memory and with just four wins, a draw and eleven losses, 'Sarries' were in grave danger of being relegated to the second division. The club had made a major investment in luring rugby league international forward Andy Farrell across to union but, playing in the centres, he had yet to make his mark, and the pressure was mounting. With Saracens missing the play-offs of the European Cup and sitting fourth from the bottom of the premiership table just seven points from the lone relegation spot, director of rugby Steve Diamond was sacked. Saracens' CEO Mark Sinderberry, Eddie's former boss at the Brumbies, made a plea for him to fly in for a six-week consultancy to help coach Mike Ford in a desperate bid to stay up in the top league. With Eddie and former league international Ford working tirelessly, Sarries won their next four matches and climbed the table to the point that there was even some hope of them finishing sixth and qualifying for the next season's European competition. Two losses to end the season – one by a point to Leicester Tigers – saw them finish in tenth spot but safely out of danger. Club owner Nigel Wray made Eddie a substantial offer to stay on, but even though he had yet to sign a contract, he elected to honour his commitment to the Reds. It was a decision that all concerned would come to regret.

With departing coach Jeff Miller struggling through the 2006 Super 14 season, the Reds finished in twelfth place with four wins and nine losses, ahead of just the Cats and competition newcomers Western Force. The team's last match under Miller was a morale-boosting 22-16 win over the Highlanders on 12 May 2006. Eddie moved into Miller's office at Ballymore two weeks later.

As always, Eddie hit the ground running and, after some promising results in a series of pre-season matches, expectation was high. The Reds had moved their home games from the much-loved but outdated Ballymore to the state-of-the-art 50,000-seat Suncorp Stadium. It put added financial strain on the Reds but such was the faith QRU chairman Peter Lewis had in his new coach, nothing was too much trouble. Previewing the upcoming season in the 2006 annual report, Lewis noted: 'After taking a deep breath we put considerable resources into our team by way of new players, staff and facilities suggested by our new coach, Eddie Jones, as being essential if we were to be competitive. Eddie's impact can't be underestimated. By any measure our young team now has the respect of competitors and renewed interest from our long-suffering supporters.'

As a final warm-up for the Super 14, Eddie took the team to Japan, where they played the national team. The game ended with a 29-22 win to Queensland, but its greatest historical significance was the debut appearances of two youngsters who were given a run late in the second half: Will Genia and Quade Cooper.

In keeping with his commitment to foster young talent, Eddie had taken the promising playmakers, both just weeks out of school, to give them a small taste of big-time rugby before they began their apprenticeships in the Reds Academy. That scrum-half Genia would play off the bench in the first match of the Super 15 competition – a 25-16 win over the Hurricanes in front of 22,654 at Suncorp – and fly-half Cooper would be thrown into the cauldron against reigning champions the Crusaders in Christchurch a week later, gives an indication of how fast Eddie's plans went awry as injuries sidelined one experienced player after another.

It would be 2011 before Eddie's prophecy of a Reds Super Rugby championship would come to fruition and, just as he had predicted, it would be on the back of the youngsters he had blooded as eighteen-year-olds in 2006. Genia scored the clinching try in the 18-13 win over the Crusaders, and some of Cooper's sleight-of-hand during the season had to be seen to be believed. In that respect the Reds' 2006 season could be regarded as having at least one positive, but for Cooper in particular it proved a painful baptism of fire.

Born in Auckland, New Zealand, Cooper moved to Brisbane when he was aged thirteen in the hope that his precocious talent at rugby would bring him opportunities he would never get in the small North Island town of Tokaroa, where he lived with his mother, stepfather and two sisters. Two years later the QRU arranged a scholarship at the exclusive private Anglican Church Grammar School ('Churchie'), where he would get top-class coaching. Playing in the centres alongside future Wallaby back-rower David Pocock, Cooper inspired Churchie to an undefeated GPS premiership and represented Australian Schoolboys for two years.

Signed by the Reds in his last year of school, Cooper's talent wasn't in doubt, but there were question marks about his temperament. He would do something breathtakingly exceptional one moment and something incredibly stupid the next. Eddie did his best to bring him along slowly, shielding him from the media and trying hard to keep his feet on the ground. It proved a losing battle. In round eight against the Waikato Chiefs at Suncorp it all came unstuck. The Chiefs had been Cooper's local team growing up. He had dreamed of playing for them as a boy and, when he was named at number ten in the starting side to face them he was determined to make an impression. He did, but not the way he'd planned.

'It was one of the worst games I've ever played. I couldn't catch the ball; it was like a cake of soap. I was too excited. All my family had come out: lots of family from New Zealand, lots that lived here. Guys I'd grown up with. I think I wanted it too much. I was seeing big holes, I was like whoa, I'm going to go through here, I'm going to step this guy and score a try . . .'

Making it even worse was a hyped-up Cooper choosing the wrong game to display the cocky side of his personality for the first time on a big stage. Even though his own performance was going from bad to worse as the Reds stumbled to a 33-22 loss, he continued to sledge the New Zealanders. On one occasion late in the match when one of the Chiefs forwards gave away a penalty, Cooper ran up and patted him on the head. When he mouthed off at Chiefs halfback Byron Kelleher, the thirty-one-year-old fifty-seven-Test All Black just looked at him in stunned amazement and shook his head. Eddie was not impressed and let Cooper, and anyone else within earshot, know it in the dressing room after the match.

Cooper's game that night could have been an allegory for the Reds' entire season. The harder they tried, the worse they went. From the first-round win over the Hurricanes, they lost their next nine matches. A win over the Cheetahs broke the streak, but they finished the season with another two losses, leaving them in last spot with a record of two wins and eleven losses, the worst season in Reds history.

That was on-field. Off-field it was equally disastrous. Eddie, still upset about his sacking, believed the ARU was purposely making it hard for him to succeed at the Reds. Gary Flowers felt Eddie was being paranoid and denied any vendetta. Adding to the mess was the fact that new Australian coach John Connolly and Eddie simply didn't get along. It was a recipe for distrust, rumour and innuendo. It seemed as though a week couldn't go by without newspaper reports of one blow-up or another.

The first was over Eddie's attempts to recruit Clinton Schifcofske, a rugby league fullback or winger who had played over 200 games in the NRL, most recently with the Canberra Raiders. While not a headline act like Sailor, Rogers or Tuqiri, the thirty-one-year-old Schifcofske was a very reliable first-grader and an excellent goal-kicker. He had also played two State of Origin games for Queensland, most notably converting Darren Lockyer's last-gasp try in Game III, 2006 to win the series. Eddie was keen to have him at the Reds and asked the ARU to help with funding. They refused. Eddie persevered, and the QRU ended up footing the entire cost of the contract. Eddie would later use the Schifcofske case as an example of his poor relationship with ARU powerbrokers disadvantaging the Reds.

'If it was any other team, the ARU would have helped. Because it was me, they wouldn't give us a cent. That cost us a lot. I'm sorry that the baggage I brought with me hurt the team but personally it doesn't worry me. If I think I'm doing the right thing, I just get on with it. I don't worry about what other people think.'

Flowers uses the same issue to give weight to his claims that Eddie was being paranoid.

'Schifcofske was a reasonable player, and I could see him being a handy addition for the Reds, but he wasn't going to play for the Wallabies. It wasn't a personal thing against Eddie, but there was nothing in it for us. Why would we help get him across? Those conspiracies that Eddie talks about didn't exist.'

The biggest public spat between Eddie and the ARU came after the Reds' third-round 3-6 loss to the Brumbies at Suncorp – at the time the lowest-ever scoring match in the supposedly free-flowing Super Rugby competition. In a televised sideline interview immediately after the game Eddie said that the Reds had dominated the Brumbies early, but that referee Matt Goddard had 'decided to even things up in the second half'. He made the same accusation at the post-match media conference and again on radio the next day, using the words 'ludicrous' and 'disgraceful' to describe Goddard's officiating of the scrums. After the third occasion, Eddie was cited to appear before a judiciary hearing to face charges of breaching the SANZAR code of conduct. If found guilty, possible sanctions included a maximum fine of $10,000 and suspension.

A joint venture of the South Africa, New Zealand and Australian unions, SANZAR was, at the time, administered by each country on a two-year rotational basis. In 2007 the administrative body in charge happened to be the ARU, which, Eddie believed, was the reason he was being hounded for his comments.

'I think it's the ARU, not SANZAR,' he told reporters. 'In the history of the competition there have been a lot of comments by coaches about referees. The ARU has decided to pick on my comments. If they want to punish people for speaking out all I ask is that it is due, consistent and legal.' He then went and hired a lawyer.

Flowers, himself a lawyer, denied that there was anything personal in the pursuit of Eddie, despite a story in a Sydney newspaper claiming 'ARU sources say Jones is to be made an example of.'

'I can tell you there has been no instruction to "get" Eddie Jones,' he told a reporter. 'There is no get-square going to happen here. From my personal perspective, regardless of what has happened in the past, I want Eddie to be successful in Queensland. What is happening now is not between Eddie Jones and the ARU. It is a SANZAR matter. We are simply fulfilling our responsibilities as administrators. Sometimes you can understand someone saying something in the heat of the moment – it happens – but in this case he repeated the comments the next day. It was like he was challenging us to do something, and we have.'

The original hearing date was postponed to allow Eddie's counsel more time to prepare his case, giving Eddie another opportunity to taunt his accusers.

Walking up to a pack of reporters after Reds training, he smiled and said, 'You'll have to find your own headlines today, guys – I'm going to be very well behaved.' He then showed his knowledge of English football by claiming he would follow the lead of then-Chelsea manager José Mourinho and coach the Reds by remote control if he was suspended by the judiciary.

Mourinho had received a UEFA sideline ban preventing him from attending his side's Champions League quarter-final tie against Bayern Munich in 2005. It was suspected by some that he had got around the suspension by watching the game on TV and transmitting instructions via a hidden earpiece to Chelsea's fitness coach Rui Faria, who was noticed wearing an ill-fitting woolly hat and regularly scratching his ear.

'We've got all the technology in place if worse comes to worst,' Eddie said. 'I'm not concerned one way or the other. I was doing the right thing by my team, and I think that's my duty, to get them a fair go.'

In the end there was no need for earpieces, woolly hats or lawyers. Eddie pleaded guilty and was fined $10,000, with the money going to charity.

An issue that couldn't be fixed by writing a cheque was Eddie's deteriorating relationship with the man who had taken over from him at the Wallabies. John Connolly had always considered the Queensland coaching job rightfully his. Eddie felt the same about the Wallaby job. They were both strong-minded men well practised at working the media to put their case. It wasn't long before unsourced reports began appearing in newspapers hinting that Eddie was in regular contact with his former Test players, undermining Connolly and virtually coaching them from afar. At the same time 'unnamed sources' speculated that Connolly was campaigning to have Eddie sacked at the Reds so that when his contract ended after the World Cup he could assume the position of coaching director with his protégé Michael Foley appointed coach. Gary Flowers started to feel like a teacher trying to deal with bickering schoolboys.

'Eddie and Knuckles were at loggerheads pretty quickly. John is not one to back off. He goes full throttle, and Eddie is the same. Eddie was let go by us and he had a point to prove. There was no way he was going to cooperate with Knuckles and he did us no favours at all in terms of aligning the Reds with the Wallabies' interests. In those days we were trying to get strength and conditioning aligned nationally so the Wallabies and state players were working on the same programmes. That proved problematic for Eddie. He saw it as his show and he wanted to do things his way. It didn't make for an easy relationship.'

And it didn't make for an easy environment for the players, says then-Reds and Wallaby hooker Stephen Moore.

'I won't say it was a memorable season. Eddie is a coach who enjoys working with some of the best players and assistant coaches in the world. He sets very high standards for himself and for others. He likes working with people who think similarly to him. That very high level is his sweet spot, and that's the level he'd been operating at for quite a few years before he took over at the Reds. To come down from that was tough for him. We had a lot of inexperienced guys at the Reds that year. It was like Eddie had gone from working with some of the best in the world to working with club players.'

For ten months the pressure built. The team staggered from one loss to another. Morale was at rock bottom. Reds chairman Peter Lewis was continually called upon to refute speculation that Eddie was about to be sacked. Eddie admitted his daughter Chelsea had not enjoyed leaving her friends in Sydney and moving to Brisbane, but that he was still committed to seeing out his three-year contract. Eddie and Connolly were said to be 'not on speaking terms' after Test fullback Chris Latham was injured in a Reds training drill. From the first home game of the season to the last, crowds had dropped by over 10,000. By the time the Reds flew to South Africa for their last two matches of the season against the Stormers and Bulls it was with a sense of relief that the nightmare was nearly over. In fact, it was just beginning. The Reds lost to the Stormers 36-24 in Cape Town then headed to Loftus Versfeld Stadium, Pretoria, for what would prove the blackest day in Queensland rugby's 124 years. Stephen Moore says he doesn't remember much of the match. He has blocked it out.

'The one thing I do remember is standing in line behind the posts a lot of times. In saying that, that Bulls team was one of the best ever. They won the title that year, and then South Africa won the World Cup with a lot of those Bulls players in the side. It was pretty much a bunch of kids against some of the greats like Fourie du Preez, Bakkies Botha and Victor Matfield. When they started to pile on the points it was hard to stem the flow. Back then they used to sell out Loftus, and the crowd was right into it. It was daunting at the best of times, let alone in a game like that, when there was a cascade of scoring against us. You learn a lot from something like that, but it's pretty hard to take at the time.'

The final score was Bulls 92 Reds 3, the worst loss in Queensland rugby history.

Old-time players were aghast. Former Reds and Wallabies hard-man Sam Scott-Young went so far as to suggest that the players might have 'tanked' in order to get rid of Eddie.

'I can't believe it. It's an absolutely incredible scoreline and an absolute disgrace. There's obviously something deeply wrong with Queensland rugby, something that goes beyond the scoreboard. How can a team that pulls on the Queensland jumper get beaten like that? Could it be a player revolt? Have they lost confidence in the coach or even not like the coach?'

When the team's return flight from South Africa landed at Brisbane airport the media were waiting; reporters and camera operators gathered around the bottom of the escalator like hungry birds of prey. As the players emerged from customs and began slowly descending towards the pack it wasn't a pretty picture – although it did make a striking one for the next morning's front pages. In a spectacularly poor decision at the end of a season full of them, they had decided that, as their playing commitments for the year had ended, they shouldn't have to wear official team uniforms on the trip home. They came down the escalator dressed in a motley assortment of jeans, shorts, t-shirts and hoodies. In the words of Andrew Slack, writing in the *Sunday Mail*, 'looking for all money like a bunch of tourists just returned from a beach holiday'. One by one they stepped past the cameras and headed to the carousel to collect their bags. When it became obvious that there were no more to come, it dawned on the waiting media horde. 'Where's Eddie?' The coach wasn't with the team. He had left them to face the music alone.

'He's gone to England,' said one of the players. 'On holiday.'

That being the case, it was a working holiday. Eddie headed straight to Watford, and the offices of Saracens. Was their offer still open? Unfortunately not. Eddie's former assistant at the Wallabies Alan Gaffney was already installed in the coaching director's role, but they could offer a three- to six-month consultancy in the lead-up to the 2008–09 season. That was the official line anyway. Cynical observers believed Gaffney was really just warming the seat for Eddie until he arrived. Either way Eddie agreed and sent word to the QRU that he would not be returning. The horror of the 2007 Super Rugby season was behind him, but he would never be able to live down the stain of that day at Loftus Versfeld.

Asked by the *Japan Times* newspaper in 2014 to describe his most embarrassing moment, he answered: 'Experiencing a big loss while coaching the Queensland Reds. The Bulls beat us 92-3.'

He acknowledges that the entire Queensland experience was a mistake.

'I shouldn't have stayed in Australia,' he says. 'Once you have coached the national team, if you want to keep coaching you have to get out of the country.'

12

INSIDE THE BOKS

South Africa dealt Eddie the most embarrassing loss of his career. It also offered him a lifeline.

The close relationship between Eddie and Jake White took root in 2000. White was on the staff of Springboks coach Harry Viljoen and visited the Brumbies on a fact-finding mission along with Viljoen and fitness trainer Chris van Loggerenberg. It was an immediate meeting of minds. White, like Eddie a former teacher, was a student of the game, always eager to learn and exchange ideas. And, like Eddie, he admits he is obsessed with rugby.

'I'm not someone who can detach himself from the game. I'm always in rugby mode. I think about rugby when I wake up and I think about it before I fall asleep. Sometimes I dream about it. I don't know what I would've done if I wasn't part of rugby, but I'm sure I would be a miserable person.'

What began as a professional relationship soon developed into friendship. Whenever Eddie was in South Africa, or White in Australia, they got together for a beer or coffee and a chat about rugby. Even when they were opposing each other as national coaches they remained close – not that it was evident from the way they bickered and baited each other in the media. Prior to a 2005 Test in Sydney Jones predicted that White would attempt to turn the week leading up to the match into a 'sideshow' and labelled him 'Sideshow Bob' in reference to the character on the TV show *The Simpsons*.

White's involvement with the Springboks set-up began when he was appointed technical advisor to national coach Nick Mallett in 1997. He had been an assistant to Viljoen in 2000–01 and coach of the South African Under-21s for two years before replacing Rudolf Straeuli in the top job in 2004.

Coaching the Springboks is one of the most high-profile, and high-pressure, jobs in South Africa. Public expectation and scrutiny are enormous, and the Springbok coach has the added complication of having to tiptoe through the minefield of the country's racial sensitivities. While in 2004 South African rugby was still a long way off the recently introduced quota system that will see all Springbok teams made up of 50 per cent black players by 2019, White's selections still had to be ratified by South African Rugby Union president Brian Van Rooyen.

In his seventh Test in charge – a vital Tri-Nations clash against New Zealand at Ellis Park, Johannesburg – White had his selected team handed back to him because it contained only one black player, winger Breyton Paulse. Although the selected players had already been informed they were in the side, White was forced to replace scrum-half Fourie du Preez with black player Bolla Conradie before Van Rooyen would approve the team. The Springboks won 40-26 and would go on to beat Eddie's Wallabies in Durban the next week to secure the Tri-Nations, but the question of 'merit versus colour' would continue to be a thorn in White's side throughout his tenure. On that year's tour of the UK, black winger Ashwin Willemse broke his foot against Ireland, ruling him out of the England Test at Twickenham. Replacing Willemse with white winger Jaque Fourie would leave just one black player in the side, prop Eddie Andrews, so White asked permission from Van Rooyen to make that call. Permission granted, White announced the team to his players and began training them as per selection. The next day Van Rooyen told White the decision had been reversed and that Breyton Paulse must be brought into the starting XV. Paulse, a respected fifty-Test veteran, was understandably angry and insulted to be considered a 'quota player' and had a poor game in South Africa's 16-32 loss. Jaque Fourie was equally upset to have lost a hard-earned Test cap due to a blatantly political selection. White was finding himself in an increasingly frustrating no-win situation. Not for the last time he turned to his friend Eddie Jones for support and advice.

The Wallabies were also touring Britain, with Eddie's side due to face Scotland at Murrayfield on the same day the Boks played England. The chance to compare notes was an opportunity White wasn't going to miss.

'On our day off I flew to Edinburgh to meet with Eddie and discuss tactics against both England and Scotland. He shared some insights on the Scots, and I shared insights on the English, as the following week we would swap opponents. It was great to meet, because we didn't normally get to see much of each other during the year, and I was still learning about what was required to beat these teams in their own backyards.'

It proved an illuminating meeting for both men. Eddie's Wallabies won both their upcoming Tests, beating Scotland 31-14 and inflicting England's first defeat under Clive Woodward's replacement, Andy Robinson, 21-19. The Springboks finished off their tour with a dominant 45-10 win over the Scots, but as much as a chance to exchange intelligence, the get-together gave Eddie his first insight into the enormity of the outside pressures that White was up against.

'It's hard enough being an international coach of one of the top four or five nations. The expectations are massive, especially in a country like South Africa, where the Springboks are revered. You're playing with slim margins as a top international coach, so if there is any interference in team selection or any other aspect, it can be destabilizing. Jake had those normal pressures as an international coach, and then another layer other coaches don't have to endure. I understand why, in a young democratic country, certain decisions are made for South African rugby, but it makes life incredibly tough for a good coach.'

The spectre of political interference over selections was just one of the challenges facing White when he took on the job. Straeuli had left under a large, dark cloud after the Springboks limped their way through a disastrous 2003 World Cup campaign. Playing in Pool C along with eventual tournament winners England, the South Africans fell at the first hurdle, Clive Woodward's men beating them 25-6 in Perth. Finishing second in their group, they were then sentenced to a quarter-final against the All Blacks, who brushed them aside 29-9. Big wins over Uruguay, Georgia and Samoa were meaningless. When push came to shove the Springboks had failed to score a single try in their two 'top-tier' matches and were headed home. But it was not the team's on-field performances at the World Cup – or even reports of racial tensions within the team throughout the tournament – that dragged the reputation of South African rugby through the mud. It was what happened in the lead-up.

After the tournament the Johannesburg newspaper *Sunday Times* published sensational claims about a military-style training exercise known as Kamp Staaldraad (Camp Barbed Wire). According to an anonymous whistle-blower (later identified as video analyst Dale McDermott), players had been subjected to four days and nights of 'training' at a police camp that bordered on physical and psychological torture. Ongoing newspaper reports – supported by photographs taken from McDermott's video – revealed that, under the supervision of armed instructors, naked players were forced to crawl through gravel and stand in freezing water up to their necks while pumping up footballs. Hooker John Smit later claimed that when he and team captain Corne Krige had tried to leave the water, bullets were fired over their heads. Smit told of back-rower Joe van Niekerk 'hyperventilating' when forced to kill a chicken with his bare hands. Van Niekerk became so distressed that another player stepped in to help. Worked up at the sight of van Niekerk's botched attempts to despatch the poor bird, when Smit was ordered to carry out the same task with another chicken he ripped its head from its body. Photographs also supported claims that players were made to huddle naked in a pit while recordings of *God Save the Queen* and the All Black haka were played continuously at full volume.

The fallout was dramatic, and ultimately tragic. Straeuli, after initially trying to defend the camp, was forced to resign along with many of his staff. McDermott, unmasked as the whistle-blower, was sacked from his job. When Jake White was appointed Springbok coach he tried to have him reinstated, but SARU refused. McDermott was later found dead from what the police described as a self-inflicted gunshot wound to the head.

It was in this climate of global public humiliation, team disharmony over revelations that prior to the World Cup white players had refused to room with black team-mates, political interference and tragedy that Jake White was given the task of putting together a cohesive, winning rugby team. A team capable of doing the seemingly impossible: lifting the 2007 Rugby World Cup in Paris.

White made some key changes, appointing John Smit as captain, bringing 1995 World Cup-winning front-rower Os du Randt back into the fold and introducing Bryan Habana to Test rugby.

'I had wanted to change things when I took over, but I can't take credit for the way in which we changed. I think the players had wanted change. And after 2003 it was a logical time to move forward. We couldn't continue the way we had been, and all the senior players realized that. The new players felt the positive energy, and that set us up for the future.'

At the start things went well. There was the 2004 Tri-Nations victory and wins over Wales and Scotland on the Grand Slam tour, but on-field results were only half the battle as far as White's future was concerned. In 2005 he came close to losing his job when he refused to drop IRB Player of the Year Schalk Burger for a series-deciding Test against France in order to include black flanker Solly Tyibilika as a tribute to a recently deceased black local administrator and former player. The SARU backed down when the Springboks won the Test and the series, but the incident was typical of the political climate in which White had to operate. In 2006, the wheels came dangerously close to falling off.

During long, and at times heated, negotiations over a contract extension, it emerged that White had been approached to apply for the position of director of rugby by England's powerful Rugby Football Union. White informed the SARU of the approach, but when the story appeared in the media there was a perception that he had leaked it to put pressure on SARU. Poor on-field results fuelled public dissatisfaction and toxic press coverage. There was a bitter breakdown in communications between White and the media, and when the Boks suffered a 0-49 thrashing at the hands of the Wallabies, his chances of taking the team to France plummeted.

The South Africans ended the season with two Tests against the Andy Robinson-coached England at Twickenham. Both coaches came into the series under similar pressure. The World Cup-winning reign of

Clive Woodward was proving a hard act to follow, with Robinson said to be on his final chance after England had lost a home Test to Argentina for the first time. That the series was drawn – England winning the first Test 23-21 thanks to a late Phil Vickery try after the Boks had led 13-6 at half-time, and South Africa taking the second 25-14 – wasn't enough to secure the future of either man. Robinson was forced to resign four days after the second Test. White survived, but only after he had to fly back from England to put his case to the SARU board following a vote of no-confidence. Relieved, but far from confident about the backing of his employers, he set about preparing for the World Cup.

On the field the World Cup year started well. The Bulls pipped the Sharks 20-19 in the first-ever all-South African Super 12 grand final before the Boks met an under-strength English touring team in a two-Test series. Newly appointed England coach Brian Ashton was without thirty of his top players due to injury and unavailability, with Leicester, Wasps and Bath all involved in European cup finals. Future England captain Dylan Hartley was ruled out due to suspension. Hopelessly outgunned, England went down 58-10 and 55-22. The opposition might have been second-rate, but White was not complaining. His team had performed well, and confidence was building. Off-field, things were not as rosy, with yet another political storm creating tension. On this occasion White wasn't pressured to change his initial forty-five-player squad for the season. Rather, SARU simply added the name of black flanker Luke Watson to the list and announced it without telling him. To avoid further disruption White agreed to play Watson in a Test against Samoa, then never picked him again, believing he was not up to international standard.

Following the Tri-Nations, in which South Africa won just one match – against the Wallabies 22-19 in Cape Town – and lost 6-33 to the All Blacks at Christchurch, White cut his squad down to the final thirty for the World Cup. After a long and at times arduous journey, he was ready to head to Paris. He just needed to make one final addition to the squad.

As the 2007 World Cup approached, Eddie's career was at its lowest ebb. Within minutes of the Wallabies losing the 2003 final to England he had spoken about plans to go one better four years later but, sacked as Wallaby coach at the end of 2005 and leaving the Queensland Reds after just one enormously disappointing season, his chances of being involved in a successful World Cup campaign in 2007 seemed non-existent.

Eddie's many detractors within Australian rugby circles had taken pleasure in his fall from grace, but Jake White had never lost faith in his friend's ability and continued to marvel at the depth and breadth of his knowledge.

Prior to the Springboks Test against the John Connolly-coached Wallabies at Brisbane's new Suncorp Stadium in 2005, White had met with Eddie for coffee. As a recently departed Wallaby coach it would not be proper for Eddie to give White any inside information about the Australian team but as a coach whose teams had played at the old Suncorp many times, he did offer a warning, White recalled.

'We chatted about rugby and kept the conversation fairly general, as he obviously still had links with the Australian camp, but one thing he said to me was interesting. He said, "Jake, Suncorp is a multi-phase stadium, so it's very quick. The tempo of the game is much quicker than at any other stadium." He meant that it is a ground that's conducive to quick, flowing, running rugby, with as few scrums and lineouts as possible, which is exactly the way Australia like to play it. While I regarded Eddie highly, I thought he was a bit off the mark with his deduction. I thought, "Geez, Eddie, how can you make a statement like that? You already know what kind of game it's going to be between two teams playing on any given Saturday in the middle of July." I didn't quite buy it. It's a stadium with four lines and grass, but Eddie was spot on.'

The Australians played the game at top speed and ran the Springboks off their feet in the record-breaking 49-0 victory.

It was that kind of analysis and attention to detail that other coaches might not even consider that moved White to invite Eddie to attend a few Springbok training sessions prior to the World Cup. Eddie, who was in Japan, was due to join Saracens and agreed to stop over in Cape Town for a week on his way to England. White was impressed at how quickly the Springbok players responded to Eddie's ideas.

'In that week I saw how much value Eddie added. He took existing ideas that we had and put a different spin on them. It was a fresh approach, and I could see the guys responding to him very positively.'

While Eddie was in Cape Town the Springboks' technical advisor Rassie Erasmus told White that he had accepted the job as head coach for the Stormers Super Rugby franchise from the start of the 2008 season and would be unable to go to France. Initially angry, White saw a ready-made replacement close at hand.

'After pondering for a few days, I said to Eddie, "How would you feel about staying on to the end of the World Cup?" He didn't hesitate with his reply: "I'd like to, Jake." He was genuinely excited because he thought South Africa had a chance to win the World Cup and he saw a good opportunity to be involved with a potential world champion team.'

Eddie received permission from Saracens chief executive Mark Sinderberry to delay his arrival, but getting SARU to sign off on the appointment was not as straightforward. The idea of a non-

South African being involved with the Springboks' World Cup campaign did not sit easily with the national body, plus there was the fact that Eddie was not the most popular person amongst South African rugby fans. His outburst over the Bakkies Botha–Brendan Cannon incident, in which he'd called the Springboks 'a disgrace', had earned him the nickname 'Eddie Moans'. White persisted, however, and Eddie was added to the coaching team – with one stipulation from SARU: he was not to be considered a full member of the squad and would not be issued a Springboks blazer. The closest he could come was a team tracksuit, but even that caused controversy. The first time a photograph of former Wallaby coach Eddie wearing a Springboks emblem over his heart appeared in the media, the outcry in Australia was loud and overwhelmingly negative.

One of the first to weigh in was John O'Neill, only recently returned for a second stint at the ARU after three years as CEO of Football Federation Australia. O'Neill described Eddie's decision to join the Springboks as, 'not something you would really expect of a former Australian coach'.

'Eddie was still coaching Queensland until a couple of months ago. The argument would be, "Oh well, it's a professional game now, you go to the highest bidder, a job is a job." That's a pretty clinical and a rather sad reflection of where the game may have ended up. It's a very curious decision by Eddie. This is a quite definitive, eyes-wide-open move by Eddie to go and advise the Springboks on how to beat the Wallabies, amongst other things.'

A man whose sharp tongue could rival Eddie's, O'Neill could not resist a dig.

'I'm not sure whether Eddie is going to be able to offer any particularly useful insights, and I think the combination of Jake White and Eddie

Jones is an interesting one – Sideshow Bob and the Beaver. I don't think that in any way it should alarm the Wallabies. It might help them.'

Prominent Sydney rugby writer Spiro Zavos was less light-hearted in his condemnation. 'Is there something wrong with Eddie Jones getting into Springboks gear and helping out in coaching the side in its pre-World Cup training?' he asked in his column.

'I reckon there is. Jones has been paid big money to coach Australia and Queensland. He has picked up a great deal of intellectual rugby property from the Australian system. He should not be passing this on to a side that could well be facing the Wallabies some time in the World Cup tournament. It doesn't seem right for Eddie Jones to be so supportive and helpful to the Springboks. There seems to be an element of payback in all of this. A former Wallaby coach should not be making it harder for Australia to win the 2007 World Cup than it already will be.'

Not surprisingly, Eddie hit back, taking special aim at his former boss O'Neill.

'John is entitled to his opinion, but it's a bit like the pot calling the kettle black. He went from being the chief executive officer of Australian rugby to being the chief executive officer of Australian soccer, which is a direct competitor. That was okay in his eyes. He is being hypocritical: when he was running Australia's national soccer side he appointed a Dutchman, Guus Hiddink, as manager.'

In 2008 O'Neill would also appoint Australia's first 'foreign' coach, former All Black Robbie Deans. Not only that, but after Deans came on board, he admitted to a journalist that he had in fact tried to employ him in the role while Eddie was still in the job.

'We met at a Salvation Army function in Christchurch after the 2003 World Cup. I was deeply concerned after England beat us in the final. While I felt Eddie did a great job taking us to the final, I couldn't see him taking us to the next level. I had a feeling he wouldn't see out his contract. I wanted Robbie then but he wasn't interested at the time.'

Eddie never knew about the moves going on behind his back so soon after the 2003 final, but regardless, he had no second thoughts about accepting the job with the Springboks.

'While you'll always have the softest part of your heart for the country where you were brought up, the fact is you move on if you have opportunities to coach in other countries. I don't have a guilty conscience. My coaching knowledge has been accumulated over a number of years and it has been the result of my own work. It is not nation-specific. If South Africa plays Australia in the World Cup I will be supporting South Africa 100 per cent. Some say that's disloyal. I don't. I think I've been a loyal servant to Australian rugby. I had eleven seasons as a professional coach in Australia. Some were pretty good, a couple not so good, but I don't have any regrets. I've lived my life to a set of values and will continue to do that. People can think what they like. I'll just get on with it.'

And get on with it he did. Eddie's role with the Springboks was primarily to work with the backs, but the entire squad appreciated his input. Team captain John Smit described White's decision to appoint Eddie as, 'a stroke of genius'.

'Jake had based a lot of his coaching ideas on Eddie's philosophies and the Brumbies' style of play under him. We would watch videos of the Brumbies and Wallabies and focus on things like their lineout structures and three-phase moves from scrums. We weren't replicating what those teams were doing; it was more a case of Jake wanting us to see the benefits of a phase game based on our strengths. This resulted in a structured game based around our forwards. Eddie had often told Jake in the past that he wished he had South African athletes to play the kind of game he wanted. Now he did.

'I thought getting Eddie involved with the Boks just before we left for Paris was an excellent idea, because we'd get an injection of fresh ideas and energy from someone who had been involved in a World Cup final. Eddie was welcomed with open arms by all the players, which perhaps wouldn't have been the case with previous Bok squads when foreign coaches were viewed with suspicion.'

The Springboks soon learned the high expectations that Eddie would be bringing to the table. At the first training session that he attended the team ran through their set plays. Afterwards Smit asked Eddie, 'What do you think? What would you give us out of ten?'

'If I'm being generous, about four,' he said.

Eddie has always tried to downplay the part he played in South Africa's 2007 World Cup victory, saying his advice to the players was little more than, 'Just keep doing what you're doing, but do it a little better.'

'The team was together four years. I was with them for thirteen weeks, so my contribution has to be gauged in those terms. I just tried to add a bit of detail and finesse. The systems were in place. All I did with the Springboks was paint over the cracks. I think the isolation [during the Apartheid sporting bans] had held them back and they were a little insecure. I look at my time there when they won the World Cup as being a house painter and fixing up the bits that needed a little bit of extra attention. I gave them confidence, added subtlety to their attack and taught them how to manipulate attacks.'

Eddie may be being overly modest, or perhaps he really does believe that his part in the Boks' World Cup success was relatively minor, but White and the players certainly don't. In the space of just a few months his individual work with key players, such as fly-half Butch James, took their play to a different level, Smit recalled.

'For Butch in particular, Eddie was a godsend. Even before we left for Paris, Jake wasn't convinced that Butch was the answer at fly-half and he said to me in the week of the World Cup opener against Samoa that he thought Andre Pretorius would be his fly-half for the big World Cup games. But in France Butch just grew as a player under Eddie. He hung on every word Eddie said. He got better and better every week and was running the show by the time we got to the end of the World Cup final. At that stage Jake thought Butch was God.'

Winger Bryan Habana, who ended the tournament as top try scorer, crossing eight times in seven games, is another who benefited from Eddie's knowledge and advice.

'He played a significant part in improving us on what we did. He did not introduce Australian-type changes but rather aimed at bettering our own game. I have enormous respect for him.'

But much as he might have helped improve the confidence and competence of individual players and, as Boks' centre Jean de Villiers noted, 'helped with the backline's creativity by fixing running lines and minor details that you sometimes miss', some, such as back-rower Bob Skinstad, believe Eddie's greatest contribution to the Cup win was his steadying influence on Jake White.

'I think Eddie's contribution was twofold. He helped the team to refine certain aspects of our play and he took the load off Jake. If I was to say which was more important I'd say it was weighted towards Jake. He was less experienced than Eddie and it is very tough in that situation. As the tournament goes on everyone wants something from the coach. He has to deal with the players, the media, the other coaches, the officials. There is only so much time in the day and Jake was only one man. Reporters might be saying, "Can we meet for coffee and talk about where the team is at the moment?" and Eddie would say, "I'll do that if you want." Having him there meant that they could spread the load. It took a lot of weight off Jake's shoulders.

'Eddie came along at the perfect time for Jake. At that stage in Jake's career it was all about learning the nuances of the job and surviving as a head coach. I remember talking amongst the senior players, and we said that the coaches who won World Cups were always the ones who had weathered storms. Clive Woodward had been under the microscope after 1999, and Jake had been under a lot of pressure in 2004. Eddie had had a tough time of it after 2003, and we felt that he added the value of having been through that. He was able to say to Jake and the rest of us, don't worry about this, don't try to fight that. We were able to benefit from his experience. In saying that, the team was already quite organized when Eddie joined us. We went into the World Cup feeling pretty confident. We'd had two South African teams in the final of the Super 12 so we knew we had good players, but luck plays a part. Going into that tournament, who would have predicted that we would play Fiji in the quarter-final and Argentina in the semi-final and miss out on the All Blacks thanks to France and a couple of forward passes? To win a World Cup all the stars have to be aligned. Eddie was part of that.'

For which White will always be grateful.

'Eddie brought many things, but for me the most important asset was that he had the experience of coaching a team in a World Cup final. Okay, he never won the Cup, but he knew about the pressures of the tournament, and other than Os du Randt no one in our set-up had that kind of experience, so Eddie's role was vital. South Africans aren't very good at learning from people who haven't been there before, so it wasn't just about Eddie saying, "Run deeper, go wider and maybe run this play." It was that he offered me insights that you can only gain from experience. He'd been a drop-kick away from being a World Cup-winning coach and he wanted another shot at it. He built my confidence, and that was great for me. After all my battles and selection issues, it was good to have an outsider who was able to take an objective view. Sometimes he'd tell me to relax, because he'd been through similar situations too. At other times he'd reaffirm what I'd been thinking or doing. It was a great comfort.'

One example of Eddie being a calming influence on White was when the Springboks were struggling early in their opening match against Samoa.

Concerned and edgy, White asked, 'Eddie, what's happening here?'

'I don't know, mate,' he answered. 'I've never been in this position before. Let's hope they're in the lead by the time we get to the shed and then we can work it out.'

The response brought a laugh from White, and by the time they got to the shed the Boks were indeed in the lead. They won 59-7.

The Springboks were drawn in the same pool as England. Defeating the defending world champions and finishing top of the pool was a vital part of White's blueprint to lift the Webb Ellis Cup. Both teams started the tournament with wins, although England made hard work of putting away USA 28-10 while after their scratchy start South Africa looked very strong in despatching Samoa, Habana scoring four tries.

On 14 September over 77,000 spectators flocked to Stade de France for what was expected to be a close tussle between two teams at the top of their game. It was anything but, with injuries and suspension to key players making England's preparation a shambles. The week before the game the media was full of speculation over whether 2003 cup final hero Jonny Wilkinson would play. In the end he succumbed to an ankle injury sustained at training. Not only that, England were without back-up fly-half Olly Barkley, who was also injured in a training mishap. Coach Brian Ashton attempted to fill the massive void by alternating centres Mike Catt and Andy Farrell in the number ten position, but with the backline severely disrupted and the team missing captain Phil Vickery, suspended for tripping in the USA game, England were brushed aside 36-0.

White doubted he would see the English again, but somehow they regrouped. With Wilkinson and Barkley both available for the next match, England beat Samoa 44-22 and then Tonga 32-20 to finish second in the pool. South Africa made hard work of Tonga 30-25 after resting key players but finished strongly, beating USA 64-15 to top the pool undefeated.

The first day of quarter-finals was one of the most incredible in the history of the World Cup. First England, rank outsiders, beat Australia 12-10 in Marseilles, Jonny Wilkinson once again the destroyer, scoring all his team's points through penalty goals. Eddie refused to comment on his former team's early departure from the tournament, but Jake White had no reservations. The following day, as South Africa prepared for their quarter-final against Fiji, he was asked why Australia had lost to England. Referring to Eddie, he answered, 'He's standing in our dressing room downstairs.' That same day in Paris France pulled off one of the all-time rugby upsets. Beaten 17-12 by Argentina in their opening pool match, the French added to twenty years of Kiwi World Cup misery and eliminated the mighty All Blacks 20-18. New Zealanders cried foul over referee Wayne Barnes missing what appeared to be a forward pass that led to a French try, but the All Blacks were given the benefit of the doubt on a similar ruling. Either way, England and France would meet in one semi-final with South Africa, after beating Fiji 37-20, up against Argentina, 19-13 victors over Scotland, in the other.

By now Eddie 'Moans' was one of the most popular people in South Africa. Even former Springboks coach Nick Mallett – a highly competitive man with no love for Australians after his side was knocked out of the 1999 World Cup semi-finals by Rod Macqueen's Wallabies – acknowledged Eddie's positive influence. In an acerbic and perceptive newspaper column written late in the tournament Mallett might have taken a subtle dig at Eddie's willingness to give television interviews, but he couldn't ignore the way the Springboks had responded to his knowledge and personality.

'Jake White's inclusion of Eddie Jones in South Africa's coaching squad is proving to be a masterstroke. Jones is permanently cheerful as he clatters along in his tiny rugby boots from coaching session to TV camera. He also brings the knowledge of a coach who has taken his team to a World Cup final. And, of course, Jones has that ridiculous Australian belief that he is a winner. You cannot underestimate the importance of all that to this South African team. The Afrikaans-speaking South African is habitually portrayed as arrogant and insular. But as so often with this business of being human, the bravado is a façade for a pretty rickety interior. Your average Afrikaner is insecure, hiding behind his siege mentality with a show of aggression.

'Eddie Jones has become Uncle Wallaby to this South African team. He has told them how much they are respected by Australia and the rest of the world. South Africans just don't tend to hear enough of that sort of thing. Suddenly the players are becoming as confident on the inside as they are on the outside, and it is coming through in their rugby.

'Mr Jones has also brought a great deal of Australian know-how to South Africa's back play. He may have lost his job as Australian coach when the scrum came down around his ears, but Jones's backlines, from the Brumbies to the Wallabies, have always been brilliant. Jones is teaching those methods to the South Africans. The Aussie's positive outlook is a major boon for Jake White, who is himself gregarious and a natural optimist. One of the main reasons behind New Zealand's failure to win a World Cup since 1987 is the saturnine way that the camp tends to turn in on itself. The Aussies like to say that they are smarter than the Kiwis, but I tend to think that they do well on the big occasions because they are more cheerful.

'But I don't want to give the impression that this South Africa team is the Eddie Jones show. Jones remains White's appointment. It is one of several shrewd decisions made by South Africa's coach.'

As was his decision to play Skinstad off the bench against Argentina ahead of big Wikus van Heerden because he believed the Pumas would kick a lot in the hope of turning the gigantic Springbok forwards around. White gambled that Skinstad's extra athleticism would prove decisive late in the match, and it paid off. South Africa won 37-13 to book their place in the final. In the other semi the French could not replicate their miraculous performance of a week earlier against the All Blacks and went down 14-9 to England. Written off after their one-sided loss to the Springboks in their pool match, the English had earned a rematch and the chance to defend their title. No one was more surprised than White.

'I never expected to play them again. After the pool game they had the deflated look of a side heading home. I'd watched them closely in the media mixed-zone session after the game, and they appeared to be on the brink of collapse. When we later climbed into our bus, I noticed the England team bus was parked next to ours. It looked like a morgue. I never thought England had it in them to win four consecutive games and claw their way into the final, but I respect how they fought back. It was a great achievement.'

It was in the week leading up to the final that Eddie's experience of 2003 really came to the fore. White was nervous and edgy. Eddie was able to calm him down.

'Eddie kept reminding me, "They need to hear your voice. It's about what you say and how much you say. They draw confidence from what you say and your body language." So although I delegated to my coaching staff, I did a lot of the talking in the last week. In retrospect, it was a good thing.'

White says there was another recurring thought during that week, and it went back to a conversation he had with Eddie at the start of their World Cup journey.

'When I'd initially asked for his assistance as technical coach at the World Cup, he asked me a question. "Can you turn silver into gold, mate?" Eddie had quipped. He was only half joking but now that we were on the brink of fulfilling a dream I had another reason to avoid disappointment. I didn't want Eddie to leave a World Cup with another silver medal.

'I had a lot of nervous energy, and Eddie eventually said, "Jake, the players cannot be better prepared. They cannot have a better understanding of what they have to do on the field. They cannot be better off athletically, so stop worrying." We had thirty fit and healthy players without one niggle, and Eddie reminded me of how rare this is. "That is an incredible thing," he said. "It's not like we're carrying one player who is a fifty-fifty call." He was right.'

Eddie managed to convince White that with all the hard work done and a fit squad, there was nothing that could go wrong – but he knew better than to believe his own words. He had been in a similar situation just a week out from the 2003 World Cup final, and the best-laid plans had conspired to go awry. First the Wallabies had lost Ben Darwin and then, wanting a dry, fast track for the final, Eddie could only stand and watch as the heavens had opened. If that wasn't enough, Stephen Larkham, the Wallabies' key playmaker, was on and off the field for much of the game due to a head cut.

So when the players and coaching staff had their day off on the Thursday, two days before the final, he was ready for anything. Or just about anything.

'That day I had a conversation with a senior team official who was very unhappy with selections. He wanted more black players in the twenty-three. He was quite aggressive and wanted me, as a team consultant, to pass this on to Jake.'

Eddie chose to keep the complaint to himself, but Bob Skinstad remembers one key piece of advice that Eddie did pass on to the team that week: things don't always go as planned. Be prepared.

'He said, "You have the best lineout in the world. Everyone knows that. You are probably going to win all your lineouts. But what if you don't? England are going to attack your lineout. What are you going to do if they win one of your throws?" Basically he was telling the forwards to be prepared, that if something went wrong they shouldn't stand around wringing their hands and thinking, "Woe is me." It was the next bit that was the most important. He said, "If something goes awry, stay calm. Be the athletes you are." During the game England did win one of our throws, and Victor Matfield didn't hesitate, he charged across and made a perfect covering tackle on Mathew Tait in midfield. That was the sort of thing that Eddie brought to the team. He could be very succinct, very clear. I wouldn't say we wouldn't have won the World Cup without him, but he was very much a part of the whole team effort.'

The players made Eddie well aware of that fact after the tournament.

England had entered the final full of hope, but the Springboks were never really troubled, apart from a moment early in the second half that will forever spark debate. Unlike in Sydney four years earlier, the weather was perfect, the field dry and the South Africans' set piece was rock solid. England had plenty of ball but could not breach the Springbok defence until the forty-second minute, when, with the score 9-3 to South Africa, England centre Mathew Tait made a superb break and was pulled down a metre from the line. Scrum-half Andy Gomarsall threw wide, and Jonny Wilkinson flicked the ball into the hands of winger Mark Cueto, who dived for the corner. As Cueto placed the ball over the line Springbok number eight Danie Rossouw attempted to drag him over the sideline. At first glance it appeared Cueto had scored, but Irish referee Alain Rolland was not convinced.

'Just confirming,' he asked the television match official, Australian Stuart Dickinson. 'Is there any reason I cannot give a try please?' The TMO viewed the play from every available angle and ruled that Cueto's left boot had gone into touch a split-second before he grounded the ball. No try. It was as close as England would come. In the end it was a tryless match, much to the disappointment of spectators and TV viewers, but White and his team were ecstatic. Despite an injured knee, Springboks fullback Percy Montgomery kicked four goals from four attempts, and his team-mate Francois Steyn one from two against Jonny Wilkinson's two from two. With a winning scoreline of 15-6, South Africa were World Cup champions, and Jake White had turned silver into gold.

'The players walked up to receive the medals. The coaches were at the back of the line, and Eddie moved out of the way for me. He said, "You go first, mate." I refused and told him to go in front. Eddie has often tried to stay in the background, but I wanted him to feel an integral part of South African history that he had helped shape. He deserved his gold medal.

'When he was asked at a press conference if he had wanted to exact revenge for the 2003 Rugby World Cup, he gave a typically Eddie response. "It's not about revenge against England, but I might throw my silver medal away."'

The fate of Eddie's silver medal is unknown, but at the end of the 2007 campaign he was presented with something of equal significance. Bob Skinstad recalls that after the final the entire South African playing squad got together and decided that, in defiance of SARU's directive, Eddie should receive a Springbok blazer.

'It was a team decision. We were very much like that. We were a very tight group, and we saw Eddie as part of that group. He wasn't an outsider. Giving him a blazer wasn't sanctioned by the authorities, so we didn't have one to give him, and Bryan Habana said, "I'll give him mine." On the night of the World Cup presentation dinner we said, "If Eddie can't wear a blazer, none of us will." We wore our suits. That was the whole concept of our team, and that shone through.'

As it happened, Habana didn't have the opportunity to present his blazer personally, as Eddie recalled in his newspaper column the next year.

'On the day after the final Bryan wanted to see me to give me something, but I was flying off to Japan, so we never caught up. Three weeks later at the Saracens office a parcel arrived the size of John Smit. It was Bryan's blazer, framed – a lovely gesture from a wonderful player.'

The blazer remains a lasting reminder of a special time in Eddie's career.

'I used to experience great hostility when I went to South Africa but I really enjoyed my time with that team. They were outstanding, very humble, hard-working and open to ideas. They had a very strong team spirit, and everybody saw that. In the end, without being arrogant about it, South Africa won the World Cup pretty easily, although it was always going to be a tough final. That was the only game they didn't score thirty points. That shows they weren't only talented, but very unified to achieve a goal that everyone wants but is very hard to attain.'

Victor Matfield described Eddie as 'a great addition who made a real difference' to the Springboks and made a very telling observation about a man who has often been criticized for being 'too hands-on'.

'It suited Eddie to be assistant coach,' Matfield said. 'He could just concentrate on rugby. It brought out the best in him.'

*

There was more to Eddie's next job than 'just rugby', and it proved to be an unpleasant experience. In fact, he calls it his worst time in the game.

After a short visit to Japan to look in at his old club Suntory, where he still had a consultancy deal, Eddie headed to Saracens to take up his appointment as coaching consultant. It should have been a dream assignment. His six-week rescue mission in 2007 before taking on the Reds had been a great success. With the unqualified backing of Sarries' generous benefactor and chairman Nigel Wray and the support of club CEO Mark Sinderberry, with whom he had a harmonious partnership at the ACT Brumbies, Eddie and coach Mike Ford had staved off relegation and set a platform for the future. Now with the disastrous season at the Reds behind him and his involvement with the Springboks' World Cup win to restore his sagging spirits, he arrived at Saracens' Watford base reinvigorated for this next stage in his career.

Once again his high hopes would end in disappointment.

Alan Gaffney, Eddie's former assistant coach at the Wallabies, had taken over as Saracens' director of coaching when Eddie's short-term contract had ended twelve months earlier. With Mike Ford leaving to join the staff of England coach Martin Johnson, another Aussie, Richard Graham, had been appointed coaching coordinator.

Gaffney and Graham had built on the work done by Eddie and Ford. Saracens finished fourth in the 2006–07 premiership before being thrashed 50-9 in the semi-final by Gloucester. The following season they had a great run through the Heineken Cup, going down 16-18 to eventual winner Munster in the semi-final, and finished eighth in the premiership.

Eddie arrived three months later to take up what was to be a short consultancy position under Gaffney, but their positions soon changed. Eddie signed a three-year contract as director of coaching, with Gaffney becoming the consultant. Gaffney eventually left to join the Ireland national team as backs coach, leaving Eddie and Richard Graham to prepare Saracens for the 2008–09 season.

Graham, who had been part of Eddie's Australia A team that had scored an historic win over the 2001 British and Irish Lions, had been coaching at Bath for five years before joining Sarries. Like many before and since, he was staggered by Eddie's work ethic.

'Eddie would meet with the coaching staff at 6 a.m. to discuss how we were going to run the day, and again at 6 p.m. for a post mortem. I set myself a goal of beating him into work. I'd have my alarm set for 5 a.m. and get in there thinking I could be sitting at my desk when he walked in. It didn't matter what time I got in; he was already there. In over a year I never beat him once.'

Eddie mapped out a three-year plan to take Sarries to the top of the game in England and Europe. One of his first major moves was to entice England lock Steve Borthwick across from Bath, where he had played for ten years. Borthwick would then have another six successful seasons at Saracens before moving into coaching and becoming Eddie's right-hand man with Japan and England.

Under Eddie and Graham, Sarries began the 2008–09 season with two three-point losses to Harlequins and Sale Sharks before roaring to life with a 44-14 win over Newcastle, the start of a three-match winning streak. They would enter January with a respectable five from ten record, but from then on it would be the games being played off the field that would be of major interest to Eddie and the Saracens supporters.

Six months before the start of the season Saracens owner Nigel Wray had sold half of the club to South African billionaire Johann Rupert for £10 million. For Eddie the idea of a benefactor with deep pockets willing to bankroll his ambitious plans seemed like a match made in rugby heaven. It soon proved to be Eddie's idea of hell.

Wray, who had made his estimated £300 million fortune by investing in media, property and the British arm of Domino's Pizza, was a sport fanatic who had bought his local club Saracens for £2 million in 1995 and sunk many more millions into propping it up with little prospect of financial return.

Rupert, reputedly South Africa's richest man, had less altruistic ideals in mind when he set his sights on Sarries in early 2008. Chairman of the Swiss-based luxury goods company Richemont, which owned the iconic brands Cartier, Mont Blanc and Dunhill, along with other interests, Rupert saw Saracens as the ideal vehicle to capture the lucrative untapped 450,000-strong South African ex-pat market in the UK.

It was a plan that he had tried unsuccessfully to implement in 2004, when a bid to buy lower-division side Wakefield, rename it

London Tribe, staff it almost exclusively with South Africans and win promotion to the top league was knocked on the head by the RFU on the basis that a club's league status should not be for sale.

But with Saracens already in the top league, and the 50 per cent sale deemed a 'merger' rather than takeover, there was nothing to stop Rupert buying into the club. It was a move that eased the financial drain on Wray but raised concerns for Saracens' long-time supporters, who feared that their club would soon become a transit lounge for aged Springboks or young South Africans learning their trade before joining one of Rupert's Super Rugby franchises, the Bulls or Stormers. Local wits suggested that the club's name would be changed to Saraboks or Saffacens. Their fears were not eased when Rupert's daughter Caroline and former Springboks Francois Pienaar and Morne du Plessis were installed onto the Sarries board. Always optimistic, Eddie pushed on, but in December 2008, when his former Brumbies boss Mark Sinderberry announced that he was stepping down as Saracens CEO to 'pursue other career opportunities', the writing was on the wall.

Sinderberry's replacement was Rupert appointee Edward Griffiths, a former journalist, author and TV executive who, as CEO of the South African Rugby Union had coined the promotional slogan 'One Team One Country' for the 1995 Rugby World Cup.

In his time with Eddie at the Brumbies, Sinderberry had found that the best way to work with his coach was to give him what he wanted and keep out of his way. It had paid dividends with the 2001 Super Rugby title and Sinderberry – and Eddie – saw no reason why it shouldn't work just as well at Saracens. Griffiths was a different style of manager, one who expected to have his say on every part of the process. One, in other words, who was guaranteed to clash with Eddie.

Griffiths took over as Saracens CEO on 10 December 2008. On 9 February 2009, Eddie announced that he would be leaving the club at the end of season, with two years still to run on his contract. Former Springbok Brendan Venter was announced as his replacement.

Claiming the reasons for his departure were 'entirely personal', Eddie said, 'My wife and daughter have always given me unqualified support, but it is now time for me to put the family needs first. I have greatly enjoyed my time with Saracens extending back to 2006 and I wish the directors, staff and players well in the future.' He added that he was committed to coaching Saracens for their remaining six matches of the season and finishing on a high note.

He wouldn't last that long.

Two weeks later Venter contacted fifteen of Saracens' contracted players and informed them they would not be part of his plans for the next season. Included were former All Blacks lock Chris Jack, front-rower Nick Lloyd, who, at thirty-two, was told he was too old, and, most upsetting for supporters, centre Kevin Sorrell, who had played close to 300 games for Sarries and twice been voted 'Clubman of the Year'.

Eddie was incensed, describing it as 'the worst week I've ever had in rugby' and launching a broadside at Griffiths and Venter.

'You've got to treat people well, and I don't think that happened,' he said. 'I've never seen anything like it. Some of the guys have been in tears all week, and yesterday there was a meeting with lawyers. I'm 100 per cent disappointed. I brought my family here and I wanted to build a strong club, the best in Europe. There's never a right time for this. The impact of culling so many of your best players has a massive effect on the club.'

Within days he was gone, headed once more to the land of his ancestors. The land of reinvention. Japan.

13

RUGBY SAMURAI

To commentators and spectators the key moment in Japan's stunning 2015 Rugby World Cup win over South Africa in Brighton was when Japanese captain Michael Leitch rejected a kickable penalty goal which would have tied the game and opted for a scrum. To Eddie Jones, it occurred three years earlier when another Japanese captain, Toshiaki Hirose, made the mistake of laughing during a press conference following Japan's 21-40 loss to the French Barbarians.

When Eddie was appointed coach of the Japanese national team in April 2012 following three seasons with Suntory, he inherited a team with a long and, surprisingly, proud record of mediocrity. In over thirty years of trying the Brave Blossoms had never beaten a top-tier rugby nation. Their average score against the top teams was 85-0. In seven World Cup campaigns they had won just one match, against Zimbabwe in 1991. Four years later they were beaten 17-145 by the New Zealand All Blacks. Their overall World Cup record was twenty-four matches played with one win, two draws and twenty-one losses. Points scored for: 428. Against: 1158.

When Eddie announced in his first day on the job that he intended to make the quarter-finals at the 2015 World Cup, few took him seriously. Japanese players were too small, too slow and technically naive. Most of all, they were accustomed to losing. When American Football coach Vince Lombardi said, 'Show me a good loser and I'll show you a loser,' he could have been talking about the Japan rugby side.

Eddie's tenure in charge started well. Playing against weak opposition, the Brave Blossoms ran up some huge scores and breezed through the Asian Five Nations tournament, beating Kazakhstan 87-0, UAE 106-3, Korea 52-8 and Hong Kong 67-0. With a step up in class to the Pacific Nations Cup, they continued to acquit themselves well, losing 19-25 to Fiji, 20-24 to Tonga and almost causing an upset against Samoa, going down by a point, 26-27 in Tokyo.

By Japanese standards, it had been a great tournament. They had tried hard and gone down honourably to teams that were expected to beat them. All was how it should be. To Eddie, that attitude was precisely what he was trying to stamp out. The loss to the French Barbarians, eight days after the Samoa game, provided him with the perfect springboard from which to turn things around.

Eddie's former deputy at Saracens, Richard Graham, felt Eddie's 'sprays' were so good that he could have rehearsed them beforehand. His forwards coach at the Wallabies, Ross Reynolds, agreed, saying, 'I wouldn't be surprised. He's a very scripted person.'

Questioned about the infamous French Barbarians press conference by Spanish football journalist Guillem Balague in January 2018, Eddie admitted that on occasion he did pre-prepare his outbursts, but this was not one of them.

'I definitely didn't plan that, but it was the best thing I did because it helped change the mindset of the Japanese. They were a team that was happy to try hard and get beaten. If they got beaten fifty to twenty-five, everyone would clap and smile at the end because you'd put in and it was accepted that you'd lose.'

The media conference began ominously, Eddie sitting staring straight ahead, arms folded and his eyebrows already at attention. Speaking through an interpreter, necessitating long pauses which appeared to magnify his growing rage, he blasted his team's performance.

'We showed no fight. Physically in the first half we let the French Barbarians do what they wanted to do. We were completely outplayed in the set piece, and I was really disappointed with the players' attitude today so I have to have a real rethink about selection. A lot of those players today showed that they probably don't want to play for Japan. That's the reality. We had young blokes out there in the first half that should have been going out there and been smashing their opponents. So I had to yell and scream at half-time like a school teacher. Why? Players don't want to win enough. They don't want to change enough, so I'm going to have to change the players. Simple. We cannot have performances like that for Japan. There was nothing brave or courageous about that today. It was really disappointing. I've been praising the efforts of the players, but today we took a massive step back against a competent team but not an outstanding team. You know, if I was a young player playing today you'd want to be making a mark, and you didn't see too many of those players do that today. So we either find Japanese players who want to do that or we might have to go back to the old selection policy and pick ten foreigners, because that was bad today, a really bad indictment on Japanese rugby. I apologize for the performance. I'm responsible for it so I take full responsibility for the performance. My coaching is not up to the standard it should be, but I can guarantee I'm going to change things.'

It was then that a reporter asked a question to the captain Hirose, who leaned towards the microphone, sighed and half-smiled, almost as if to say, 'How do I follow that?' It was a moot point, because he never got a chance to open his mouth before Eddie saw an opportunity and pounced.

Eddie's former coach Bob Dwyer has described what happened next as 'so savage it was embarrassing'. Eddie considers it a crucial turning point in the history of Japanese rugby, and if Toshiaki Hirose was collateral damage, so be it.

'He was a great little bloke. I'm still friends with that guy. I have coffee with him every time I go to Japan but I knew that one of the most important things I had to do was change their mindset, so when he laughed I thought, "Shit, here we go. I might as well give this a twirl."'

And give it a twirl he did.

'It's not funny. It's not funny. That's the problem with Japanese rugby. They're not serious about winning. If we want to win we've got to go out and physically smash people, and we didn't do it. In reality some players today will never play for Japan again, unless they change. That's reality. You've got players who didn't want to make tackles. They're never going to play for Japan again, unless they change. You know, we've got to grow up. The options in front of us, what do we want to do with Japanese rugby? Do we want to grow up? Do we want to produce players who are international players, or do we want to continue down the track where we're a half-pie New Zealand side? We need players to grow up, to take responsibility, and it's got to start happening quickly, because we've only got three years until the World Cup. There's just no sense about winning, and we've got to get it into the players quickly.

'It's tradition in Japan. Look at it historically, all big games Japan has played they get beaten in the first half and then try in the second half. We have to change the mindset. The French players were grabbing us, stopping from defending and we're letting them do it. Every time we've put out a team this year against strong opposition it's in the back of my mind that it's going to happen. We need to find the players that aren't like that. It was disgusting today, No other way to look at it. We had fifteen players out there who did not want to put their bodies on the line. Players understand the game plan but they weren't physical. How can you play rugby and not be physical? I have to find players who are going to be physical.

'We've got a real problem in Japanese rugby. I just watched the Under-20s nearly get beaten by Zimbabwe. Players aren't strong enough, they're not fit enough, they haven't got the right attitude. We have to change things considerably and that's why I'm being so aggressive about how we played today, because we can't accept it because nothing is going to change otherwise. The players have to understand that. The players have to take responsibility for it. The players come in and say, "We didn't do this, we didn't do that . . ." that's a load of rubbish. What we didn't do was play with any sort of spirit or physicality tonight. Why have we got players at the end of the game racing out of the line and wanting to make tackles? Why weren't they doing that at the start of the game? They seemed frightened. We've got to change that mindset, just like the Japan soccer team has changed their mindset. They go out there and try to win the game. We go out there and all we want to do is just compete. They've all been in the squad for six to eight to ten weeks. They all know what is expected of them. There's no excuse.'

Before Eddie's blast, when it came to rugby, Japan was a country full of excuses. As one publication had said of a twenty-point loss by the national team, 'Japan won the second half and ended up losing honourably.' No journalist would dare describe another Japanese loss in such terms after sitting through Eddie's onslaught, which was directed as much to them as it was to the players.

'The chairman [of the Japan Rugby Football Union] came up to me at the end and said, "It's about time someone said that," and it did have an effect on the team because then it became evident that it was never good enough to lose. We became all about winning, and it helped change the way the Japanese thought about rugby. The spectators as well, and the media, because when you get those sorts of mindsets about a losing team or a losing country, it's not just the team and it's not just the players. It's the media and the fans. It becomes a self-fulfilling prophecy, and you've got to break that.'

After the French Barbarians tour Eddie called his coaching staff together and set them a task: tell me what is wrong with this team. They came back with three main points. The players were too small, they weren't fit enough, and they had what the coaches termed 'a farmer's mentality'.

As a player who had overcome his small stature with hard work and attitude, Eddie understood the first two. The third was not so obvious. It got back to Japanese culture, a riddle that Eddie would have to unlock if he was to turn around a team that reflected centuries of tradition.

'I think what they meant was, seventy years ago 75 per cent of Japanese grew rice, so they lived in villages and grew rice and in the village, there was one boss, and that boss told everyone what to do. If anyone stepped out of line they were kicked out of the village in disgrace and they had nowhere to go, so no one stepped out of line, everyone did what the boss told them to do. It meant that Japanese had no leadership skills. I couldn't accept that. How can one nation have no leadership skills? How can one nation that after World War II was an absolute mess and rebuilt the country to be one of the powerhouses of the world have no leadership skills? There's got to be leadership skills there. So what we did was create situations to develop leadership. We'd set up a team meeting in a nice room. We'd have a video camera in each corner, and the coaches wouldn't turn up, and we'd see what happened. We'd see who took charge, who ran the meeting. We'd set up training sessions where the coaches wouldn't turn up, and the players would have to lead. We kept on disrupting the environment and developing opportunities for the players to lead, and they did. They developed the skills to lead.'

And instead of the farmer's mentality Eddie set out to instil the mentality of the most famous of all Japanese warriors: the samurai.

'I commissioned a thesis on samurai culture, because I wanted to work out what were the non-negotiables of Japanese culture. Young people don't associate with samurais, but there are underlying characteristics and values in any society, and I wanted to understand them. What came out of it was the three characteristics of loyalty, trust and hard work, so those were the things that we really emphasized and kept hammering.'

With a Japanese sports psychologist employed to help the players with the cultural aspects, Eddie concentrated on the on-field preparation.

'If you're not big enough you can be faster, you can be fitter and you can be smarter, because nothing stops you from being that. I got the best fitness and conditioning coach in the world, because not only could he make them fitter, he could make them faster. We had about six months together and we were going okay, but if we were training the same way everybody else was training we might get as fit and as fast as everyone else, but we weren't going to be faster, we weren't going to be fitter. So we got together again and said, "Most teams train twice a day. If we are going to be a team that beats a tier-one country, we've got to train three times a day."'

Eddie introduced a 5 a.m. session.

'The players hated it. Most players couldn't sleep the night before because they were so worried they wouldn't wake up in the morning. Most of the coaches were the same. They couldn't sleep either. I'm lucky. I get up that time anyway, so it suited me. People said, "You can't do that." I said, "Why? No one knows what the body can do." So we had the players training at 5 a.m., 10 a.m. and 3 p.m. and we got them fitter and faster and we increased their body weight.'

But it wasn't all about the quantity of the training that the players did, it was about the quality. Part of Eddie's masterplan for the small Japanese players to outplay their larger, more experienced opponents was to make better use of the ball. There was no point trying to bash their way through the defence, they needed to get themselves into positions where the defence wasn't.

In studying the way teams in other sports managed to do that, Eddie became a big fan of Barcelona FC, and its coach Pep Guardiola. In 2013, with Guardiola then with Bayern Munich, Eddie arranged a visit.

'We had a small team and what we needed to do was find or create space, and I thought I might as well go and see the best coach in the world whose team played like that. I managed through one of the sponsors to arrange a meeting with him. He was very giving of his time. We sat down and spoke about the principles of finding space, and it really helped how we played as a team.'

But it was on the training field that Guardiola made an even greater impact on Eddie and the way he worked his players.

'I went and watched Pep's session. He was coaching some of the best players in the world, and it was minus five. It was freezing. They did quite a traditional warm-up, and I thought, "Maybe I'm not going to learn anything today," but then they had twenty-one players and they were in three teams of seven, working on getting into space. Pep was out there running the session and speaking in four or five different languages, telling guys like Arjen Robben what to do. It was just really enlightening how hard they worked in that twenty minutes and how he was embedding his philosophy on that team and how the players had bought into it.

'I remember them coming off, and they had sweat pouring off them. I have watched many football teams train, and they were down here and he was up there. It definitely changed the way that I coach. I came out of that session embarrassed about how I had been coaching. When I was a young coach I used to coach pretty hard and I probably got criticized a bit for it. I work the players a lot harder now, but for shorter periods.'

When he returned from Munich, Eddie cut the length of the team's training sessions from two or three hours to a maximum fifty minutes of high-intensity, high-quality work.

'I said to the players, "If I say train at 100 per cent, and you're not giving me exactly what I need, you're not going to train. You can go back to the hotel. You can drink green tea, you can eat nice mochi [rice cakes], you can do whatever you want to do but you're not going to train." The first couple of sessions we kicked players out of training, and the Japanese players hated it, but it sent the message that if you didn't come to training with intent of improving, then you weren't going to be there. We had players who would train long periods to impress the head coach, but with no intent to improve. So now we had fifty-minute sessions where the players had to come with intent to improve and we became the best training team in the world. We've got data to prove it. The speed of our training, the intensity of our training, was better than any team. So we were able to change the mindset of the whole team from being a traditional slow-training team to be being fast, intensive, competitive, going at each other. There was no senior versus junior any more. Everyone was competing with each other.'

These were all innovations that Eddie would adopt, refine and later bring with him to England. Coaching the Japanese national team was both a crossroads and a finishing school in his career. In the decade since he had coached Australia to the World Cup final, Eddie's CV had been far from glowing. He had been sacked by the Wallabies, had a disastrous season with the Reds, clashed with management at Saracens and been banished to coaching club rugby in Japan. Other than his success in a short-term consulting role with the Springboks in 2007, he was yesterday's man. Japan changed that. For Eddie it was very much the right job at the right time. The country of his ancestors offered him a clean slate that no tier-one nation could. The Japanese players might not have been as big or strong as Kiwis, Aussies or Brits, but they were compliant. They respected authority and were prepared to follow instruction without question. Likewise, the administrators running the game in Japan were willing to bow to Eddie's judgement, unlike the powerbrokers at the ARU. They allowed him to experiment and implement training regimes that more established unions would baulk at. If he berated his players or assistants in public, it was accepted as necessary, rather than a potential HR incident. All they asked for was results, and that is what Eddie gave them.

In November 2012, five months after the French Barbarians debacle, Eddie took Japan to Europe, where they beat Romania 34-23 and Georgia 25-22. The next year they again stormed through the Asian Five Nations undefeated, scoring 316 points and conceding just eight. There were also wins against Spain, Russia, Canada and the USA. The New Zealand All Blacks beat Japan 54-6 in Tokyo to reinforce the difference in class between the top side in the world and the rest, but it was another 2013 loss, 21-18 to Wales in Tokyo, that Eddie credits with providing a key ingredient to his arsenal, as the Brave Blossoms finished their World Cup preparation in 2014 with wins over Samoa and Italy.

'I was so angry when we got beaten by Wales. We made a simple mistake at the end of the game. I couldn't get to sleep that night and then I just came up with one phrase that encapsulated how we had to play, and we never looked back.'

Japan beat Six Nations champions Wales 23-8 in the return match to tie the series. It was Japan's first-ever win over a top-ten rugby power, although the achievement was downplayed internationally, as Wales was missing fifteen players who were touring Australia with the British and Irish Lions under Welsh head coach Warren Gatland, and stand-in coach Robin McBryde had made five changes to the side that had beaten Japan in the first Test. Even so, the win gave the Japanese players enormous confidence in their coach and the direction in which he was taking them. The phrase that had come to Eddie that restless night became an ingrained catchcry: a new mindset.

'It was a phrase that was simple to understand, but it changed the way we played. Sometimes you get it right, sometimes you don't. It was just about not letting a side recover. We had to make sure that when we were on the attack, as soon as we had the defence on the back foot we had to keep them on the back foot. It was as simple as that.'

14

EDDIE-SAN

The Japanese squad that arrived in England to contest the 2015 Rugby World Cup was a very different beast to the one that had started the campaign three years earlier. So was its coach.

In the time it took Eddie to turn a team of rugby neophytes into a force to be reckoned with, he had undergone his own journey of self-discovery. During that period he developed a spiritual affinity with the country of his ancestors, spoke at length to his mother for the first time about her struggles with cultural identity, lost his father and faced his own mortality.

Through all that he emerged a better football coach and, according to those who knew him well, a better, more balanced person. In the words of former Wallabies assistant coach Andrew Blades, 'Eddie got his mojo back in Japan.'

For Eddie, the journey really began in 2009 with his second stint at Suntory Sungoliath after his tenure at Saracens had ended in acrimony. For a rugby coach whose last three full-time positions had ended badly, it could have been seen as the Last Chance Saloon. His first experiences in Japan had been relatively brief, and their influence cursory. He and his wife Hiroko had dropped in on their way back to Australia after his six-month playing sabbatical at Leicester; there had been eighteen months at Tokai University, and one season at Suntory before climbing the heights with the Brumbies and Wallabies – and falling back down again.

The coach who returned to the Suntory clubhouse at Fucho, half an hour by train from central Tokyo, was a far cry from the cocky, self-assured Napoleonic figure who had clashed with officialdom from North Sydney to Watford over the previous decade. Suntory president Junichi Inagaki says Eddie was initially unsure of himself as he began his second stint at the club and obviously affected by the battering his career had taken since 2003.

'I would say he wasn't as self-confident then,' Inagaki told *Telegraph* writer Tom Cary. 'Now he is more confident and he has the experience and the reputation. He has become almost a monstrous character, but certainly at first he was a bit milder. He was always quite aggressive in terms of his passion for rugby, but particularly after the World Cup final against England, when Jonny Wilkinson kicked that drop-goal. Eddie struggled a bit after that, moving from job to job. The connection with Japan, and Suntory, probably worked well for him at an unstable time. Japan provided some continuity for Eddie-san at an unstable time. Japan was maybe lucky to get Eddie during that period when he was trying to get back to the top. But maybe Eddie was lucky to have Japan, too.'

By the time Eddie left Suntory to take on the role as Japan head coach in 2012, the Sungoliaths – spearheaded by Wallaby George Smith and Springboks' halfback Fourie du Preez – were back-to-back national champions. He was undisputedly the top coach in Japan, but by international standards that meant next to nothing. To the major nations, Japan remained a rugby backwater; a place for big-name Australians, Kiwis and South Africans to play a few seasons of second-rate rugby and pick up first-rate wages. There is a joke amongst rugby forwards: wingers only score a lot of tries because they are marked by other wingers. To the uninitiated the same could have been said of Japanese club rugby teams. They only won games because they played other Japanese teams.

When he took over as Japan coach, Eddie had been in the country long enough to know where he had to start if he was to implement change. To understand the national team, he had to understand the nation.

'The national team is always affected by the society. One of the things you try to do is understand how society operates and historically what has worked and what hasn't. I did a coaching clinic for 160 Japanese coaches and I was talking about the need to individually get the best out of each player, and one of the coaches put his hand up and said, "No, in Japan we want to harmonize everything. We want everyone to be treated the same way." You can't do that. If you want people to be high-performing, you can't be like the society. Society rules are put together for people to live together, not necessarily to win. To win you have to have certain principles that are different to society.

'The more I've travelled the more I've understood the psyche of teams and how it's affected by their culture and their society. If you energize the good parts of each of those cultures then you've got a good culture. One of the things you learn working in different cultures is the value of discernment, of understanding in that culture what is absolutely non-negotiable and what is negotiable, and keeping the things that are non-negotiable and changing the things that are negotiable.'

One of the things that Eddie did not try to change was himself.

'My wife is pretty clued-up and she said, "Just remember, you will never be accepted as a Japanese, so don't ever think you will be." That really stayed with me, so I never cared whether I was liked or not. All I was looking for was respect.'

Part of that process was being able to better communicate with the players. Eddie began learning to speak Japanese during his time at Tokai University. He was far from fluent according to Tokai vice-captain Toshihiro Miyano, but that did not prevent him from displaying the sledging skills honed at Matraville High and Randwick Rugby Club.

'He was learning some basic Japanese at that time. He was particularly good at making fun of people.'

By the time he was appointed national coach Eddie's Japanese language skills had improved markedly, but that didn't mean he always chose to display them. Like many bilingual people he often found it useful to downplay his fluency, preferring to use a translator while monitoring what was being said around him. The translator given the job of passing on Eddie's remarks to the Japanese players was Hidenori Sato. A specialist in working with foreign-born rugby coaches for over ten years, Sato considers translating for 'Eddie-san' the toughest assignment of his career.

'Just once I tried to tweak something he said to a player to make it less harsh, but Eddie understood enough Japanese to pick that up, and I never did it again, that's for sure. I would just be adding subtitles to the conversation because most Japanese understand English swear words, and I did not have to put in any emotion because he was doing plenty of that. Towards the end, some of the players started to dislike me because his words were coming out of my mouth.'

With the improved language skills, Eddie found it easier to assimilate. Heeding Hiroko's advice, he would never try to become Japanese, always considering himself an Australian ex-pat. Even so, he immersed himself in the Japanese lifestyle, regularly visiting the *onsen* (hot springs) at Odawara, 80 kilometres south of Tokyo, and developing an interest in Japanese baseball, especially the fortunes of his favourite player, Tohoku Rakuten Golden Eagles' never-say-die pitcher Masahiro Tanaka. It all helped him understand the culture he was dealing with on the training pitch, but Hiroko was right: he might earn respect, but he would always be an outsider.

That realization moved him to speak to his mother Nellie about how she had dealt with returning to Japan after spending much of her youth in the US.

'She had a tough life. Her family went to America and then, when World War II broke out, all the Japanese who had been working in the country, basically as Americans, were told they weren't wanted. They were put in internment camps. She went to one camp with her mother, while her father went to a different one. They exchanged letters, but these were censored by the government. When they went back to Japan after the war they were ostracized again. Outcasts. They never fitted in anywhere. So my mother made a deliberate policy when she went to Australia that we would be brought up 100 per cent Australian. When you are half and half, people don't treat you the same, but you have to be tough to survive. I never grew up feeling isolated, but it did make me think about what makes people tick.'

Thinking about what makes people tick became a key element of Eddie's coaching platform. To him a team was more than just a collection of talented players thrown together. They had to be carefully selected, each with individual strengths and qualities, in order to create the best possible outcome: a winning unit.

'You have to understand what your team needs to win. What are the roles you have to have, what are the responsibilities each role has, and be able to identify the talent to fill those roles. In rugby we have fifteen players. I am generally looking for thirteen players that can give me absolutely budgeted performance. That each week they are going to give me about seven out of ten, because then I know that we are going to be consistent, because if we have thirteen of the fifteen players playing seven out of ten, we are going to be in the ballpark, we're going to be in the game. Then I allow the team to have two X-Factor players. The X-Factor player is someone who can play absolutely brilliantly, but unless they are a freak, like a Lionel Messi, they can't play at that level every week. The brilliant players might give you a nine out of ten performance but then the next week they might drop to a four out of ten, so we allow to have two of those players. You can't have more than those because you get too much variation in your performance and therefore your chances of winning become less. So identifying talent is so important. The other two areas I find important are closely connected but different. One is being able to give your team absolute and complete clarity on how you want to be seen as a team, so for us it's how we want to play, how we want to train, how we want to behave, making sure you have very clear messages about what is expected and what they need to do. There's common language. There's no discussion about what everyone has to do, because in our game, when you're under pressure you have to make a decision. You don't have time to think, and the decision has got to be based on all the factors that are around you. You've got to weigh up those factors quickly and you've got to make the right decision. To do that you need to have a clear head. You can't be thinking, "Is this the way we do it?" You've got to be very clear about what you have to do. So clarity is enormously important to us. The other important area is cohesion: making sure that people work together, and again that comes back to understanding their roles and responsibilities, understanding the values and the expectations, what's tolerated and what's not tolerated. You want to have a self-driven team. As leader of your team, if you're doing a great job, you should almost make yourself redundant because your team is setting the standards themselves. If someone is not doing what they should do, your team is telling them so. It shouldn't be up to the leaders. If you're a leader and every time you see your team you are telling them what they are not doing right, then you're not doing a proper job as a leader. You've got to get your team to be self-regulating, because if you've got a self-regulating team it allows you to step back and look at the bigger picture. It gives you time to make the good decisions. You want your team to be operating by itself.'

When he first took over the Japan side Eddie was committed to using Japanese players instead of foreigners as his predecessor, John Kirwan, had done. The All Black legend was criticized for turning the Brave Blossoms into a virtual New Zealand B side. Although he ended his four-year tenure as Japan's most successful ever coach with a win-rate of over 58 per cent from fifty-five matches, Kirwan could manage only two draws against Canada at the 2007 and 2011 Rugby World Cups and at times had as many as eight former New Zealand or Tongan players in his side.

Eddie started out with the best intentions, talent scouting the Japanese junior sides in the hopes of spotting up-and-coming players who would be peaking for the 2015 World Cup. He was to be disappointed. Three months after taking over as national coach he fumed on the sideline as the Japan Under-20 side was beaten by Wales.

'Wales beat them 125-0. Three months in, I've thought, "This is a great job I've got. I've got no young players coming through, they're hopeless."'

Soon afterwards the same team barely avoided the ignominy of losing to Zimbabwe. Many of the best young Japanese players were in the side that went down to the French Barbarians in 2012, sparking Eddie's press conference meltdown. It was then that he embarked on his campaign to change the mindset of the Japanese players, but he realized that goal could not be achieved by working from the outside in. Any realignment of attitude had to start from within the team itself. He needed foreigners to show the way.

Suntory had taught Eddie a valuable lesson. By bringing in the likes of Smith and du Preez and integrating them with the Japanese players, rather than having the locals play a mere supporting cast role to the big-name imports, he found a successful balanced approach that he would use with Japan and, ultimately, England.

Overseas-born players who had been dropped from the side, such as New Zealander Luke Thompson, were recalled. Others, who Eddie felt had something to offer, were brought in. One was former Australian rugby league star Craig Wing.

Wing had grown up in Sydney playing both rugby union and rugby league. In 1997 he was a member of the Australian Schoolboys rugby side alongside future Wallabies George Smith and Phil Waugh that played an England Schools team containing Jonny Wilkinson and Steve Borthwick at North Sydney Oval. When he left Sydney Boys' High School, Wing had the chance to play rugby with the NSW Waratahs or league with South Sydney.

'The Waratahs said I wouldn't play in the top grade until I was twenty-three or twenty-four. At Souths I was training with the first-grade team when I was still at school. I signed with them and was playing first grade a month later.'

When Souths were thrown out of the competition temporarily two seasons later, Wing was approached by Eddie to join the Brumbies.

'He was a great rugby player as a schoolboy. Smart, strong, aggressive. He would have revolutionized the way the Wallabies played.'

Eddie met with Wing and his father Allan at a Sydney steak restaurant but couldn't convince him to make the move back to the fifteen-man game. After also knocking back an offer from the Brisbane Broncos rugby league team, Wing signed with the Sydney City Roosters. It proved a good move. Over the next eight seasons he played in four grand finals, winning a premiership in 2002, and became a regular in NSW Origin and Australian Test sides before returning for a final two years with the Rabbitohs.

'In my last season I made the Origin side after a few years out but I'd had a couple of shoulder reconstructions and started to realize I was human and couldn't defy time. I'd lived in Randwick or Bondi all my life. I was in that Sydney bubble and I thought I'd just like to go somewhere different. The idea was I'd play two years of rugby overseas, see a bit of the world, then hang up the boots, come home and find a job. I was talking to a couple of French clubs for four or five months, but it was going backwards and forwards, and then an offer came to play in Japan. I didn't even know they played rugby in Japan, but I did the deal, and it was a great experience. There are some things that you'd love one day, and the same things would get to you on different days, but overall it was incredible.'

In 2010, his first season in Japan, Wing's NTT Shining Arcs took on Eddie's Sungoliaths.

'Suntory were the top team, and we were right down the bottom but we nearly beat them. I think that was when Eddie thought I might still have something to offer. He told me, "You know after three years you can play for Japan?" It was the first time I'd even thought about it, but when he became the coach he gave me a call.'

Wing believes that even though Eddie at first talked the talk about fielding a national team made up primarily of Japanese-born players, he always knew he would have to play the foreigners.

'I'm sure it was part of the plan from the beginning. The way the Japanese players are brought up is to always follow the rules, never step outside the box. On the field they are good at playing the role of soldiers, but you also need generals. You need people who can be creative, score tries, get you out of tough situations. You can't always be inside the box.'

Other overseas players that Eddie brought into the side, and who would play a major role in its success, were forwards Hendrik Tui, born in New Zealand, and Tongan junior Amanaki Mafi, and former Otago winger Karne Hesketh. His most controversial move was appointing twenty-five-year-old Michael Leitch captain ahead of Toshiaki Hirose.

New Zealand-born Leitch had lived in Japan since he was fifteen and spoke the language fluently, but to Japanese rugby officials and supporters he was still a foreigner. Having imports coach and play for the Brave Blossoms was one thing. Having one lead them was another. The irony was that Eddie's only concern was that Christchurch-born Leitch was 'too Japanese'.

'He wanted me to get rid of the Japanese attitude that "almost winning is good enough" and to set Kiwi and Australian expectations. He kept drilling into me that I had to take responsibility on the field rather than waiting to be told what to do.'

One member of the squad who needed convincing of the value of bringing foreigners back into the fold was one of Eddie's 'X-Factor' players, goal-kicking fullback Ayumu Goromaru. Tipped to be the future of Japanese rugby when he made his Test debut aged nineteen in 2005, Goromaru had never fulfilled his potential at international level, being dropped after just three caps and missing selection for four years. He didn't make John Kirwin's squad for the 2011 World Cup and was considered washed up when Eddie offered him a lifeline in 2012. That three years later Goromaru would be named in the Rugby World Cup 'Team of the Tournament' is testament to the success of Eddie's transformative process.

Recalled Eddie: 'When Goromaru first came in he didn't like foreigners. He hated foreigners. He'd always sit at the back of the room. By the end of the tournament he was sitting at the front of the room and he was asking questions. The change in behaviour was enormous.'

With the core of his team in place and the process of changing the mindset of the players well underway, Eddie worked as he always did: flat-out with no thought of rest. It was all falling into place, the highpoint being the 23-8 win over Wales in which Craig Wing, playing in the centres, was the standout player.

'That was the start of the belief,' says Wing. 'That was the game when we started to think that we were moving up into the league of the bigger international teams.'

Nothing, it seemed, could stop Eddie. Nothing, but his own body.

On Tuesday, 15 October 2013 Eddie and members of his coaching staff were returning to Tokyo by car after inspecting facilities at a training camp site to be used in preparation for their 2 November match against the All Blacks. On the journey Eddie began to feel unwell.

'I hadn't really slept for a few days, then during this long drive I got a headache. When I got out of the car I was limping on the left-hand side, then I realized I couldn't touch my nose with my hand, which is one of the tests for stroke, so that was it, they packed me off to emergency.'

Eddie was diagnosed as having suffered a stroke and placed in intensive care. When the Japan Rugby Football Union issued a statement announcing that Eddie had been hospitalized, it sent shockwaves through the rugby world. One of the first to contact Hiroko was Jake White, who told reporters in South Africa that Eddie was experiencing paralysis, but able to speak.

'Typical of Eddie, he's talking about the challenge of the All Blacks and the subsequent European tour.'

Messages of support came from Eddie's former players such as Matt Giteau, and New Zealand coach Steve Hansen and the All Blacks players. Back in Australia, Eddie's friend and former Wallabies cameraman 'AJ' George was in constant communication with Japan backs coach and ex-Wallaby skills coach Scott Wisemantel.

'I was in shock. I was texting all the time. Scott kept me in the loop. It was a frightening time, but in the end it probably helped Eddie. He learned to let go a little bit, get other people to do things for him. I think it made him enjoy himself more.'

Former ARU boss John O'Neill also noticed that a change had come over Eddie.

'We had always maintained a civil relationship, and I met up with him in Japan after the stroke. I think it had been a Road to Damascus moment for him. The intensity of the bloke was extraordinary. I've never seen a coach work harder, but he had to learn that working sixteen hours a day is not what it is about. It is about being productive. I think he had a good look at life after the stroke. I detected a more at-peace Eddie Jones when we met.'

Former kicking coach Ben Perkins is another who believes Eddie is a more relaxed character since his stroke, but for Eddie himself it was a terrifying experience.

'I was paralysed down the left side, and it was frightening. I was in hospital for six weeks. By probably week four I had full mobility back but I did an extra two weeks of intensive rehab. I was driving the nurses mad, up at eight o'clock at night walking around for fifty minutes, trying to get better. When I had the stroke the first thing I thought when I woke up was: "We have got the All Blacks on

Saturday. How am I going to get out of the hospital?" The doctor said no, you'd better slow down, and I did. Since then I have taken every day as a bonus. I had coached officially for seventeen years, and it was the first time I had actually had a break. The doctor said, "If you recover fully you can coach until you're seventy," so I might keep him to that. It probably gave me renewed focus, how lucky I was to coach. It made me realize what fantastic opportunities I've had and to appreciate them fully.'

With Eddie still in hospital, the Brave Blossoms were caned 54-6 by the All Blacks. It was a loss that brought the Japanese players back to reality after their big win over Wales and one that still rankles Craig Wing.

'We were in that game until the last twenty minutes. We had some opportunities and we didn't take them. I was personally upset that the score blew out and we didn't score a try. Deep down I think we were intimidated. I'd watched the All Blacks over the years and during the game I remember thinking, "These blokes looked bigger and scarier on TV." I know it was the first game of their tour, and maybe they were taking us a bit lightly, but it would have been interesting to see how we would have gone if Eddie was there. He was very good on game day at getting you to focus on your task. I think the Japanese players in particular missed him.'

That being the case, when he returned it was as if he had never been away. For the five months leading up to the World Cup Eddie put the squad through a punishing training regime, including a camp at Miyazaki on the island of Kyushu at the southernmost part of Japan, which was a popular tourist spot due to its proximity to the ocean and nearby mountains. But there was nothing relaxing about the schedule Eddie mapped out for the players, recalls Craig Wing.

'I played nineteen years of professional football, and that was the toughest training of my life. It wasn't so much the physical side of it. It was more the intensity. As a rugby league player, I was used to training for two hours at a time, getting flogged on road runs and things like that, but Eddie was more scientific. Everything was well thought out. We didn't train for too long, but we trained many, many times. For five weeks we didn't get a day off. I think we probably set a record for the most sessions ever in a day. Everything was worked out in half-hour blocks. You went from one thing to another; skills, gym, meetings. I think Eddie thought if the Japanese players had too much free time they'd head off into the mountains or something, so every minute was taken up. We were pushed to the limit. It was all about going to the next level.'

The schedule at Miyazaki was varied, and punishing. Players worked on traditional rugby skills such as handling, kicking and scrummaging, but also on cross-sport training like wrestling and boxing. They cycled and hurdled. To ingrain the Randwick style of straight, close running they ran passing drills tied together with elasticated rope. Eddie even brought in former UFC fighter Tsuyoshi Kohsaka to teach his players how to stay low in contact. It might have seemed random at the time, but, as always, there was method to Eddie's madness, says Wing.

'People who have never seen Japanese club rugby have this idea that foreigners can just go over there and run around and cut the locals to shreds. That's not how it is. Some of the international players excel, but some don't. Eddie had a Springbok player with him at Suntory called Danie Rossouw. He was a formidable player, one of the best forwards in the world, but he was nothing special in Japan. He made no impact because he thought he could play the way he always had. He charged in with high body height thinking he could bash his way through the defence, but the little Japanese players would chop him down low around the legs. Eddie saw that, and I think that was a key to the way we played the Springboks in the World Cup. Keep low and chop them down. That was very much part of the game plan.'

The time at Miyazaki was so successful that Eddie has booked the same facility as England's training base prior to the 2019 World Cup. Wing says the camp not only took Japan's fitness and skills to new levels, but also served to bring the foreign and Japanese players closer together.

'I think the Japanese players carried the foreigners through it. They were used to following instructions. They could work for twelve hours without batting an eyelid, but even so I remember them saying, "This Eddie Jones, he works so much." That was the thing about Eddie. He was there every bit of the way with you. I've had a lot of coaches in my career and I put him right up there with the best of them. He tried to think of everything. He was really good with the older guys. He knew that we couldn't do it every day, so he was like: "Just make sure you're right on game day," and I appreciated that. He was tough on the younger guys, though. He broke them down and rebuilt them. He broke a few, but I suppose he'd tell you that if they couldn't take it they weren't tough enough for the job. And he wasn't one of those coaches that you'd think, "What would you know? You wouldn't understand," because he did understand. No one worked harder than Eddie. I remember during that camp I had days where I'd be up at 5 a.m. and after physio I wouldn't finish until 10 p.m., and then I'd be up at 5 a.m. the next day. One morning I've come out, and Eddie has said, "Did you watch the Melbourne Storm [rugby league] game on TV last night?" I've said, "Are you serious? I was asleep," but Eddie would have watched it. He was unbelievable.'

It was while Eddie was, as ever, working tirelessly at his goal of making a rugby team better in Japan that, 8000 kilometres to the south, his father Ted passed away in Sydney. Two years later he spoke to reporter Matthew Syed of *The Times* about his loss.

'He must have been very proud of you, I suggest,' Syed wrote. 'There is a long pause. "He was a good guy," he says finally. There is another pause as he seeks the right words. "There is one thing I regret. I should have spent more time with him towards the end, but I was working in Japan. The greatest song is the one by Harry Chapin where he talks about bringing up his son. It is so true. The first bit is about him not having time for his son because he is working hard. But when he retires, and has plenty of time, his son has grown up and hasn't got time for him. It is so true about life, I reckon."'

On 11 September 2015 the Japan rugby side departed from Haneda airport in Tokyo, bound for the UK and the Rugby World Cup. Craig Wing recalls it was hardly an auspicious send-off.

'There was no one there. Not one reporter, no officials, no fans. Eddie said we had to wear our suits. I said to him, "Eddie why do we have to wear these suits? We'll only be getting into our tracksuits when we're on the plane. No one's here. Who's going to know?" He told me, "When we leave here we're going out in our suits with our heads held high, because when we come back we will have changed history." A month later, when we came back, we were rock stars. It was like those old videos of The Beatles. There were thousands of reporters, fans, people crying, cameras everywhere. It was like nothing I'd ever experienced, not playing Origin or winning the grand final with the Roosters. Everyone wanted to be near us, they wanted to be part of it. There were people there like politicians and corporate bigwigs who just wanted to be associated with it all. It was just like Eddie had said it would be. It was all part of his plan from the beginning.'

15

THE BLOSSOM
AND THE ROSE

There were two matches at the 2015 Rugby World Cup that transformed Eddie's life. In the first he engineered the greatest upset in the tournament's history. The second, he had nothing to do with.

Japan's 34-32 win over the Springboks in Brighton was so unthinkable that no one could have tipped it with any conviction. Not even Eddie, who admitted, 'I woke up on Saturday morning believing we could live with the Springboks for sixty minutes but did I honestly believe we could beat them? I had my doubts.'

Two weeks later, when Australia humbled England 33-13 at Twickenham, the result wasn't as unexpected as Japan's win over South Africa, but the ramifications for Eddie were just as great. The Wallabies' victory opened the door to one of the plum jobs in world rugby. The Japanese win enabled him to walk through it.

Just like with the All Blacks at the 2003 World Cup, Eddie had targeted the Springboks as vulnerable. Together with his assistant coaches, Steve Borthwick in charge of the lineout and Marc dal Maso the scrum, he put together a plan and drilled it into his players over and over until it became second nature. Do exactly as I say, Eddie told them, and you will win. Australian football legend Leigh Matthews, the AFL's 'Player of the Century' and a four-time-premiership-winning coach, once said of coaches, 'We're salesmen. We sell hope.' Prior to the Springboks game Eddie was selling more than that. He was selling belief, and his players were buying.

As Eddie explained after the match, 'We'd prepared for this game for a very long time, having implemented a routine in training we called "Beat the Boks", which we'd run through time and again for twenty-minute spells in training leading into the tournament. It was the way we believed we had to play to beat them. The Springboks are an incredibly physical side but they don't like being turned around, and it was critical that whether we were kicking, passing or running we kept on moving forward at all times. The plan seemed to instil confidence in our players. The Japanese can be inclined to go into their shells but they never did. I could sense something was different before kick-off. The Japanese tend to get quite frenetic before games but this time they were very calm.'

At the start of the match it appeared they might have been too calm. South Africa won the coin-toss and elected to kick off. The ball went to Japanese back-rower Hendrik Tui, who was tackled only 15 metres out from his line. Fullback Ayumu Goromaru's clearing kick was taken over the halfway by Springbok fullback Zane Kirchner, who slipped a tackle and passed to Bryan Habana. The champion winger headed down the sideline untouched as the Springbok supporters roared. This was going to be a cakewalk. Then, as if someone in the Japanese coaching box had flicked a switch, the Brave Blossoms clicked into gear. Japan outside centre Male Sa'u pinched the ball off his opposite number Jesse Kriel at the breakdown, and Japan swung it wide, making 40 metres and showing that anything the Springboks could do, they could do just as well. And one thing they could do better: tackle. Part one of the 'Beat the Boks' defensive plan was to go low. Part two was to defend in numbers. Whenever one little Japanese player would dive at a Springbok's ankles in what the media dubbed a 'chop tackle' another two or three would come in around his waist and chest. It succeeded in both bringing the big South Africans straight to ground without off-loading and slowing their recycled ball. The longer the game went, the more Japan won the battle of the breakdown. At the scrum, where Japan gave away 128 kilos to the South Africans, the tactic was for a quick strike from hooker Shota Horie in order to avoid a pushing contest and, with ball in hand, everything was done at pace, giving the Boks no time to settle. At the six-minute mark, following a Japanese scrum win and a quick pick-and-go, Goromaru stepped inside the South African defence and made a clear break well into Springbok territory. With winger Akihito Yamada unmarked outside him, he threw the dummy and was cleaned up by Kirchner. Again the Japanese cleared quickly, catching the Springboks offside, and Goromoru calmly stepped up to kick the penalty goal for a 3-0 lead.

As the TV camera captured the deadpan face of Eddie in the grandstand, commentator Joel Stransky, who kicked the field goal that won South Africa the 1995 World Cup, perfectly summed up the state of play.

'You've got to love the contrasting styles: South Africa big, strong and powerful playing the one-off running game, trying to almost bully Japan into submission, this man Eddie Jones, his team playing fast and furiously; pick-and-gos, moving it quickly and certainly dictating the speed of the game.'

Eddie might have been concerned that his team would be able to match the Springboks for only sixty minutes before height, weight and experience would begin to take its toll, but if anything it was in the last quarter of the match that Japan's superior fitness, courage and refusal to accept defeat carried them home.

The teams had gone in at half-time with South Africa leading 12-10 after both sides had turned down kickable penalties, gone for the lineout and scored from driving mauls. Goromaru put Japan back in the lead with a penalty soon after the break before Springbok lock Lodewyk de Jager burst onto a pass 30 metres out, stepped through a rare missed tackle and scored next to the posts. The conversion made it 19-10 to South Africa, but the Japanese wouldn't go away, forcing the Boks into continual errors. Goromaru put on a kicking masterclass to level it up at 19-19 and then 22-22, before replacement Springbok hooker Adrian Strauss bullocked and stepped his way across the line for a converted try and 29-22 lead with twenty minutes left to play. This was where Eddie thought his team might wilt. Instead it was where they dug deeper than ever before.

Except for one miscued penalty in the first half it had been the kicking of Goromaru that had kept Japan in the game. Now it was time for his pace to stun the South Africans and send the Japanese supporters into a frenzy once more. With eleven minutes to play, after working their way up-field from their own line, Japan won a lineout and produced a perfectly worked set move from 40 metres out. With the ball swung wide, centre Harumichi Tatekawa gave an inside pass to blind-side winger Kotaro Matsushima, who made the break before linking with Goromaru to score wide out.

As the TV coverage showed Eddie giving the slightest of smiles, Stransky called it 'an Eddie Jones set move'. Added his Australian co-commentator Gordon Bray: 'The Ella brothers would be proud of that one, Eddie.'

From 7 metres in from touch Goromaru landed his toughest kick of the afternoon to lock it up again at 29-29. Two minutes later South African replacement Handre Pollard kicked the Boks back in front

32-29, setting up arguably the greatest five minutes in Rugby World Cup history.

From the restart the South Africans kicked deep, hoping to play out the game in Japanese territory, but the Brave Blossoms would not be dictated to, throwing themselves at the Springbok defence in wave after wave. Every time the South Africans cleared, the Japanese would counter-attack, and when their backs were pulled down with desperate tackles, the forwards would control the breakdown, recycling fast and cleanly. The game might have been played at Brighton Community Stadium, but Operation 'Beat the Boks' was being put into practice with all the precision and confidence of a training session at Miyazaki.

With less than two minutes of the match remaining, after nineteen phases of play, Goromaru charged for the line and was brought down centimetres short. In a calculated bid to slow down the Japanese recycle, Springbok replacement front-rower Coenie Oosthuizen lay across the back of the maul and made no effort to roll away. French referee Jerome Garces had no hesitation in reaching for a yellow card, sending Oosthuizen off for the remainder of the game and awarding a penalty to Japan.

Eddie reached for the water bottle as replacement scrum-half Atsushi Hiwasa kicked for touch and former Springbok Joel Stransky put the situation into perspective for the TV audience.

'South Africa are in serious danger of losing a game and it becoming one of the biggest upsets in the history of rugby union – one of the most famous victories in the history of sport I would go so far as saying. And if it were to happen, as a South African we would be mortified. The other side of that is what would this do for the belief of the tier-two rugby playing nations?'

From the lineout win Japan set the driving maul, with the entire team rushing in to lend weight. The Springboks were pushed back over the line but in the mass of bodies referee Garces could not determine if the ball had been grounded. The Television Match Official reviewed the footage and ruled a 5-metre scrum to Japan.

With a minute left to play, Springboks coach Heyneke Meyer, the prospect of the most humiliating loss of his country's proud rugby history unfolding in front of his eyes, sent out front-rowers Jannie du Plessis and Tendai 'The Beast' Mtawarira, with 132 Test caps between them, to strengthen the seven-man scrum. Eddie made his own substitution, putting on winger Karne Hesketh for the dying moments of the game.

With thirteen seconds left in regulation time the scrum was set. Hiwasa fed the ball, the Springboks tried to apply pressure, and the front row collapsed. Garces put the whistle to his mouth and raised his arm. Penalty Japan.

The way Goromaru had been kicking, it was an almost certain three points which would surely give Japan a 32-32 draw, a more than laudable result. Captain Michael Leitch walked towards the referee. Up in the grandstand Eddie sent down a message to the sideline: take the kick.

'I was screaming, "Take the three, take the three," but I had coffee with Leitchy in the morning. We went down to Brighton Beach, it was sunny, and I said, "Look, mate, we've got nothing to lose. If you think we should have a go, have a go."'

In making his decision, Leitch remembered Eddie's words.

'The last thing Eddie said to me before the game was, "Go with your heart," and my heart said to take the risk. I chose to scrum rather than kick because they were one man down and we could use the advantage. I decided that we wanted to win rather than draw. I didn't want to disappoint the boys.'

Or the Japanese supporters in the 30,000-strong crowd, who were beside themselves with excitement, chanting, waving national flags and in some cases so overcome with emotion that tears were streaming down their cheeks.

The scrum was set and reset four times before Hiwasa off-loaded left to Leitch going down the short side. From a quick clearance at the breakdown it went back to the right. The Japanese forwards took it up four times, the play moving from one side of the field to the other, stretching the exhausted South African defence, before Leitch looped wide and headed for the corner. Dragged down by Strauss a metre out and a metre in from the right-hand touchline, Leitch laid the ball back for Hiwasa, who swung it wide to centre Tatekawa in midfield. Tatekawa passed to replacement back-rower Amanaki Mafi looming up on his left. Mafi drew in three defenders and pushed off Jesse Kriel before sending a perfectly timed pass to Hesketh who dived over inside the left-hand corner-post with Springbok replacement winger J.P. Pietersen arriving too late.

The winning try set off amazing scenes of joy, excitement and, in the case of the South Africans, shock and bewilderment. Gordon Bray called it 'a rugby miracle'. His co-commentator Stransky said of the Brave Blossoms, 'At the end of the day they have worn their hearts on their sleeve. They have defended like Trojans. They have made 122 tackles. When it looked like a lost cause they have stood up and won what will become one of those folklore games that will become an example to all the underdogs: the David and Goliath of rugby union.'

As the Japanese players lined up along the sideline and bowed to their delirious supporters, Eddie shook hands with his coaching staff and headed down the steps to join his team.

'When Karne Hesketh crossed for the try it was the most emotional I've been since coaching the Wallabies to a semi-final win over the All Blacks at the 2003 World Cup,' he said. 'I couldn't be more proud of my players and coaching staff. When the final whistle blew even my fellow coach Steve Borthwick, one of the toughest competitors you will ever meet, was showing his emotion. When we got down to pitch level it seemed as if everyone was crying. I've never seen more grown men in tears. It was an absolutely unbelievable scene which will live with me for the rest of my life. I'll never cease to wonder at the Japanese psyche. These guys seem to cry when they're happy and laugh when they're nervous – it's almost the opposite of western behaviour – and the tears were flooding out on the pitch. It was an amazing place to be. The South African supporters are usually not great losers but they were actually happy for the Japanese supporters. They went down to Brighton train station, and the South African supporters clapped the Japan supporters onto the train. There is no other sport where that happens.'

Even Sir Clive Woodward, now a respected media analyst, was impressed with Eddie's achievement, tweeting, 'Wow – biggest calls in history of World Cup – Japan no kicks for goal / totally best game ever in World Cup history – Eddie Jones brilliant.'

And in his post-match media conference Eddie had some words for Sir Clive.

'We've made a splash today but we want to make a real dent in the tournament. We are not done. If we make the quarter-finals, then I can retire from coaching. I can be like Clive Woodward and tell everyone what to do on television. Tell Sir Clive I want to be like him. That's my dream.'

The Brave Blossoms didn't make the quarter-finals. After just four days' rest they lost their next match against Scotland 45-10 before going on to beat the other two teams in their pool Samoa 26-5 and USA 28-18. They finished level with South Africa and Scotland on three wins but missed the play-offs due to their lack of bonus points. It was a disappointment, but just as Eddie had told Craig Wing, they returned to Japan as heroes. Not that their coach would stay there long. Twelve years on from his greatest disappointment, Eddie was back in the big time. Just three days after Japan's win over South Africa the Stormers Super Rugby franchise announced that Eddie would be taking over as coach from the start of the 2016 season. Eddie issued a statement saying how excited he was to be joining the Cape Town organization, 'one of the biggest franchise jobs in world rugby'. What wasn't made public was that Eddie had negotiated a 'get-out clause' in his contract, just in case something even bigger came along.

*

While the Brave Blossoms had been enjoying their best ever Rugby World Cup, the men wearing the red rose of England were suffering through their worst. Which, given how they had gone in 2011, is saying something.

Despite making it to the 2007 final, where his team was beaten by the Springbok side coached by Jake White with Eddie as his technical advisor, England coach Brian Ashton returned home under extreme pressure to keep his job. Throughout the World Cup, stories had been leaked from inside the England camp that claimed the players were virtually running the team and that there was widespread dissatisfaction with Ashton's coaching style. It was widely felt that if England had not made the World Cup final Ashton would have been sacked immediately. Even so, he wouldn't last long.

With wins over Italy, France and Ireland and losses to Wales and Scotland, England finished second behind Wales in the 2008 Six

Nations – its best result for five years – but it wasn't enough for Ashton to keep his job. He was sacked amidst speculation that the RFU would follow the lead of Australia, which had just hired its first 'foreign' coach, Kiwi Robbie Deans, and pursue Jake White, with Eddie as his assistant, to replace Ashton. Former chief rugby writer for the *Independent* Chris Hewett says that was never going to happen.

'The RFU had this policy of "English coach for English people". They would never even look at a foreign coach.'

Even before Ashton had been sacked, chairman of the RFU Martyn Thomas instructed Elite Performance Manager Rob Andrew to pursue former England captain Martin Johnson for the role of team manager. Johnson had become a national hero following the 2003 World Cup win, and Thomas believed he could reignite the magic of England rugby's greatest achievement. The problem was, Johnson had never coached a team in his life.

'It was an absolutely bone-headed decision,' says Chris Hewett. 'Rob Andrew did the negotiations and admits that he ended up hoping Martin would turn the job down. Martyn Thomas had said, "We want Johnson," and Andrew followed that instruction. Getting Martin Johnson was a high-level RFU project, but it was never going to work.'

To be fair to Johnson, his appointment did work up to a point. That point being the 2011 World Cup. Taking over in July 2008, he found himself on the steepest of learning curves. England had been on a catastrophic tour of New Zealand the previous month under the control of caretaker manager Rob Andrew. The team had lost both Tests to the All Blacks, 20-37 and 12-44 and been rocked by allegations of player misbehaviour. Following the first Test in Auckland, an eighteen-year-old barmaid claimed in a newspaper article to have been sexually assaulted by Topsy Ojo, Mike Brown and Danny Care. No official complaint was made, and an internal investigation found they had no criminal case to answer, although Ojo and Brown were fined for staying out all night.

That Johnson should take over the team at a time of off-field media scrutiny was a portent of what was to come. His tenure was marked by a series of running battles with the press, more often than not over events occurring off the field.

Johnson's first Test in charge was a 39-13 win over a Pacific Islanders team at Twickenham, followed by three losses to Southern Hemisphere touring sides: 14-28 against Australia, 6-42 to South Africa and 6-32 to end the season against the All Blacks. It was a tough introduction to international coaching for Johnson. In the three losses his team conceded 102 points and scored just one try. Things could only improve and, to a degree, they did. In 2009 England again finished second in the Six Nations, this time behind Ireland, with wins over Italy, France and Scotland. There was also a 2-0 series win over the touring Argentinians, but more losses to New Zealand and Australia at Twickenham.

In his first full year as England manager Johnson could boast a 50 per cent winning record. It was neither a pass nor a fail, but his many critics, including former World Cup-winning team-mates Josh Lewsey and Will Greenwood, who had now joined the media, didn't hold back in slamming their ex-captain's safety-first tactics or his team's pedestrian style.

Johnson admitted it was a lot harder ignoring the negative comments as a coach than it had been as a player.

'No one likes getting criticized, but you put your balls on the line when you play or coach. Whatever people say, it does get to you, but you've got to take everything with a pinch of salt. You don't get carried away with yourself or too down on yourself.'

The next year Johnson, and the team, achieved a major breakthrough. While England dropped to third in the Six Nations with only two wins and a draw, they did manage their first success over a Southern Hemisphere team under Johnson. A 21-20 win over Australia in Sydney was followed five months later by a 35-18 victory against the Wallabies at Twickenham. The two wins were bright spots in a season that saw England's winning percentage drop below 45.5 per cent and included losses to Ireland, France, New Zealand and South Africa, but they were enough to raise hopes at RFU headquarters that Johnson and his side were about to turn the corner.

The early signs in the 2011 World Cup year were promising. England won their first Six Nations championship since 2003 when Johnson had captained the team under Clive Woodward, an omen that wasn't lost on long-suffering supporters. Only a 24-8 loss to Ireland in the last match prevented a Grand Slam. The side then completed their World Cup preparation by splitting a two-Test series with Wales and reversing the Six Nations result against Ireland, winning 20-9 in Dublin, before heading to New Zealand for their first pool match against Argentina.

England won that match 13-9, but it wasn't the result or the less-than-convincing performance of Johnson's men that made the headlines. It was what the players got up to after the game. With the match played in Dunedin on the Saturday night of 10 September, the next day the team headed to Queenstown, where the RFU paid for dinner and drinks at the venue Pub on the Wharf. Afterwards some players, including team captain Mike Tindall, who six weeks earlier had married the Queen's grand-daughter Zara Phillips, kicked on to the Altitude Bar nightspot. Three days later the front page of *The Sun* was filled with a headline that ticked every box on a British tabloid editor's wish list: 'Mike Tindall Gropes Blonde – Zara's Hubby Puts Head in Girl's Boobs at Dwarf-throwing Contest'.

Supported by photographs taken from the venue's Facebook page, *The Sun* reported that the England players were 'watching a light-hearted dwarf-throwing contest' when 'scores of women made a beeline for the strapping lads'. An unnamed source was quoted as saying, 'One particularly beautiful blonde went straight for Mike. But rather than reject her advances, unfortunately he was extremely responsive. They were flirting with each other and getting very touchy-feely. Then they went into the doorway, where the girl gestured Mike towards her chest. She pulled his head towards her breasts and she rubbed the back of his head as she did so.'

The paper said there was no suggestion the pair left the nightclub together, and Altitude Bar manager Rich Deane made a statement defending his establishment and the behaviour of the players. 'Firstly there was no dwarf throwing,' he said. 'That's just not cool.' The little people had, in fact, been star attractions at the bar's always popular 'Mad Midget Weekender' event, and their feet never left the ground.

'The English rugby players were great lads, not throwing the midgets. It was all light-hearted, good-humoured fun. This is the tabloids taking photos out of context and telling silly stories.'

Perhaps, but even so, it was not the kind of publicity Johnson had wanted to be dealing with in the first week of the World Cup. He faced the media stony-faced and did his best to defuse the situation.

'It was guys out having a few drinks, as other teams have done in the same town during the World Cup,' he said. 'There is no difference. It is just the way it has been reported: Rugby player drinks beer. Shocker.'

But if Johnson thought the 'boys will be boys' defence was going to wash with the British tabloids, he was naive. The London editors instructed their reporters to track down any young women who had been at the bar on the night in question. Failing that, an interview with any dwarf who felt he had been unfairly thrown would suffice.

The England team continued its way through the group stages, beating Georgia 41-10, Romania 67-3 and Scotland 16-12, but the rugby seemed almost secondary in importance to what the red tops dubbed 'Dwarfgate'. The 'mystery blonde' reportedly seen flirting with Tindall was revealed as being twenty-nine-year-old Jessica Palmer, a former girlfriend of the England captain. Tindall was forced to revisit his earlier statement that he had gone straight back to the team hotel after leaving the Altitude Bar when CCTV footage emerged showing him and Ms Palmer together later at another nightspot. The early arrival of Zara Phillips to join Tindall in New Zealand, a trip planned months earlier, was reported as 'the Queen's grand-daughter flying in to support her husband'. News websites asked readers to report any sightings of the couple. Ms Palmer was tracked down in Queensland, Australia, where she had fled to avoid media scrutiny.

Meanwhile Johnson fought a losing battle trying to keep the press, and his players, focused on the rugby. Team management was censured by the RWC organization when numbers on players' jerseys peeled off in the first match against Argentina. Two of Johnson's assistants were then banned for switching footballs in order to aid kicker Jonny Wilkinson in the game against Romania. Any more on-field indiscretions, the RFU was told, and England would be expelled from the tournament. Off-field it was just as bad, with front-page reports in local newspapers that a female hotel employee in Dunedin had been subjected to 'lewd banter' by England players James Haskell, Dylan Hartley and Chris Ashton.

It all added to an impression of chaos within the ranks, and when the team meekly bowed out of the tournament with a sloppy 12-19 quarter-final loss to France, it almost came as a relief to management and supporters, who felt the scandal-ridden campaign was finally over. Not quite. The next day, with their playing commitments ended prematurely, team members went on a day trip to nearby Waiheke Island. On their return journey across Auckland Harbour, centre Manu Tuilagi jumped off the ferry and swam to a nearby wharf, where he was arrested by police and detained for an hour before being released. He was fined £3000 by the RFU.

Tuilagi wasn't the only member of the squad to be punished for a lack of discipline. Back in England, after an investigation by RFU Elite Performance Manager Rob Andrew, Haskell and Ashton both received suspended fines of £5000 for their part in the Dunedin hotel incident, but it was team captain Tindall who paid the highest price. For his night out in Queenstown he was fined £25,000 (reduced on appeal to £15,000) and thrown out of the England Elite Player squad.

It was all too much for Johnson. The giant former lock who had taken everything that opposition forwards could throw at him in eighty-four Tests for England, three British and Irish Lions tours and 362 games for Leicester, was a beaten man. Two weeks after New Zealand downed France in the World Cup final and six weeks before his contract was up, he announced he was quitting.

For the fourth time in six and a half years England were on the hunt for a coach. Once again foreign names were mentioned, with former Springboks mentors Nick Mallett and Jake White, and Kiwi Graham Henry, who had just stepped down from the World Cup-winning All Blacks, said to be in the frame. There was even talk that Sir Clive Woodward would make a return despite ongoing friction with Rob Andrew. Pushing Woodward's case was an unlikely ally – Eddie Jones – who said the input of his former rival was imperative if England was to again become a force in world rugby. Asked if he would be interested in the role himself, Eddie answered, 'I'd be crazy not to. It is one of the top jobs in world rugby.' As the RFU weighed up its options, it looked in-house and appointed Stuart Lancaster as caretaker coach for the Six Nations campaign.

Another schoolteacher-turned-coach, for three years Lancaster had performed the dual roles of RFU head of elite player development and coach of the Saxons, England's B team. Appointed as his assistants were former dual international Andy Farrell as defence coach, and Graham Rowntree, who had been England scrum coach under Martin Johnson. According to Chris Hewett, Lancaster was seen as a safety-first short-term fix until the RFU could sign a big name to take England through to the 2015 home World Cup.

'He was really low-profile. People were worried that we'd ended up with a low-level technocrat. He was only ever supposed to be a caretaker coach but then he strung together some good results and got the job.'

The son of a Cumbrian farmer, Lancaster moved into coaching at second-division club Leeds aged thirty after his playing career ended abruptly when he was injured in a training accident. A meticulous planner and keen student of the game, he eventually gave up his job as a physical education teacher when appointed Leeds full-time director of coaching. His efforts in leading the club to the top flight in 2008 brought him to the attention of Rob Andrew, who lured him to the RFU at the end of the following season.

When appointed England caretaker coach, the quietly spoken, even-tempered Lancaster immediately set about mending the team's culture and reconnecting with the English public. Two of his first acts in the job were to hold public training sessions and leave Danny Care out of his Six Nations squad after he was arrested and charged with drink driving.

The public, and the players, responded.

England's first Test under Lancaster was a 13-6 win over Scotland at Murrayfield, followed by another away win, 19-15 over Italy. A 12-19 loss to Wales at Twickenham was followed by a 24-22 win over France in Paris, making Lancaster's side the first England team in the history of the Six Nations to win all three away legs. A resounding forward-dominated 30-9 win over Ireland at Twickenham that secured England second place behind Wales was enough evidence for the RFU's new CEO Ian Ritchie to call off the search. Lancaster was appointed full-time coach on a four-year contract through to the end of the 2015 World Cup.

It proved a popular move. While leading contenders Nick Mallett and Jake White had the international experience that Lancaster lacked, the public and the RFU were still in favour of having an Englishman in charge of the team at the home World Cup. The Six Nations success made the local man an obvious choice and, it seemed at first, the right one.

Following the Six Nations Lancaster took his team to South Africa, where they lost the first two Tests but came away from the third with a creditable 14-14 draw. Back at Twickenham a 54-12 win over Fiji was followed by close losses to Australia and South Africa, before the final Test of the year, against the All Blacks.

If the team's mixed results after the Six Nations had raised any doubts over whether the RFU had done the right thing in appointing Lancaster, they were dispelled with England's emphatic 38-12 win over the world champions, who had been unbeaten in their previous twenty matches.

Praised as one of England's greatest-ever victories, the record seventeen-point winning margin would have been even greater if not for a late consolation try to All Black Julian Savea after England replacement Mako Vunipola had been yellow-carded with six minutes remaining.

It was England's first win over the All Blacks in nine years, and only their seventh in history. Most exciting for the home supporters amongst the 82,000 at Twickenham and the many more watching on television, Lancaster had fielded a young side with just 206 caps between them, against the All Blacks' 788. The future looked bright. The World Cup couldn't come fast enough.

England would finish second in the Six Nations in each of the next three seasons, including a Triple Crown in 2014. There were also two wins against Australia – 20-13 in 2013 and 26-17 in 2014 – and a one-point loss to the All Blacks in Dunedin in 2014. Plus an amazing 55-35 win over France in 2015 when they fell just one converted try short of the 27 points needed to pip Ireland for the Six Nations championship.

It should have made for a relatively smooth approach to the 18 September start of the Rugby World Cup, but by then Lancaster had brought a new face into his squad. One who, in the words of Chris Hewett, 'poisoned the well'.

Sam Burgess wasn't well known to the majority of rugby union followers in the early part of 2014, but he was one of the biggest names in rugby league. Born in Dewsbury, West Yorkshire, in December 1988, the 196 cm (6 feet 5 inch), 116 kg (18 stone 4 pound) forward was playing first grade for Bradford Bulls in 2006 at the age of seventeen and made his debut for Great Britain against New Zealand a year later, scoring a try and terrorizing the opposition in attack and defence in the 20-14 win at Huddersfield. It was a performance that moved reporter David Burke to write in the *Telegraph,* 'The last 18-year-old to make such an impact on his first Test appearance was Andy Farrell, also against the Kiwis in 1993. Farrell went on to lead his country, win

34 Test caps and receive the Golden Boot as the world's best rugby league player in 2004 before switching to rugby union.'

YouTube footage of 'Slammin' Sam' sitting Kiwi wrecking-ball Fuifui Moimoi on the seat of his pants was viewed over one million times. One of those who watched the video was Oscar-winning actor Russell Crowe, owner of the South Sydney Rabbitohs NRL team. Crowe invited Burgess to visit him on the set of his movie *Robin Hood*, being filmed in Derbyshire. It was there that Crowe offered Burgess the chance to star in his own Hollywood-like scenario.

The big kid from Dewsbury, the film star said, would come to Australia, join the worst team in the NRL, and help turn them into the best. Together they would scale the battlements and taste the ultimate victory in the final scene.

Which is exactly what happened. Burgess, along with his brothers, Luke and twins Tom and George, joined Souths on a three-year contract, beginning in 2011. In his last game for the club, the 2014 NRL grand final, he suffered a fractured cheekbone in the opening tackle of the match but remained on the field to inspire the Rabbitohs to their first premiership win for forty-three years.

It was a man-of-the-match performance that enhanced Burgess' reputation as one of the best forwards in the game. Former champion player turned respected media commentator Peter Sterling went so far as to rate him the best Englishman ever to play in Australia, ahead of the likes of Cronulla pair Tommy Bishop and Cliff Watson and Manly legends Malcolm Reilly and Phil Lowe.

It wasn't just the South Sydney faithful who were ecstatic at Burgess' grand final heroics. It was Stuart Lancaster and Andy Farrell. At the start of the 2014 season Burgess had announced that he had accepted a huge four-year contract to play rugby union for Bath, with a view to making the England team for the World Cup. Lancaster and Farrell saw Burgess as their X-Factor, the missing piece of the puzzle that would see the home team crowned world champions at Twickenham on 31 October 2015. Others weren't so sure.

The difference between Burgess and other league converts such as England's Jason Robinson and Wallabies Wendell Sailor, Lote Tuqiri and Mat Rogers, who had all played in the 2003 World Cup final, was that while they had the luxury of several seasons and numerous Test matches to learn the nuances of the game, he would have just eleven months. And it wasn't just the coaches and selectors Burgess would have to win over. As with Sailor and Co. in 2001, he was arriving in a blaze of publicity about his high-profile and massive pay packet. With established players desperate to snare a place in the World Cup squad, the risk of affecting team harmony was high. Then there was the question over whether his skills would be transferable anyway. The player that he was most likened to – former NRL forward Sonny Bill Williams, who had developed into a star centre with the All Blacks – was a far more elusive runner than Burgess and possessed one of the best passing games in either code.

Burgess arrived at Bath exactly one year out from the World Cup final, but complicating matters was his broken cheekbone, which kept him off the training paddock for another month. Bath coach Mike Ford kept a packed media conference guessing over whether he would play Burgess in his rugby league position of the back row or at centre, where Lancaster and Farrell – who had made the same positional change in his code swap – saw him playing for England.

Regardless of where he played, says Hewett, the experiment was doomed from the start.

'He was not a union man. He had barely watched a game of union, and he was the highest-paid player in the country straight away.

'England assistant coach was ex-league player Andy Farrell, and Lancaster was a northerner, well versed in league, so they were very excited about Burgess. Stuart had all the stats. He was saying, "He does thirty-two carries a game," but that was in rugby league, where there was no need for quick ball from the tackle area, which in rugby union is the keys to the palace. He had no experience of what was required in rugby at all. That didn't seem to worry anyone. He was a big name, and all the tabloids wanted him to do well and be the big story. Ultimately it proved calamitous, and Lancaster and all who sailed with him sunk to the bottom.

'They played him in the centres, where he was seriously useless. Because that's where Lancaster and Farrell wanted him, that's where Mike Ford played him at Bath, but it came to a point where he was on the bench against Toulouse, and Ford played his son George and Jonathan Joseph in the centres, and they carved it up. Burgess was watching and he went up to Mike after the game and said, "I'm not a centre, am I?"

'Mike said, "No. We're going to play you in the back row for the rest of the season."

'So even though he wasn't playing in the centres for his club, he goes straight into the England side as a centre.

'No one had ever done less for an England jersey.'

At the end of January, after a total of 313 minutes of rugby union, Burgess was brought into the England set-up for the Saxons game against Ireland's B side, the Wolfhounds, at Cork. The media descended on the team's training sessions, quizzing Burgess on how he felt he was adapting to the new code. 'It's a lot harder than it looks on TV,' he said.

Lancaster arrived on the afternoon flight to watch his star recruit in action. The match programme had a photo of Burgess on the cover with the headline 'Opportunity Knocks'. As one reporter wrote, 'Well, if it did, it was very quietly, and it left before Sam heard it.'

In Australian rugby players' vernacular, Burgess had a 'Barry Crocker', rhyming slang for shocker. The first time he touched the ball he was penalized for not releasing when tackled. From there on, things only got worse. In the first half he threw a looping pass over the touchline, slipped over when wrong-footed in defence and tried a backhand flick-pass that went to no one, costing his team 10 metres. The final straw came late in the second half when he dropped a pass cold without an Irishman within metres. He was replaced soon afterwards.

As representative trials go, it could not have been less impressive but Lancaster was not discouraged. He stood above Burgess' aisle seat on the flight back to London, talking quietly in his ear, advising and encouraging, not wasting a moment in his desire to have his star signing ready in time for the big show.

Eight months later Burgess played his first full international for England in a 19-14 World Cup warm-up win over France at Twickenham.

Even though he had been playing flanker for Bath, Burgess paired with Henry Slade in the centres and showed he had made enormous strides since his performance in Cork. His defence at number twelve, where he bowled over French captain Dimitri Szarzewski with a thumping head-on tackle only two minutes after kick-off, was a feature of the match, but there were still big question marks over his attack.

'He couldn't pass,' says Chris Hewett. 'Every time England had the ball at the set piece, at the scrum or lineout, Slade would move from thirteen to twelve so they could play some moves. When it was France's ball, Burgess would go back to twelve. On the basis of that, Lancaster said, "This man is the answer." It was ridiculous.'

Ridiculous or not, when Lancaster named his thirty-one-man World Cup squad two weeks later, Burgess was in it, with Northampton centre Luther Burrell the man to miss out. It was a tough decision, with Lancaster admitting to shedding tears when informing Burrell, whom he had known since his school days, that he had not made the squad.

England had one final warm-up – a 21-13 win over Ireland in which Burgess went on as a replacement for Brad Barritt with eleven minutes remaining – before going into camp for their World Cup opener against Fiji. All host countries enter their home World Cup under pressure, but for England the task in 2015 was even greater than usual. With the draw determined on world rankings as they stood three years out from the tournament, England found itself in Pool A, the so-called 'Pool of Death', alongside international heavyweights Australia and Wales, as well as Fiji and Uruguay.

England got off to a nervous start, the 35-11 win over the Fijians marred by poor decision-making, a shaky scrum and a lack of cohesion in the midfield. If Fiji had not missed a possible eleven points through off-target kicking and had a player sin-binned for an illegal tackle, leading to a penalty try, the home team could have been in trouble. In eight days, they would be. Big trouble.

Lancaster made three crucial backline changes to his side for England's second match against Wales, dropping fly-half George Ford for Owen Farrell, moving Brad Barritt from twelve to thirteen to replace the injured Jonathan Joseph and elevating Burgess to starting inside centre. Critics questioned whether Lancaster was being barmy or brilliant.

'If we win the game, it will be judged a success,' he conceded. 'If we lose, well, the selection is already being questioned. It comes down to the next two games. I understand the consequences, I understand the stakes. It's a World Cup. I'm in charge, and it's a difficult pool.'

Sitting back and enjoying England's discomfort was Wales coach Warren Gatland. Asked if he would be preparing any special treatment for the inexperienced Burgess, Gatland said simply, 'No, we'll be going out to smash him, just like everyone else.' Gatland did suggest that England would miss the footwork of Joseph, a thought echoed by livewire Welsh centre Scott Williams, who said he would much prefer to mark Burgess than Joseph. When this was put to Burgess at a pre-match press conference he answered innocently, 'Who's Scott Williams?'

It didn't take him long to find out. In his short time on the field Williams was electrifying for Wales, finding Burgess out of position and stepping his way through the England defence on one long scything run before a serious injury saw him stretchered off.

The match started well for England, with the home side up 19-9 soon after half-time, and 22-12 with half an hour remaining. The Welsh scrum seemed disorganized, their injuries were mounting, and strong England defence had their joyous, singing supporters confident of the win needed to guarantee a spot in the quarter-finals. And then the momentum began to shift. Keeping the ball in play to avoid lineouts, Wales started winning the battle of the breakdown. England conceded penalties, with Welsh kicker Dan Biggar cutting down the deficit. With eleven minutes left, and England leading 25-18, Lancaster replaced Burgess with his Bath team-mate Ford, who went to fly-half with Owen Farrell moving out to centre. Less than two minutes later, England's World Cup fell to pieces.

From a maul 40 metres out the ball went wide to Wales replacement Lloyd Williams. Usually a scrum-half but thrown on the wing due to the Welsh injury crisis, Williams scooted down the left touchline and kicked low into centre-field. Wales number nine Gareth Davies picked up the bouncing ball at full stretch and dived over between the posts. Biggar converted to tie it up at 25-25.

With seven minutes remaining, England fullback Mike Brown was penalized for holding the ball on the ground, and Biggar, who hadn't missed a kick all game, slotted it over from just inside halfway. England had an opportunity to snatch a draw at the death when Wales gave away a sideline penalty 25 metres out. England captain Chris Robshaw was faced with the same options as Japan's Michael Leitch against South Africa a week earlier: take the draw or go for the win. England's kick was more difficult than Japan's, but the decision was the same. Robshaw instructed Ford to kick for touch. England won the lineout but Wales gave them no chance to replicate Japan's miracle win. They drove the English over the sideline, and the game was lost. England's World Cup dream, years of work by the organizers, and the hopes of hundreds of thousands of fans now rested on eighty minutes against the Wallabies in seven days' time.

The pressure on England in the lead-up to the match was immense. Everyone had an opinion on Lancaster's handling of the side and the value of Burgess, including Eddie. Writing in his Australian newspaper column he said, 'Does clarity of game style matter? It sure does. The Wallabies are clear in how they want to play: keep the pace up, play ball-in-hand and make good decisions on kicking to keep the opposition back-three deep. England is like a bag of mixed boiled lollies, sometimes expansive, sometimes set piece-driven. It's seen simply in the change at number ten, where George Ford, the runner and passer, has been shunted for Owen Farrell, the very good kicker and tough defender.

'Confusion reigns as coach Stuart Lancaster seems to be affected by media pressure. Lancaster is a Harvard School of Business manager-type. He creates a good high-performance environment but is strategically poor and that's a big advantage for Australia.

'As for Sam Burgess, is he boom or bust as a centre? He was a non-event in the loss to Wales. "Lost" would be the most accurate term for him. However, if he sticks to rugby he will be outstanding in two years.'

Lancaster stuck with Farrell over Ford for the do-or-die match against the Aussies and, with Joseph cleared to play, moved Barritt to twelve and benched Burgess. It was, as Eddie had suggested, a mixed bag selection: the defence-oriented fly-half and the fancy-stepping centre. The critics lambasted the side as neither one thing nor the other. Did Lancaster want them to shut the Wallabies down or out-run them? In the end it was academic. On one of the most important nights in English rugby history, the men in white came up against an Australian team that was simply unstoppable. In their best performance since Eddie engineered the RWC semi-final win over the All Blacks in 2003, the Wallabies blew England off the park 33-13, with fly-half Bernard Foley contributing a record twenty-eight points.

Australian coach Michael Cheika had come into the World Cup with a similar selection conundrum to Lancaster. Like the England coach, who agonized over which of his two talented fly-halves to pick, Cheika was blessed with David Pocock and Michael Hooper, along with the All Blacks' Richie McCaw, two of the three best number sevens in the game. Who to choose? His solution was brave, and spectacularly successful: he played them both, moving Pocock to number eight. What the Australian pack now lacked in height it more than made up for in speed at the breakdown. The Pocock–Hooper tag-team totally dominated the England loose forwards on the ground, and the Wallaby backs did the rest.

For the England supporters it was a night to forget. For Bernard Foley, one to be savoured forever.

'The thing I remember was the anticipation and the build-up. All week we tried not to read anything about it or get caught up in the hype, but it was impossible not to sense that anticipation in the public and the media. We all knew the significance.

'We were staying in a hotel at Westminster, and it was a long bus drive to Twickenham through London. Everywhere we looked there were people wearing England jerseys all over the footpaths and crossing the road. We drove past the Fan Zone at Richmond Park, which was all kitted out, and then, when we got to Twickenham, the amount of people walking around, and the car park and the sponsors' signs . . . it was amazing.

'We knew that the pressure was really on England and that's why we knew that we had to play a smart game and not allow them to get into it.

'There were some significant points straight away. There was a centre-field scrum, and I kicked into the corner, and Mike Brown juggled it and took it over the sideline, and I knew that he was feeling the pressure.

'We were the underdogs because we had lost the last two times we had played them and we'd won only one from four under Cheik when we'd toured in 2014, but there was belief amongst the squad. We'd been together a long time and we knew we had the potential, so it was good that we backed our preparation and showed what we could do.'

The first of Foley's two tries came just after nineteen minutes when he dummied and stepped his way through the England defence from 10 metres out. The conversion took the score to 10-3 and increased the pressure on Lancaster and his men, but it was the second try, five minutes from half-time, in which replacement fullback Kurtley Beale took a no-look inside pass from Foley, drew the defence then sent it back to him, that was most significant.

Just like the 'Beat the Boks' plan that Eddie had drilled into his Brave Blossoms before their showdown with South Africa, Michael Cheika and his staff had long been working on a strategy to beat the men in white. It didn't have a name, but it could have been 'Eliminate the English'.

'A lot of preparation went into that game,' says Foley. 'Cheik and the coaches had studied England's games and they must have seen something there that they thought we could capitalize on. They came up with the return play down the short side after the lineout. We worked on it for three or four months after Super Rugby finished. We had a trial match against the USA and the World Cup games against Fiji and Uruguay. Cheik told us not to show that we had it in our arsenal. We didn't want England to know. The instruction was that even if we could score off that play in the early matches, don't do it.

'We practised that play a lot at training in the week before the game but we couldn't get it right. The pass was too shallow, or there were people in the way. Kurtley Beale didn't start at fullback, but when Rob Horne went off Israel Folau moved from fullback to wing, and KB went to fullback.

'KB ran the perfect line, went through the gap and gave it straight back. That typified the whole journey of the previous two or three months. There was the fitness, the runs up hills and stairs, the road runs, the sessions in the heat at our training camp in the US, but it really came down to smarts and getting that play right just for England.'

Soon after half-time Lancaster brought on Ford and moved Farrell into the centres in a desperate attempt to spark a comeback. For a moment there was some hope when Anthony Watson scored a converted try and Farrell kicked a penalty to bring the home team within seven points with fifteen minutes to go, but then Farrell was sin-binned, and Matt Giteau scored a late try for the Wallabies to end England's hopes, and its World Cup.

The contrasting reactions of the two coaches as Giteau dived over in the corner said it all, Cheika jumping to his feet and giving a fist-pump salute, Lancaster staring straight ahead, composed but shattered. His team had just become the first England side – and the first home nation – not to advance out of the pool stage. There was still one match to play against Uruguay, but England's tournament was effectively over, and so was Lancaster's time in charge.

The recriminations and blame-game began immediately. Burgess was the scapegoat, especially when it was revealed that he had already decided to turn his back on rugby and return to South Sydney. Disgruntled players began making anonymous complaints to reporters about Lancaster's selections. He was forced to deny that he had been unduly influenced by Andy Farrell to choose Burgess and prefer his son Owen ahead of George Ford.

'The decisions we make on selection are collective and they're ultimately mine and my responsibility,' he said.

As RFU chief executive Ian Ritchie headed a five-man panel holding an investigation into the failure of the team, which had now dropped to eight in the world rankings, Lancaster's sacking seemed a formality. Criticism of the job he had done – and of the RFU's decision to appoint him – came from all quarters, including Eddie Jones in South Africa.

'Every Union that's successful, every national team that's successful, has a guy that's experienced, has a guy that understands rugby,' he said in a statement that could have been a job application. 'The non-negotiables are simple, and the Unions that falter are the Unions that don't follow those non-negotiables, like England, who picked a rookie coach to coach a home team at a World Cup. When you're a home team, the pressure on that coach is enormous. You need a guy that's got experience, has been through the loop; someone who understands how to manage his team in that quite hostile environment.'

Asked if he would consider the England job if it was offered to him he answered, 'Of course I would, but whether the RFU part ways with Stuart Lancaster is a big and difficult decision.'

On 15 November, just over two weeks after the All Blacks had beaten the Wallabies to win their second successive World Cup, Ritchie presented his report to the RFU board. He then booked a flight to Cape Town, South Africa, to meet with Eddie. His instructions were clear: don't come back without him.

16

NO DAME EDNA

One month after Eddie's appointment as England head coach, the RFU invited members of the media to a hotel at Twickenham for early-evening drinks. Six days before Christmas, it was an informal, off-the-record occasion; an opportunity for journalists to meet and greet the man who would be guiding the fortunes of the national team for the next four years.

Since the official announcement of his appointment on 20 November, Eddie's name had rarely been out of the British newspapers. Every day there was a different story, a new angle. Profiles of the intriguing half-Japanese-half-Australian workaholic who had become England's first-ever foreign coach competed for space with news articles speculating on how he would go about restoring pride in the white shirt with the red rose emblem. There was speculation that Eddie felt the English players were too gentlemanly, that there was not enough 'mongrel' in the side. Which players would he bring into the team, which would he discard? Who would be his assistant coaches? Most of all, there were questions over the future of England captain Chris Robshaw, whom Eddie had described in a scathing newspaper column during the World Cup as little more than 'a good workmanlike player'. Previewing the England–Australia match for the *Daily Mail*, Eddie wrote, 'Chris Robshaw wears No 7, but he is a six-and-a-half at best. He's not hard over the ball and he's not quick. He's a useful player but he's definitely not an out-and-out open-side. To me, Robshaw is an outstanding club player but at international level he just doesn't have that point of difference. He carries OK, he tackles OK, but he's not outstandingly good in any area.'

It was hardly a ringing endorsement of the man who had captained England forty-three times, and there was talk that it wouldn't just be the captaincy that Robshaw would lose under Eddie, but his place in the team entirely. At the media conference held to announce his appointment Eddie defended his comments by saying, 'I wasn't the coach of England then, I was a newspaper columnist. I was being a bit naughty. One of the first things I have to do is sit down with Chris and chat to him. As with all the players, he's starting from zero. There's always an opportunity to change things, and he's in that position.'

It wouldn't be the last occasion that something Eddie said or wrote without considering the consequences would come back to bite him. The next time would be less than a month later at the informal Christmas meet and greet.

Eddie had first fronted the British media as England coach exactly one week after Ritchie and he had met in South Africa. He had just started as Stormers coach and had told local reporters that he was committed to three years in the job, but Ritchie had made an offer too good to refuse.

'It's funny how things work out,' Eddie said at the press conference held at Twickenham to announce his appointment. 'Last week I was in Cape Town, looking at Table Mountain through my sunglasses. Now I'm here, with my overcoat on. People who know me understand that I'm always 100 per cent committed to the team I'm with and that I don't like to let people down. I don't feel good about what I did to the Stormers, but this was a once-in-a-lifetime opportunity and I had to take it. Sometimes the bus only goes past your stop once and you have to get on it.'

Apart from a minor glitch over gaining a work visa, all went smoothly. He and Hiroko moved into the Pennyhill Park Hotel until they could buy a home nearby, and Eddie looked forward to a few rare days off over Christmas before beginning work in earnest in January. The get-together with the media was seen as part of that relaxed familiarization process.

The media invitees had arrived at the appointed time and were milling around the bar when Eddie arrived late, accompanied by Rob Andrew. Both men were friendly, loquacious and in high spirits. It soon emerged that they had come straight from the RFU Christmas party, where they had been enjoying the hospitality to the full. Eddie was at his disarming best, displaying the side of his personality to which only his closest associates are usually privy. Walking from group to group, glass in hand, he was witty, outgoing and forthcoming. When asked late in the evening whether he would be sticking with Chris Robshaw as captain, he answered openly, 'No, mate, I'm going with Dylan Hartley.'

As rugby scoops go, this was about as big as it gets. For the previous month journalists had filled thousands of centimetres of column space speculating over who Eddie would choose as his captain, and Hartley's name had barely rated a mention. One columnist went so far as to suggest that Eddie should choose a different captain for each of England's Six Nations matches and make his final decision after that. Hartley was not one of the five he named in the article.

It was hardly surprising. No one questioned Hartley's skill or toughness as a player – the New Zealand-born hooker had played for England sixty-one times – but his disciplinary record was appalling. Between 2007 and 2015 he had been suspended a total of fifty-four weeks after being found guilty of a range of on-field charges including eye-gouging, biting, punching, elbowing and abusing an official. That Eddie would consider him to lead England was a shock, but it was also a symbolic gesture. In choosing Hartley, Eddie was sending a message: no more Mr Nice Guys.

The journalists to whom Eddie had revealed his plans were placed in a moral dilemma. As a group of them sat down for a meal after the function, the discussion inevitably moved to the Hartley bombshell. This was a story too good to sit on, they agreed, but the invitation to the RFU drinks had been clear: it was an informal, off-the-record function. Anything said by Eddie was not for publication. Well, yeah, but . . . what about if Eddie wasn't quoted? Better still, what about if they could get confirmation from Hartley? One of them rang him at home in Northampton.

'So, Dylan,' he said. 'How do you feel about being appointed England captain?'

'I don't know what the hell you're talking about,' Hartley replied truthfully.

The reporters weren't put off. Their stories appeared, without sources, and created a storm on several levels. Reporters who had stuck to the off-the-record edict were upset that the others had not played by the rules. Editors were angry that they had missed the story, and Eddie would never be as trusting of the English press again.

Not that Eddie was out to win any popularity contest. As he said six months into the job, 'I don't want to be Dame Edna Everage, a popular Australian. I just want to give English rugby a winning team.'

The first steps towards achieving that goal were taken long before the players arrived to begin work at Pennyhill Park. First he needed to settle on his coaching staff. If anyone needed confirmation over who was calling the shots at the top of English rugby it came when the RFU backed Eddie to the hilt in his bid to have Steve Borthwick released from his contract with Bristol. With Bristol boss Steve Lansdown digging in his heels and demanding £500,000 compensation, it could easily have been a case of the RFU telling Eddie to look elsewhere. Instead they signed the cheque and told their new coach, 'What else do you want?'

Next on the list was defence coach Paul Gustard, whose coaching career began when Eddie gave him a job at Saracens in 2008. It was there that he devised what became known as the club's 'Wolfpack defence', based on the saying 'the strength of the wolf is in the pack, the strength of the pack is in the wolf'. Gustard, who approached his work with Eddie-like intensity, once brought a wolf to training to inspire his players. On another occasion he brought a snake. He claimed to remember every try that had ever been scored against his team.

'Every single one hurts me,' he said. 'They stay in my head for days on end.'

Eddie believed he had the ideal pairing.

'Their personalities work,' he said. 'Paul's an extrovert, Steve's an introvert; Steve's analytical, Paul's emotional, so it's a perfect blend. You need some guys who want to be at the front of the bus and some at the back – if everyone wants to be at the front it won't work.'

In Borthwick and Gustard, Eddie had two assistant coaches who came close to matching him in work ethic and almost obsessional pursuit of excellence. His next appointee outdid them all. During his playing career Jonny Wilkinson would practise his kicking for hours every day of the year, including Christmas, and never head for home until he had landed six consecutive goals – no matter how long it took. On one occasion it almost led to an emotional breakdown.

'The more I stayed, the darker it got,' he said. 'The harder I tried, the worse it got. In the end I couldn't see anything and I was literally on the brink of running away I was that frustrated. I felt I was almost about to have a breakdown. I wanted to leave because I knew it was pointless but I'm one of those people who just can't do that. I just hate failing. It bothered me for the rest of the night. It was all I could think about.'

After a chance meeting in a supermarket, Eddie asked the not-long retired Wilkinson to come on board and work with Owen Farrell and George Ford. A few days later the two young kickers arrived for their first session with the 2003 World Cup hero.

'He seemed to have been out there a while by the time we turned up,' said Ford. 'He was kicking when we arrived. When he played, he practised and practised. He still practises now, and it rubs off on you.'

With his coaches in place Eddie set about creating the right environment for the players. One of his first instructions was that the training room at Pennyhill Park be repainted and the inspirational quotes on the walls chosen by Stuart Lancaster removed. His was to be a new era in every way, not that the players needed the smell of fresh paint to figure that out. Like Wallabies, Springboks and Brave Blossoms before them, the Red Rose soon found that their new boss was a man who set the bar very high.

Eddie's first game in charge was the 2016 Six Nations opener against Scotland. He had selected an initial training squad of thirty-three, with ten to be omitted before the first match. Notable newcomers were Jack Clifford, Elliot Daly, Paul Hill and the exciting Maro Itoje, all of whom would make their mark as the season progressed. Back into the squad after missing the World Cup due to a suspension for head-butting was Dylan Hartley, while centre Manu Tuilagi returned from injury. Tom Youngs, Brad Barritt, Tom Wood and Geoff Parling, all starters in the World Cup loss to Australia, were missing.

The squad's first training session under Eddie was an eye-opener for all concerned.

'After twenty minutes, they were just shot,' Eddie recalled. 'They couldn't run any more. They weren't fit. The basis of Test rugby is physical condition. You've got to be fit enough to play. I was thinking, "What have I got myself into here? This is going to be hard work."'

Not just for him, but the players too, as back-rower James Haskell found as Eddie cracked the whip in the lead-up to the Calcutta Cup clash.

'Eddie is a very straight-talking guy, a constant presence, and he shot me down a couple of times, but everything was spot-on, very detailed and very thought-through. The sessions were a mix of the physical, the mental and learning. You didn't know what was going to happen next. The standards were demanding. Everyone was caught up in it, wanting to impress, wanting everything to click straight away.'

After just seven training runs together the new coach and his team headed to Murrayfield still very much an unknown quantity. As his Wallaby rival Michael Cheika had done with Pocock and Hooper, Eddie got around the issue of choosing between George Ford and Owen Farrell by picking them both – Ford at ten, Farrell at twelve. He also kept Chris Robshaw in the side, but moved him from number seven to number six, bringing Haskell back into the team as open-side. Dylan Hartley was captain.

The match was tight, with England leading 7-6 at half-time before replacement Mako Vunipola did the early work for winger Jack Nowell to seal a 15-9 win. It was hardly spectacular, but it was a start and with Italy to come Eddie was able to get to work sculpting the team that he had always wanted.

When Eddie's appointment was announced three months earlier, RFU boss Ian Ritchie had spoken of the importance of signing 'an experienced international coach'. Eddie's critics claimed that was just a euphemism for 'foreigner', but either way, in Eddie they were getting someone who had accumulated more knowledge of top-level coaching around the world than anyone else in the game. He was also someone who, through often painful trial and error, knew what worked and what didn't. Much of what local media heralded as stunning innovations introduced by Eddie to transform the England side were actually techniques he had used with success in Japan.

When he took over the Brave Blossoms Eddie was frustrated by the players' lack of leadership and decision-making skills. He found a similar situation with England and set about correcting it the same way. In Japan Eddie and his coaches had called team meetings and not arrived, then secretly filmed the players' reaction. In England, he would tell the team they would be collected by buses from their hotel in order to arrive at a certain location at a specific time, then not order the buses and see how the players dealt with the problem.

The results were similar. Just as the Japanese had become more adaptable, the English started thinking for themselves and responding to different situations in the flow of the game.

'It's about players taking more responsibility,' Eddie said. 'I'm pleased when that happens because my job as a coach is to make myself redundant. Look at the best teams around the world. If the people involved run the team, the team is much more powerful because they are the ones making the decisions. England was a team dependent on the coach, and now to a large degree that has changed. I'm not redundant yet, but by 2019 it is my hope that the team just goes out there and does it. If there is a problem on the field they solve the problem, they don't have to ask for a solution. That's what you want, a self-organizing team, a team that is self-reliant, that makes decisions by themselves. One that just gets on with the job. So we do things now to equip them like that. For instance, we send them down to the gym and tell them a weight session is on and we don't send the coaches down and we see what the players do, whether they get on with the job themselves or not. You see who are the leaders and the guys who aren't leaders. We've done that with sessions on the field and with team meetings, and the progression of the team to be able to organize themselves has been really powerful. People say things about young people, how they are this and they are that, but I think like anything they are a product of their environment, and if you can create the right environment you get the right sort of people. That has been probably the most pleasing part of the English team for me.'

The most pleasing part of the English team as far as the public was concerned was that they were winning.

Following the first-up victory over Scotland, Eddie and his men headed to Rome and a 40-9 win that was notable for the Test debut of Saracens forward Maro Itoje, the England Under-20 captain. Eddie had dropped him back to club rugby in the ten-man cull of his original squad of thirty-three prior to Murrayfield but chose him on the bench for the second match.

'Maro is a young kid who has a good head on his shoulders,' he said when announcing the team. 'He's like a Vauxhall Viva now. We want to make him into a BMW. He's got a lot of work to do, but he's got potential.' Itoje, who admitted going to Google to find out what a Vauxhall Viva was, went on with twenty-six minutes remaining and showed enough in that time to convince Eddie that he should be a major part of his plans going forward.

The two wins to open the Six Nations were cause for optimism amongst England's long-suffering supporters, but the doubters were yet to be convinced. Scotland and Italy were seen as the most beatable sides in the tournament. The BBC called them 'predictable successes' and voiced the opinion of many in saying that it would be the games against Ireland and Wales at Twickenham, and France in Paris, that would prove if Eddie really was the super-coach that the RFU had painted him as.

By now Eddie was well and truly into the role. He knew his players, and they knew him. As so many had found out in the past, he was not a man to keep his thoughts to himself, or to worry about others' feelings.

Japanese magazine *Number* ran a profile of Eddie under the headline 'The Courage to Be Hated'. Eddie disavowed the quote, but not the premise behind it.

'I didn't say you had to have courage to be hated. That was the Japanese interpretation. I just said, and I believe it, if you want to be successful you have to be yourself. You've got to have certain values, and out of those values comes the way you behave. I just try to be myself, and if people don't like me that's not my concern. I just get on with it. I try to be as respectful as I can. I want people to work hard and I want people to be committed. If people don't like that, that's their problem, not mine. Japan is a country where people like to be liked. That's why it's such a good headline.'

In camp throughout the Six Nations Eddie put those policies into practice day after day. He reportedly told scrum-half Ben Youngs, 'You're too fat and not sharp enough.' Captain Dylan Hartley walked off the training paddock one day to be met with Eddie's blunt assessment of what he felt was a sub-standard performance, loud and cutting in front of the rest of the squad, while others, including

James Haskell, were left in no two minds about Eddie's views if they fell short of his expectations.

It was not unexpected. In the days after his appointment the media had reproduced numerous examples of Eddie's 'tough-love' style of man-management. Former England player and premiership club coach Dean Ryan canvassed some of Eddie's ex-players for their opinion of his interpersonal skills.

'Depending on who you speak to, you hear he was fantastic or he was horrendous,' he wrote in the *Guardian*. 'There's very little in between.'

The England players stood very much on the side of fantastic. Sick of being punching-bags after their World Cup failures and seeing Eddie as their ticket back to respectability, they took whatever he dished out and asked for more.

The criticism of Youngs' weight, and the ignominy of being left on the bench behind Danny Care for the opening match against Scotland, were taken as a challenge rather than a slap-down. The Leicester Tigers scrum-half worked hard on his fitness and won the starting role against Italy and Ireland. Likewise Hartley.

'I didn't hit the expected levels one day and I got told, "Not good enough. You should be leading by example." So the next day, you're thinking, "I need to be exceeding expectations." Eddie is always asking questions, always pushing me.'

Flanker Haskell, whose Test career had been resurrected by Eddie after Stuart Lancaster had preferred Tom Wood during the World Cup, was full of praise for Eddie's management style, despite being in his sights on occasion.

'Under this regime, I'm enjoying it more than I have ever done,' he said. 'The one-brush-sweeping-all policy, treating every player the same, doesn't work. We all have different emotional needs, and Eddie understands that. I feel for the first time in my career that there is someone who knows how to talk to players and get the best out of them.'

Some of the players who had been on the end of Eddie's blasts during his time with the Wallabies and Brave Blossoms might shake their head at Haskell's take on his style. There is no question that Eddie could always get the best out of his players, but there was very little shade in the way he got the message across. It was once all black and white, yet the Eddie Jones who arrived for his first day of work at RFU headquarters in December 2015 was a very different person to the one who took over the Wallabies in 2001 or sought redemption in Japan in 2007. He had been through a lot since then, the disappointments, losses and health scare – the Road to Damascus moment, as John O'Neill had described his stroke. But Eddie credits something else for helping change his attitudes to dealing with people. The lessons he learned from his daughter Chelsea.

'I was brought up a certain way,' he said. 'You were given a situation, and you had to fight through it. You had to work out a way. If someone told you to do something, you'd do it. You were taught to respect authority. I thought I could be tough on her, that I could impose my will. I've made a lot of mistakes with that: the way I've spoken to her, the way I've treated her, but as she grew up, I came to understand that you have to be more sympathetic. You have to engage with young people so they can make decisions for themselves. You can't make decisions for them.'

As he told Australian journalist Andrew Webster in 2016, 'My greatest weakness was that I didn't have any tolerance of people. If people weren't as driven as me, I couldn't tolerate them. I'm still like that to some extent but, particularly with the players, I am much better than what I was. The longer I coach, the more I learn it's about how you establish your relationship with people. Some players need an arm around their shoulder, some need a kick up the backside, and it's working out when they need it and in what form they need it.'

A case in point was Chris Robshaw. Eddie had belittled him in the media during the World Cup, stripped him of the captaincy and moved him from open-side to blind-side flanker. To come down hard on the former leader in the close-knit training camp environment could have broken his spirit and affected team morale. Instead Eddie took on the role of mentor. It had immediate effect, with Robshaw playing his best rugby for years and becoming a vocal Eddie disciple.

'For me he's probably got the best man-management skills out of anyone I've met,' Robshaw said at the end of Eddie's first season in charge. 'It's little bits of encouragement. You just want that support from the top guys. He gives me great confidence and allows me to go out and play. In return I want to improve, work on my game. He gives me little goals to work on, whether it's improving something like lineout jumping or lifting, rucking or whatever it might be. He knows what he wants out of the players.'

What he wanted was for them to win, and they responded.

England beat Ireland 23-10, with Itoje starting for the first time. Eddie rated his performance 'up a level from a Viva – to an Astra'. The Red Rose was now top of the Six Nations table but just as impressive for England supporters was the fact that their new coach was not satisfied. 'We probably left ten to fifteen points out there, as we couldn't always convert our attacking pressure. We weren't quite sharp enough and we were letting them get a hand in at crucial times.'

Two weeks later it was the turn of Wales. The last time the two countries had met was the World Cup debacle in which England had given away a 22-12 lead with thirty minutes remaining. At one stage it looked like Eddie's team was headed down the same path. After leading 16-0 at half-time and 25-7 with six minutes left, England let Wales back into the game. Two tries in three minutes saw the Welshmen pull to within four points and it was only a desperate lunge from England centre Manu Tuilagi on full-time that stopped Welsh flyer George North from scoring the winner. In the end it was a 25-21 win to the home team, and a relieved Eddie could look forward to Paris and the chance of delivering England their first Grand Slam since Clive Woodward's men had achieved the feat in 2003.

'It was a funny performance by us as at times we were immaculate, but then we dropped off a little bit at the end,' he said. 'You never really know what happens in scenarios like that but if you look at our first sixty minutes we were fantastic, especially after that result four months ago. Now we can't wait to go to Paris and to do the business. The Grand Slam is there for us to take. Obviously it will be hard for us with France playing their last game at home, but I think that we're good enough.'

Man of the match was Itoje. As Tom Fordyce of the BBC put it, 'Maro Itoje was compared to a Vauxhall Viva by his coach at the start of this tournament, and to an Astra after the win over Ireland, but this was a Rolls-Royce of a display from the young Saracens second-row.'

The following day Scotland beat France, giving England its first Six Nations title for seven years. The result could have seen Eddie's men take their foot off the pedal the next week in Paris, like other England teams chasing the Grand Slam had done on two previous occasions.

Not this time. First-half tries to scrum-half Danny Care and front-rower Dan Cole gave them a five-point half-time lead, but the boot of Maxime Machenaud kept the French in touch. The pressure could have got to them, but England's third try to winger Anthony Watson and a string of goals to Owen Farrell saw them comfortably home 31-21. Again, it wasn't a perfect performance, but the English players were tough, relentless and uncompromising. Just like their coach.

'I'm very proud of the boys,' he said. 'It's a great achievement by the team. I always had confidence in them. The great thing is, the best is ahead of us. We're looking forward to Australia and we're only going to get better.'

And get better they did, the outstanding 3-0 series whitewash in Australia followed by four more wins at Twickenham over South Africa 37-21, Fiji 58-15, Argentina 27-14 and Australia 37-21, to give England its first-ever unbeaten season and cement the number two world ranking behind the All Blacks.

The twelve straight wins turned Eddie into a national figure and the British media's favourite quote-machine. Reporters loved his straight-talking, rapid-fire style. The week of a Test match took on a familiar routine. In the days leading up to the game he would say something controversial. Over the next forty-eight hours the media would debate it from all angles. After the match Eddie would berate reporters for doing their job, then three or four days later it would start all over again. His press calls were like riding a carnival rollercoaster; he was friendly one moment, counter-punching the next, and anyone sitting alongside him was merely filling a chair. After one media conference when every question had been directed to his coach, England captain Dylan Hartley stood up and asked Eddie, 'Why did I come in? I should have gone to the bloody bar.'

It was that kind of belligerent, irreverent attitude that Eddie was looking for when he appointed Hartley as his captain.

'The first thing with a captain is that he has to be one of the first players selected,' he said. 'Those stories about Richie McCaw are true. In training the All Blacks go from one drill to the next, and he sprints there, he's the first there. He cleans the changing room after the game, and that's the sort of guy you want.'

Not that Eddie was looking for someone to sweep the floor or pick up the dirty jerseys when he appointed Hartley. The qualities he was seeking wouldn't win too many Best and Fairest awards, but they were imperative for Eddie's vision of a new-look England.

'I watched England's World Cup games quite closely and thought they lacked a forward that really had a bit of mongrel about him. Dylan Hartley did that previously, and it had got him in a bit of trouble, so he was an obvious choice. Dylan is an honest, hard-working bloke, and I admire his aggressive and uncompromising approach to playing rugby.'

Eddie added to Hartley's mystique by nicknaming him 'The Butcher', although not for obvious reasons.

'He looks like a butcher, don't you reckon?' he said. 'When you go down to your local butcher shop, you can see Dylan behind there. "What would you like, madam? Six lamb chops? Here you go."'

His choice of captain might not have pleased the purists, but a traditional, gentlemanly leader was the last thing Eddie wanted. Hartley's comments when England arrived in Brisbane for the first Test of their Australian tour summed up the attitude Eddie was looking for as clearly as if he had written the script himself.

'We expect to dominate on Saturday night, but why not?' Hartley said. 'We believe in ourselves, we're a good pack. There's no point in us boarding the plane if we don't believe we can do it. If you're tired and want a holiday you can go home. We've brought our best squad, a hungry squad ready to compete, a squad hungry to climb the world rankings, a squad that wants to win and believes we can.'

After Wallaby coach Michael Cheika accused England of 'niggle' in their first Test win, Hartley was far from offended.

'Niggle isn't something we practise,' he said. 'We practise being physical, confrontational. We want to dominate. If that's the way we are being perceived, that's a compliment.'

With the captain setting the tone, Eddie surrounded him with other players noted for their fighting qualities, tough competitors such as Dan Cole, Mike Brown and James Haskell. When Haskell was ruled out through injury from the 2016 match against the Springboks – a game Eddie predicted would be 'like chess on steroids' – he replaced him with the like-minded Tom Wood.

'He's got a bit of Rambo about him,' Eddie said of Wood. 'He walks around the hotel with no shoes on. He's got bows and arrows round the corner, he's got chainsaws.'

Rambo, chainsaws, aggression and confrontation? Was this really an England rugby team? Certainly not one like the 1973 version, of whom the captain John Pullin said after being beaten 18-9 by Ireland in Dublin, 'Well, we might not be any good, but at least we turn up.'

Eddie didn't want a team that just turned up. He wanted one that was the best in the world, and the English public was right behind him.

17

THE EDDIE EFFECT

Ian Herbert, who was chief sports writer for the *Independent* before joining the *Daily Mail*, was in an ideal position to view 'the Eddie Effect'. As a general sports writer, rather than a rugby specialist, he was able to monitor Eddie's impact across a broader spectrum and says his no-frills, hard-edged approach was embraced by England fans starved of international success.

'I was coming at the Eddie story from a non-rugby specialist writing background. I was looking at it more as a narrative about the Australian influence.

'I had written about the England team under Stuart Lancaster at the World Cup. Stuart was the quintessential Englishman: urbane, gentlemanly, respectful, the type of person you'd like to meet at the pub, but the 2015 RWC was a calamity for England. After all the intelligent, schoolteacherly talks of Lancaster, it turned out to be a disaster. It just looked like there was no plan.

'Eddie is the antithesis of that, and everyone loved it. He calls it straight, there's no waffle. His initial press conferences were divine after Lancaster. People immediately started buying into Eddie, but I think they were partly buying into Australia.

'For so long there was this perception about the way British teams played. The emphasis on defence, that feeling that sport was about respecting your opponent and "play the game, old chum". The problem was, we weren't winning, and people started to have doubts. It was almost a philosophical debate: "How nice should we be?" Eddie was at the forefront of that, showing us the Australian way to do things, to be more direct and more committed to winning above all else.'

Herbert says the 'Eddie Effect' crossed over to football when Gareth Southgate was appointed England manager in December 2016.

'Eddie once made a comment that English teams spent too much time worrying about being liked and "going around the world apologizing". When Gareth Southgate was appointed, someone put that quote to him, and he said, "Well, Eddie won't do that, will he?" Gareth is very mild-mannered and quiet and he has used Eddie as a role model as he tries to stop being a boring old Englishman.

'He has been to watch Eddie at work. For a while there he was talking more about Eddie than he was about football. What he is saying is that the England team has to be less nice. They have to rediscover what they had in 1966; they have to find the missing ingredient. It is almost as if we needed an Aussie to come in and show us how to play the game.'

And it was not just the England football manager who was won over by Eddie, says Herbert, but the English football public.

'The English are obsessed with football, but the game has been annexed. It has moved further and further away from the man in the street. The Premier League is full of media-managed cosmetic people; players who earn £250,000 a week and smug managers like Mourinho and Guardiola. I think people like Eddie's freedom of expression.

They sense that he is a real person, a guy who calls it straight.'

Indeed he is. Eddie's second season in charge began just as the first had ended, with great expectations, and even greater quotes.

'We are going to believe we can win Test matches and that we are going to be the best team in the world. If that is being arrogant, then it is being arrogant. To me, it is belief about what we can do. I am quite happy for the players to talk about that, because that is the way we are going to think. If you are winning and you are arrogant, it is self-belief. When you lose, it is being arrogant.'

England's first match of the season was a 19-16 home win over France followed by a 21-16 away victory over Wales. Then followed one of the strangest Test matches ever seen at Twickenham, as Italy gave England a mighty scare in a game that Eddie called 'not rugby'.

Under Irish-born coach Conor O'Shea, the Italians went into the match well drilled on exploiting a loophole in the laws of the game in order to upset their high-flying hosts, who were chasing a seventeenth straight victory. By not committing any players to the breakdown other than the original tackler, thus avoiding the formation of a ruck, the Italians could not be ruled offside. Therefore they could stand among the England inside backs, virtually surrounding scrum-half Danny Care and making it impossible for him to clear to his number ten, George Ford. While perfectly legal, the ploy completely befuddled the England players and also the crowd, who were at first bemused and then angered. As was Eddie up in the stand, his scowl growing darker and darker as the game went on. At half-time Italy led 10-5, and England clung to a precarious 17-15 lead with eleven minutes to play before three late tries saw them comfortably home 36-15.

After the match Eddie was scathing in his comments, saying the crowd should ask for their money back, and likening Italy's tactics to one of the most notorious incidents in Australian cricket history.

'I was remembering Trevor Chappell bowling underarm along the ground. Similar rules today. It's not a game of rugby. It ceases to be a game of rugby. Congratulations to Italy, strategically it was smart, so well done to them, but let's be serious about it, it wasn't rugby today. I'm not happy with what happened. I played rugby a long time ago, I've coached rugby. I understand what Italy did and I'm not angry with what they did, but I just don't think it's rugby.'

His opinion didn't mellow with time. Asked a few months later for his views on the match, he went so far as to accuse Italy of playing against the spirit of rugby.

'They did something very clever but not in the spirit of the game. When I was coaching Japan we were playing the All Blacks in 2013. Japan's last game against the All Blacks had been 145-13. Their average losing score against a tier-one country was 85-0, so we toyed with the idea of destroying the game. Legally you can destroy the game like Italy did. You can stuff the game right up, but then how could I ever say to Japan, "You can beat a big team," if you're already saying, "You can't beat that team, you've got to play against the spirit of the game"? Italy did that. When they walked out they were already waving the white flag because they didn't want to get beaten by ninety points. They wanted to get beaten by forty points. That was their target. Our players weren't slow in working out what to do, they were slow in executing. They knew exactly what to do but they just couldn't execute. It took them until after half-time to execute it, and then they did it pretty well.'

The International Rugby Board would change the law prior to the

2018 Six Nations as a direct result of Italy's tactics, but even though England had won on the scoreboard, the general feeling was that Conor O'Shea had won the tactical battle of the coaches. After the match he revealed that he had spoken to French referee Romain Poite during the week and told him what tactics he intended to employ. It was a clever move. During the first half a perplexed Dylan Hartley and James Haskell had approached Poite and asked him to explain the law that the Italians were exploiting. 'Ask your coach,' Poite had said, waving them away.

'We were just playing to the rules,' O'Shea said. 'Everything we did was completely legal. If people want us to come over here and roll over and have our tummies tickled, well, we're not going to do that. If they want us to lose by 100 points, well, why should we? Why should we be normal? We should be ourselves. I thought the game was compelling. You had players having to make decisions on the pitch, they had to deal with it. That's what rugby's about. Rugby's a game of chaos.'

Following the scare against Italy, Eddie worked his players hard in preparation for their next match, a home game against Scotland two weeks later. Concentrating on mending the issues he had detected when the team was put under mental pressure by the Italians, he wasn't his usual quotable self in the week before the match. Scottish coach Jim Telfer more than made up for it in his pre-match interview, launching a colourful attack on Eddie, England supporters and Twickenham itself.

'Eddie Jones doesn't want to beat teams, he wants to demolish them, which I find a bit disappointing,' he said. 'To me he's building his whole team on set piece and the building of the attack comes secondary. Having coached Australia and Japan, you would have thought the opposite would be the case.

'The way he speaks, it's a bit like Donald Trump. He wants to be the big man, you know? His goal is to win the World Cup in 2019, and so far it's gone well, but I think he could be a little more circumspect, show a bit more respect for the opposition. He doesn't seem to show much respect, and it could come back to bite him.

'Twickenham I find intimidating. The whole atmosphere is intimidating, there's so many of them, three tiers of them. If you ever think about wanting separation from England just sit ten minutes in Twickenham and listen to them. They think they're superior, and a lot of them will come from the southeast, bags of money and bags of this and bags of that. They don't really appreciate the other team.

'In France they just boo the other team, in Argentina they boo the other team, in England it's just disdain. It's, "Why are we playing these plebs?" I don't like Twickenham. It's a concrete jungle, there's nothing attractive about it at all.'

When it came to game time, Telfer's words proved far more incisive than anything the Scottish players could produce on the field. England won 61-21 in the team's best performance since the previous year's tour of Australia.

The result gave England its second successive Six Nations championship and a world-record-equalling eighteen straight wins. Victory over the Joe Schmidt-coached Ireland in Dublin would see Eddie's team become the first to win back-to-back Six Nations Grand Slams and also surpass the All Blacks' record for consecutive wins. Given the way they had brushed the Scots aside at Twickenham and the fact that Ireland had already lost to Scotland and Wales, many believed it to be a fait accompli.

Instead, the day after St Patrick's Day 2017 would haunt Eddie for a long time to come.

Ireland won 13-9, but their dominance was far greater than the score would suggest. Eddie was full of praise for Ireland's performance and highly critical of his own.

'We are all disappointed. Ireland played superbly. They deserved to win. They shaded us in the lineout, they shaded us at the breakdown, and we struggled to get any momentum because of that. I thought our effort was outstanding, but our execution wasn't great because of the pressure they put on us. We wanted to put pressure on Ireland, but because of the way they played – and they played the conditions superbly – they put pressure on us. We've got to accept we weren't good enough today and learn from it and move on.

'You hate losing, but when you have been winning a lot it doesn't matter what you do to stop complacency, it is always there. We were definitely complacent, and I was the worst. I didn't prepare the team well.'

Les Kiss, former Springboks defence coach and part of the Ireland coaching set-up from 2009 until 2013, says Eddie was being too hard on himself. He says he and his team wouldn't have known what hit them.

'I wouldn't say Eddie didn't prepare his team properly. He would have done everything right, said all the right things, but it was his first game as England coach at Dublin, and it's a different place. No matter how much you think you are ready for it, it can get to you, and that's what happened that night.

'There's always that old line about every game being important, but to Ireland no game is more important than England. The only thing I can compare it to is when the Springboks or Wallabies play the All Blacks, but it's deeper than that. It's not hate, but it is a different level of competition to anything else. To be able to stop the English from winning something big like the Grand Slam and taking the world record would have made it even more special.

'Joe Schmidt wouldn't have done or said anything out of the ordinary to get the players up for that game. He wouldn't have to. It's not the coaches who take the players to a different level for games like that, it's the players themselves. I saw it a lot in my time with Ireland. I was part of the coaching team when Stuart Lancaster brought England to Dublin in 2011 with the Grand Slam up for grabs. We smashed them 24-8, and then it turned out they'd already had thousands of t-shirts printed up saying they were Grand Slam champs. All that sort of stuff adds to the build-up of England games, but it's never spoken about. You never talk about history to the players; it's just part of their psyche. They've got centuries of oppression under the English to fire them up, but they don't do it with big speeches and fist shaking. You see the players in the dressing room before the game, talking quietly to each other, saying what they're going to do. All the coaches have to do is prepare them as best they can and leave them to it. Sometimes it's best just to step away.

'The Irish are different to Australians. The Wallabies want to show that they're more athletic and better sportsmen than everyone else. They want to throw the ball around and run you off your feet. The Irish want to get you down into the trenches and rip your eyeballs out.'

Things didn't stoop quite to that level in Eddie's first loss as England coach, but the Irish forwards, and constant rain, did squeeze the life out of any hopes the English had of mounting their now customary last-quarter domination. Ireland, forced to reshuffle the pack when number eight Jamie Heaslip was injured in the warm-up, were inspired, with Heaslip's replacement Peter O'Mahony producing a man-of-the-match performance. In comparison, England appeared nervous and disjointed, with basic errors and poor handling costing them any chance of achieving their twin goals. Ireland scored the only try of the match when lock Iain Henderson forced his way over from a lineout.

The England players looked almost embarrassed when they stepped up to receive the Six Nations trophy, the fireworks and streamers that were supposed to herald the Grand Slam and world record providing an ironic backdrop to their disappointment.

Eddie, not for the first or last time, reached for a cricket analogy to sum up the moment.

'We are still batting at a pretty good average. Even Don Bradman got zero when he played his last Test. At full-time I told the team, "Be proud of yourselves, boys." We are back-to-back Six Nations champions, which is a fantastic achievement. We're joint world-record-holders, but we weren't good enough today.

'We are fourteen months into a four-year project, as I have been saying. We have been chuffed with the results we have had, but realism tells us we have still got a lot to do. How many teams have a 90 per cent winning record at Test level? The All Blacks are the only ones, and we have been doing that since the last World Cup.'

As for missing the world record, the old schoolteacher was a realist.

'That's why there is a law of averages. It's so hard, you get a team on the day that plays above itself like Ireland did today, and we were slightly off for whatever reason, and you get caught. We said to the players this was like a World Cup final. We got beaten 13-9, and you come away with a silver medal. It doesn't taste good and it makes you want to get that gold medal.'

The media and public couldn't help but be impressed with the way Eddie had accepted his first loss as England coach. He had been gracious in defeat, made no excuses, congratulated Ireland, commended his players on their effort and moved on. If only he had left it at that, the loss in Dublin would have been just a minor blip in an otherwise exemplary season. Instead, Scotland coach Jim Telfer's prophecy that Eddie's lack of respect would come back to bite him was about to come true.

*

By the end of his second year in charge of the England team, Eddie was more than a rugby coach in the eyes of the English public. He was a personality, a celebrity, a public figure. He had gone from being a big fish in the small pond of Japan, where rugby was seen as something of an oddity, to a big fish in the biggest pond there is.

As former Leicester Tigers coach Matt O'Connor, who like Eddie came to England after coaching the Queensland Reds, puts it, 'London is a different league. It is the mecca of world rugby. There is so much corporate involvement, so many different opinions and different voices. The interest in rugby is like nothing else anywhere, and Eddie has to put up with that on a daily basis.'

The little hooker from Matraville High was photographed joking with Prince Harry at training; he and his wife Hiroko sat in the royal box at Wimbledon with tennis legend Rod Laver. He couldn't go anywhere without being recognized.

Journalist Chris Hewett, who struck up a relationship with Eddie when he wrote a column for the *Independent* during his time with Saracens, recalls accompanying him to Bath for a match.

'Unlike some England coaches, Eddie always gets along to watch premiership matches. He goes to two, sometimes three a weekend. He was going to watch Bath play Toulon and asked me if I wanted to go along. As we sat in the crowd, the TV camera was on him all the time, and after the game we went to a restaurant for a meal. They put us at a table near the window, and people saw him and came in to talk or have their picture taken with him. He was absolutely fantastic. He spoke to everyone, posed for pictures. He had such good grace and enormous patience for someone not known for his patience. I'm not sure he is always comfortable with it, but he realizes he is a public figure and he plays his part.'

Eddie's willingness to rub shoulders with the general public would lead to him becoming the victim of a disgraceful incident the following season, but in 2017 he was very much enjoying the fruits of his enormous popularity – as was his business manager. With on-field success came off-field opportunities. Within weeks of Japan's stunning 2015 World Cup win over South Africa, Eddie was appointed to the advisory board of the Japanese branch of international investment banking giant Goldman Sachs. Committed to two meetings in Tokyo a year, his role was to pass on his expertise in managing people of different nationalities. Another corporate heavyweight, Japan's leading investment bank Nomura, contracted Eddie for three years to work in the areas of leadership and teamwork with its clients in Europe. He was also appointed as brand ambassador for Mitsubishi Motors in the UK and took on a similar role in Australia for contentgroup, a specialist government media consultancy headed by his former ACT Brumbies colleague David Pembroke. There were also highly paid corporate speaking engagements around the world, including one that he would come to wish he had turned down.

Fuso Talks is a series of business lectures run by the Mitsubishi Fuso Truck and Bus Corporation, a division of Daimler Trucks Asia. Starting in 2015, and held at the company headquarters in Kanagawa, Japan, the talks feature guest lecturers addressing an audience made up of Fuso employees and clients. On 10 July 2017, Eddie spoke at the fifth event, on the subject of 'Leadership'. His talk centred mainly on how he had transformed the Brave Blossoms from earnest losers into a team capable of downing the mighty Springboks.

It was an inspiring story, but it would be fair to say it didn't exactly hit the mark. Eddie would have realized very early into his presentation that this was not a rugby crowd. It may not even have been a predominantly English-speaking crowd. In fact, if not for two words – and YouTube – the speech would probably never have caused a ripple of attention outside the Fuso conference room.

Taken in context, the two words that created a media storm eight months later weren't part of any diatribe against any rival team or nation. In the light of other comments by sporting coaches, such as those made by Scotland's Jim Telfer about England fans four months earlier, they weren't even heartfelt or premeditated. What they were was ill-considered and careless.

The first came when Eddie was trying to illustrate the size of the task he faced when he took over as Japan national coach. Three months into the job, the Japanese Under-20 side had lost to Wales by 125-0. Making the point that a country with a much larger population, such as Japan, should not be beaten so easily by a country with a smaller population, he gestured to a table with a glass of water on it and said glibly, 'So, Wales. Who knows Wales? Are there any Welsh people here? So it's this little shit place that's got three million people. Three million. Japan's got how many – 125 million. So Japan's the size of this table and that glass is Wales.'

A few minutes later he spoke about the progress he was making with England.

'As a leader, your prime responsibility is to get the best out of your team. We're trying to do that with England at the moment. So we've played twenty-three Tests, we've only lost one Test to the scummy

Irish. I'm still dirty about that game. But we'll get that back, don't worry. We've got them next year at home. We'll get 'em back.'

The speech given, Eddie took his bow and headed for the exit. He probably didn't give a second thought to what he had said, but, as the saying goes, there are two things you can't take back: the spent arrow and the spoken word. Especially in the age of social media. Even as Eddie was landing at Heathrow and heading home to Surrey, Fuso Talks convenor Florian Laudan, head of communications for Daimler Trucks Asia, was downloading footage of the speech onto YouTube, where it would sit barely noticed for months, like a submerged iceberg waiting for an oncoming ship.

Before Eddie and his men would have the opportunity to gain their revenge on Ireland there were still six matches to be played in the 2017 season.

The first was against the Barbarians invitational side. An uncapped international, it was really a trial game which would enable Eddie to look at some options for the upcoming two-Test tour of Argentina. With sixteen of his first-choice players chosen to tour New Zealand with the British and Irish Lions at the same time as the Argentina series, and another fourteen out injured, Eddie blooded eight newcomers. As Dylan Hartley was unavailable due to a European Champions Cup match, Eddie also took the unprecedented step of naming Chris Robshaw and George Ford as co-captains.

When asked how he felt having two captains would work, he showed the Irish loss hadn't affected his sharp wit or sense of history.

'It's not like Winston Churchill. Someone doesn't say, "We'll fight them on the beaches." There's always a discussion going on. When we get a penalty, Dylan will go up to Owen Farrell and say, "Should we kick this one? Is it in your range?" It'll be fine.'

And so it proved, with England winning 28-14. While it was hardly a classic free-running Barbarians encounter, Eddie couldn't help but be impressed by the effort shown by his young team, which had a combined 277 Test caps against the Barbarians' 812. Only five England starters, fullback Mike Brown, winger Jonny May, back-rower Chris Robshaw and halves George Ford and Danny Care, had played more than three Tests. Showing plenty of promise for England were back-rower Tom Curry and lock Nick Isiekwe, both teenagers, and twenty-two-year-old winger Nathan Earle, but Eddie reserved greatest praise for Robshaw, captaining for the first time since the World Cup.

'It was a bit of a cleansing act for Robbo. I probably started part of the discussion when I was a journalist. I probably still haven't apologized properly to him for that. But that was a different life. He gets rewarded for being a good player. It was a nice moment for him today. If we had fifteen of him we will win the World Cup with that sort of attitude and that sort of commitment.'

The following day Eddie named a thirty-one-man touring party for Argentina, with fifteen uncapped players, including New Zealand-born rugby league convert Denny Solomona. A blockbusting winger who had played Test rugby league for Samoa, Solomona had played only ten games of rugby union for Sale and passed his three-year residency eligibility just a month earlier.

It was a controversial selection. Eddie's boss, England rugby chief executive Ian Ritchie, was a vocal critic of so-called 'project players' – those imported into a country for the sole purpose of having them eligible to play Test rugby – and the RFU was a prime mover behind having the residential eligibility period raised from three years to five from 2020. During his tenure Eddie had appointed Rotorua-born Dylan Hartley his captain, and fellow Kiwis Nathan Hughes, Teimana

Harrison and Ben Te'o had all made their England debuts during his first two seasons in charge.

Questioned over whether his readiness to pick foreign-born players was poor reflection on the standard of the England talent development programme, he answered bluntly, 'That's not my problem.

'My job is to coach the national team. If England aren't producing more international players it's the development area's problem. My job is to make the national team win. If the national team wins, the game in England is healthy. If it is healthy, we get sponsorship, we get media attention, and that allows more money to be put into development. How that money is spent is not up to me to say.

'The reality is, it doesn't matter what country you go to, you want to pick the best players because you want to win. Whether they've come through because their great-grandfather was English or they've done residency here is of no consequence to me.'

But Eddie's decision to pick Solomona was made even more pointed as Solomona had ruled out playing rugby league for England, saying 'My heart's not here. It's not for England.'

Solomona convinced Eddie that he had had a change of heart when the two met at a Sale gym session, and he was added to the Argentina tour squad despite never having trained with the national side.

Eddie brushed the criticism aside.

'I think I am as desperate to coach England to a win as any England coach and I haven't been brought up in England, as you can tell by my accent,' he said. 'It's about how you feel and how much you want it.'

And, most importantly from Eddie's point of view, how well you play. No rugby coach loved rugby league players more than Eddie; none had more success with them. In Solomona, he saw a project very much worth pursuing.

'There's something about him. He finds the line. He's got that ability, when he gets the ball, to score a try. He's still got a lot of work to do on his game positionally, but we can work on those areas with him. He's got a certain amount of X-Factor about him, though. What we want from league players is that they don't forget what they were good at. We want them to run hard and be good with the ball and when the opposition get the ball we want them to hurt them, as that's what they're good at.'

Considering the hard time Eddie had given Clive Woodward over his rapid promotion of league convert Henry Paul in 2001, Sir Clive could have been forgiven for a wry smile, but it wasn't the only about-face Eddie would make over the years. During the 2003 World Cup Woodward was hounded by the Australian media over England's so-called boring tactics. Eddie tried to taunt him into a change of tactics on the eve of the final, preaching about both coaches' 'responsibility to the game'. When Eddie received the same criticism when he was in charge of England, he countered with, 'Test match rugby is about winning, it's not about entertainment. If you want entertainment, watch Super Rugby.'

Another unexpected addition Eddie made to the Argentina touring party was his old friend Glen Ella, whom he called in to work with the backline, seven of whom were uncapped.

'It was good fun, but it was hard work,' Ella says. 'England had a full team out with the Lions, and the Pumas were at full strength so it was always going to be tough, but Eddie put a good squad together, and they worked very hard. A lot of players in that campaign really established themselves over there. That's the thing about Eddie. He can spot talent and then bring it out in players. England always had the players, but they weren't being coached properly. Eddie was the right person at the right time.'

As semi-finalists at the 2015 World Cup, Argentina posed a serious threat to the inexperienced England side. Following the loss to Ireland, Eddie's side was in grave danger of going from potential world-record-holder to dropping three Tests in a row. Instead, his thrown-together team of 'strays and waifs', as one journalist called them, pulled off two memorable victories.

The first Test at San Juan was a harum-scarum affair that would have done nothing for Eddie's blood pressure, but he still described it as 'one of the best team efforts I have been involved in'. The lead changed six times, and with 100 seconds left it looked like the Pumas would win after two missed tackles by late replacement Solomona had led to tries. Then, in the final play of the match Solomona got the ball on the right wing 60 metres out, crashed through two attempted tackles, stepped in-field, palmed off a third would-be defender, outpaced the cover and scored under the posts to secure a 38-34 win.

A week later, in Santa Fe, the second Test didn't produce quite the finish of the first, but it was still a seesawing match that was in the balance until a George Ford drop-goal sealed a 35-25 victory and gave England only their second-ever series win in Argentina. The first, under Stuart Lancaster four years earlier, had been against a depleted Pumas outfit. Eddie's young men had taken on the best that Argentina had to offer and done themselves and their coach proud. With the World Cup edging ever closer, the successful tour had shone the light on some youngsters who would be pushing the more established players come 2019.

'We wanted to win 2-0, and to have a number of the young players come through really well is great for us,' Eddie said. 'A few guys have done really well. Harry Williams, Charlie Ewels, Tom Curry and Sam Underhill at open-side flanker, Mark Wilson has proved himself to be a very competent player. In the backline Piers Francis and Alex Lozowski are worth looking at. Denny Solomona too.'

From Argentina Eddie returned to England for a five-month break before a return bout with the Pumas as the first of three end-of-year Tests at Twickenham. The hiatus gave him the chance to work out how to meld his new up-and-comers with the returning stars, plot tactics for a fifth showdown with Michael Cheika and the Wallabies and, unfortunately for him, fly to Japan to speak at Fuso Talks.

The first Test of the autumn series at Twickenham was a third consecutive win over Argentina 21-8, but it was not without its challenges. When Underhill gave away a penalty inside the England 22-metre zone Eddie was seen on TV throwing his notebook and pen and dropping the f-bomb in frustration. It didn't need a lip-reader to work out what he was saying.

'F***. How f****ing stupid are we?'

The outburst brought prompt action. Not from World Rugby or the RFU. Worse. An early morning call from his ninety-three-year-old mother Nellie in Australia, telling him to watch his language.

Next up it was Australia. Eddie was on his best behaviour. It was Wallaby coach Michael Cheika who needed to have his mouth washed out with soap.

In the first of their three encounters, Cheika had done his best to keep his emotions in check and let Eddie do the talking. During England's 2016 mid-year tour of Australia that had not been hard. The Wallabies were coming off a brilliant 2015, where they had reached the World Cup final and finished the season number two team in the game.

Six months later, when he arrived in London to play England for the fourth time in the season, things weren't going so well. His Wallabies had gone down 3-0 to England at home, been beaten three times by the All Blacks, lost their number two ranking and just gone down to Ireland in Dublin. He was in no mood to let Eddie win the war of words again.

Zeroing in on Eddie's claims of media disrespect during the series in Australia, Cheika said his old Randwick team-mate had 'tarnished his legacy' in his home country.

'Eddie has always operated with a chip on his shoulder, and now that there's not a chip because he's going really well, he's got to keep looking for it,' he said. 'I think he's very respected in Australia. I don't know where that "unrespected" comes from.'

Cheika was something of an expert on disrespect at the time. He had been furious four weeks earlier when the *Auckland Herald* newspaper had published a caricature of him as a clown wearing a Wallaby jumper on the eve of the third Bledisloe Cup match, under the headline, 'Send in the Clowns'.

Eddie, asked his opinion, called it 'a bit of fun', but couldn't resist the opportunity to stir the pot ahead of the Wallabies' arrival in Britain.

'We know even now they're talking about a Grand Slam. They're obviously full of optimism and confidence. They won't be sending in the clowns.'

Before the Twickenham match the *Australian* got into the act, portraying Eddie in a cartoon as a crazy clown with a red cross of St George painted across his white face.

Eddie wasn't offended, other than to criticize the quality of the artist, but Cheika wouldn't be drawn into the discussion, saying, 'I just don't find it funny.' One thing he would comment on, and with passion, was Eddie's use of Glen Ella as assistant coach during the series in Australia.

In his new role as a contributor to a sports website, Ella had previewed the upcoming England–Australia Test as a showdown between two coaches rather than a contest of two teams.

'I know that both Cheika and Jones have been waiting for this game for some time.

'For Cheika, because inwardly he has been seething about the results in June and can't wait to get the chance to beat Eddie back on English soil – and to prove that he can coach.

'Then you have Eddie Jones, who is a little pissed off about how he and his team were treated whilst in Australia, especially by some of the media, and will want to prove that the whitewash was no fluke.'

Cheika, wrote Ella, 'would have had nightmares' over the way Eddie 'dominated him big time' during the series.

'Michael was clearly beaten badly in the propaganda battle against Eddie in June. It was a real master and apprentice show.'

When he arrived in London the Wallaby coach fired back.

'It's funny that everyone is up the front of the bus when they have had a win. A guy like Glen is always up the front of the bus for a handout when he has had a win, but when it is tough and you have to run uphill, I have not seen that bloke or a few of those blokes around.

'Any guy who would support England against Australia, especially a guy who has played for the Wallabies, there has got to be a reason why. I don't know if he is bitter. Maybe they want us to get kicked out and have a job there. It is more about your approach to your own team. I have never coached a club in the same competition I used to be in, but each to his own.'

England's 37-21 win didn't improve his mood.

A year later, when Cheika and his men returned to Twickenham, their fortunes were on the rise. In the previous ten weeks they had drawn twice with the Springboks, twice beaten Argentina, thrashed Japan and ended an eight-match losing streak against the All Blacks. The spring tour had started with a 29-21 win over Wales. Eddie said he wanted the Wallabies to 'bring their best game'. Cheika thought they had.

Yet again it was a win to England, 30-6, but not without controversy. Irish TMO Simon McDowell ruled a try to England winger Elliot Daly on the tightest of calls, Wallabies Michael Hooper and Kurtley Beale were sin-binned, and Hooper and Marika Koroibete both had tries disallowed.

When Beale was ruled to have deliberately knocked the ball down, rather than attempted an intercept, and sent to join Hooper in the sin-bin, the TV camera caught Cheika mouthing the words 'f****ing cheats'.

Eddie began his post-match media conference by apologizing for swearing the previous week and saying he would 'leave that to the other side'.

'I didn't throw a pen today, I didn't swear. I think my mother will be pleased. I don't expect a phone call at five o'clock in the morning.'

He then proceeded to turn the screws even further, pointedly praising the work done by Cheika's new skills coach, former All Blacks' assistant Mick Byrne, in improving the Wallabies' performances.

As for the fifth win in succession against his old team, he likened it to a 5-0 Ashes series win, the ultimate insult to any Australian sports fan.

While jubilant Eddie was charming the press under the grandstand, a livid Cheika was outside doing a TV interview, the steam all but coming out of his cauliflower ears.

After holding himself in check when asked about the contentious rulings against Australia, Cheika appeared stunned and then angry when the interviewer mentioned that the cameras had captured him swearing.

'It will be relayed time and again,' she said. 'You may be aware of it, but there was one reaction in which it appeared you swore and accused someone of being a cheat. Do you apologize?'

'Not at all, no. I never said . . . what are you talking about?'

'It's best to ask . . .'

'Is that really what we're going to talk about? Is that what it is coming down to?'

'It's going to be replayed on TV.'

'They can replay whatever they want. Like, if that's what it's come down to, that's it, right? I'm trying to have an interview without trying to get stuck into that, and you try to keep making it . . .'

The interviewer tried to make a point but Cheika cut her off.

'No, no, you are . . . so don't say you're not. Have the respect for me to say, "I am doing that," at least. At no stage . . . maybe I could have said something, but if that's the new thing, then, yeah, maybe I did swear. I don't know. It happens sometimes in life. I'm sure you have as well, or maybe the TV cameras weren't on you at the time . . .'

The interviewer started to say, 'I agree . . .' but Cheika had already turned and walked away.

Two days later, at an event in Monte Carlo, Eddie was named World Rugby Coach of the Year, an honour he dedicated to his fellow coaches and players, before saying that he felt it should have gone to New Zealand's Steve Hansen.

'I must admit I feel a bit embarrassed,' he said. 'We're not the number one team in the world. I think Steve Hansen should be up here, but someone has judged it another way. We want to be the number one team in the world and until we're number one we've got nothing to crow about.'

Asked what he would do with the award, he answered, 'I think my dog will play with it.'

England had one final Test for the year, a 48-14 win over Samoa, giving them a 90.9 per cent success rate for the season. The players headed off for a well-earned break, but while they were looking forward to relaxing Eddie remained cautious.

'Every day I wake up, I am worried,' he said at the Coach of the Year ceremony. 'If that ever changes I will be worried because every day potentially something could happen.'

The black-tie crowd chuckled. Just Eddie being Eddie. He had just been named the top coach in the game, his team had won twenty-two out of their last twenty-three Tests, he had uncovered a new vein of talent and he had a third straight Six Nations championship in his sights. The All Blacks and the number one ranking were coming to Twickenham in November.

What could possibly go wrong?

18

UNSTEADY EDDIE

When Eddie was appointed England coach a former Wallaby staffer received a call from a colleague at the RFU.

'How do you think he will go?' he was asked.

'He'll go very well at the start. The real question is how he'll go for the last two years.'

It proved to be a very astute answer.

Eddie's first two seasons were better than just about anyone could have foreseen. Even Ian Ritchie, the RFU chief executive who had flown to Cape Town to sign him, admitted Eddie had far exceeded his expectations.

'One felt Eddie was the right person for the job but one never thought he would win eighteen games on the bounce,' he said.

Ritchie was so confident that the team was in the best of hands that he stood down from the job at the end of the Argentina tour, saying the time was right for someone else to oversee England's final assault on the World Cup. His replacement was former RFU chief financial officer Steve Brown, who took over in September 2017, just in time to watch Eddie and his men go through the three autumn Tests undefeated.

One of Brown's first jobs in the New Year was to extend Eddie's contract until 2021. The original plan had been for Eddie to leave immediately after the 2019 World Cup. After that, he had told reporters, 'I'll be off watching cricket in Barbados.' So why the change of plan? Steve Brown said it was to ensure a smooth transition from Eddie to his successor, whom Eddie would help choose and mentor. The new coach would then take over after the 2021 Six Nations and lead the side through the 2023 World Cup in France. Eddie's version of events was that he was loving the job so much he just couldn't walk away.

'Coaching England is a dream job for me, and I was delighted to be asked to stay on after the World Cup. I have been completely focused on developing a team capable of being the number one rugby team in the world and winning the World Cup in 2019. I never take my role as England head coach for granted and did not presume I would be asked to stay on, but, once the conversations started very recently, it was not a difficult decision to make.'

Cynics suggested there was more to the decision to stay on than Eddie was admitting. The British and Irish Lions have an eight-match tour of South Africa scheduled for 2021. Coaching the world's most famous touring side would be a fitting finale for Eddie's time in England – if not his entire career.

'I'm not arrogant or presumptuous enough to think I would be offered the Lions role so it's not something I really think about,' he said, although Steve Brown said Eddie's new contract, reported to be worth £750,000 a year plus bonuses, would not preclude him coaching the Lions if he was offered the role.

But that was in January. By March, leading the Lions to South Africa was the last thing on Eddie's mind. He was too busy holding on to his job as England coach.

Before the start of the 2018 season few were predicting that Eddie's golden run was about to end. England were the hottest of red-hot favourites to win a record third consecutive Six Nations, with bookmakers quoting odds of 10/11, and 5/2 the Grand Slam.

After the first two matches it appeared the bookies were right. England beat Italy 46-15 in Rome and then returned to Twickenham to face Wales with two significant milestones up for grabs. A win would give England a record fifteen consecutive championship victories at home and take Eddie's team to twenty-five wins from twenty-six games, bettering the mark set by Clive Woodward's 2003 world champion side.

The Welsh were confident they could spoil the party. They were coming off an impressive 34-7 win over Scotland, with coach Warren Gatland boasting he had the fittest team in the championship.

Gatland also admitted that he had told Wales chief executive Martyn Phillips before the Scotland match, 'We'll beat this mob by twenty points.' He stopped short of making any such predictions about the England match but did say that Twickenham held no fears for him or his players.

Asked about Eddie's ambition to become top team in the world by dethroning the All Blacks at Twickenham in November, the New Zealand-born Gatland answered, 'The autumn is going to be interesting. You set yourself up for a big game and then you potentially become number one or someone pulls your pants down.'

Needless to say, Eddie wasn't going to let Gatland upstage him.

'Warren's been talking a lot this week,' he said. 'They are definitely confident and cocky. Everyone has been telling them how well they played last week but it is easy to play when the ball is on the front foot and going from side to side.

'We've heard how fit Wales are. If it was a cross-fit game then I'd understand why fitness was so important, but we want to be the best in the world and be good enough to beat Wales. We don't want to get our pants pulled down.'

Not content to merely counter-attack, Eddie then went on the offensive. Two years earlier he had started a firestorm when he singled out Ireland playmaker Johnny Sexton for special treatment in his pre-match interview. Now he tried it again with inexperienced Wales fly-half Rhys Patchell.

At twenty-four years of age, Patchell had played just six Tests in five years, with the Wales number ten jumper held firmly in the grip of Dan Biggar and Rhys Priestland. Eddie, after making a point of struggling to remember Patchell's name, said he would be a prime target for the England defenders.

'He's a young guy, he's inexperienced and he's their third-choice ten. He will have to find guys around him to help because he'll be under some heat. I'd imagine that when [Wales captain] Alun Wyn Jones and the guys go down for breakfast on Saturday morning they'll be looking at him and thinking, "Can this kid handle the pressure today?" He's got to get the ball wide, and that's going to be a big job. It will be different to playing against Scotland. It's a big ask. Playing in front of that Twickenham crowd with boys like Sam Simmonds, Chris Robshaw and Owen Farrell running at him, it will be one hell of an experience for the kid. When it gets a bit cut and thrust, nip and tuck, this will be a proper Test match. Then we will see if he has the bottle to handle it.'

In the end both coaches were correct to a degree. Wales were full of running at the end, the England defenders did put Patchell under pressure – although he handled it well – and two early tries to winger Jonny May proved the difference as Eddie's men held on for a 12-6 win.

As always, after stoking the fires early in the week, Eddie refused to talk about Patchell after the match. Asked if questioning 'the bottle' of the young man had achieved the desired effect, he reacted predictably.

'I made some comments before the game. I'm talking about the game now. If you want to talk about the game, ask me a question. You guys ask me to make comments before the game, and I make comments and raise issues. If you don't want me to do that, I won't do it.'

The reporter persisted.

'How do you think he stood up?'

'I don't coach him, mate,' Eddie said, bringing the media conference to an end. 'Ask Warren.'

One thing Eddie was prepared to talk about was the media's treatment of England fullback Mike Brown. In the lead-up to the match there had been talk in the press that Brown's club form for Harlequins had not warranted England selection. As he had so many times in the past, Eddie stuck with his tried-and-tested player, and after Brown was praised for his man-of-the-match performance in a post-match BBC radio interview Eddie didn't hold back.

'He was good today, wasn't he?' the interviewer asked.

'You guys tell me he can't play Test rugby, and now you're telling me he's good.'

'Oh, I don't know that's quite fair, Eddie . . .'

'You guys are unbelievable. Fair dinkum, you guys are unbelievable.'

'In what way?'

'You're always criticizing him, and now he has a good game, you're all on the bandwagon.'

'I don't think you can treat the whole media as one . . .'

'Oh, I think we can. I think we can. And I'm sick of it, mate.'

'Well you're on for three Six Nations in a row, and your record is pretty outstanding, so from your point of view . . .'

'And you guys are better selectors than we are. That's what you think you are. And now he plays a good game, you're all on the bandwagon.'

'Okay, but I think most people agree that Mike Brown was excellent today.'

'He's been excellent for twenty-three games for us, so I don't know what was different today.'

It was vintage Eddie; the mid-week controversy followed by the post-match harangue. At first the media had lapped it up, but after more than two years it had become a little tired, a little irritating. What had initially seemed fresh and honest in Eddie's dealing with journalists now seemed cocky and contrived. Still, what could they do other than take whatever he dished out, write their stories and traipse along to the next press conference? As Eddie had found out very early in life when playing alongside the Ellas in sporting teams that rarely lost: 'If you are winning, there's not much that people can say, is there?'

And at the start of 2018 Eddie was very much winning and had been for a long time. But that was about to change.

Few could have seen it coming. Wales had beaten Scotland, England had beaten Wales; surely the trip to Murrayfield would result in win number twenty-six for Eddie and his men.

Not so much. The Scots were magnificent, the English horrible in their 13-25 loss to the home side. Eddie's post-match concession that 'they were too good for us' fell way short of summing up how superior Scotland had been. For over two seasons Eddie had spoken about the work he had done on the England players' decision-making skills, turning them into an outfit that could alter direction in a trice and change the game-plan in order to suit the conditions. Against Scotland they appeared lost, as if there was no plan to change in the first place. The Scots beat them all over the park. They beat them in enthusiasm and passion. Most of all they beat them at the breakdown, stealing possession ten times, with three turnovers going to Scotland's captain, back-rower John Barclay.

As he had after his side's only previous loss, the year before in Dublin, Eddie took full responsibility for the defeat, saying he had not prepared his team well enough. If that had been all there was to it and England had simply regrouped and carried on where they'd left off, beating France and Ireland in their next two matches to win the Six Nations, all might have been forgotten. As journalist Chris Hewett said, 'He took some heat but he ain't the first to hit the rocks at Murrayfield.' But that wasn't all there was to it. The Scotland loss sent Eddie into a spiral that he would struggle to pull out of. It was if he went to sleep the night before the game and woke up living another life.

It started as he was waiting to board the 9.15 a.m. Sunday train from Edinburgh Waverley station to Manchester, where he was to be guest of Sir Alex Ferguson at Old Trafford for the Manchester United–Chelsea match. Eddie would later tell reporters that he had been taunted on the platform and abused on the train. Asked whether the abuse had been physical or verbal, he answered, 'A bit of both.' There was no need to ask what had happened next. It was caught on a bystander's phone camera and broadcast around the world via social media.

As Eddie arrived at Manchester station he was met by a driver sent by Manchester United Football Club and led outside to a waiting car. As he stepped outside the terminus he was spotted by two young men who asked for a photograph. As he did regularly, Eddie agreed, but after his earlier experiences that day, he did not look pleased or comfortable. One of the men handed his phone to the driver, and Eddie stood between them. As the photograph was being taken two more men ran up, one from behind, the other from the side. The mood quickly changed from rowdy to aggressive. Eddie tried to disengage himself from the grasp of the man next to him, but he was held tight. A railway employee, seeing the potential of the situation getting out of hand, walked over and tried to pull one of the men away. Eddie broke free, headed for the car and climbed into the back. One of the men followed and shouted through the closed window in a Scottish accent, 'What happened last night, you baldy c***?' The other three started chanting, 'You're a baldy f***ing c***.' The railway employee herded the fourth man away from the car, but he doubled back and opened the back door, repeating the abuse as the other three came closer, swearing and waving their fists. As the car began to move away, they continued chanting, 'Scot-land, Scot-land . . .'

When the video appeared on social media and was picked up by media outlets, the outcry was immediate.

Scotland Rugby issued a statement saying it was 'appalled' by the vision.

'The disgusting behaviour of those involved does not represent the values of our sport or its fans,' it said. 'The dignity Eddie and the England team showed on Saturday is in stark contrast to this ugly incident.'

Eddie said he would no longer be able to travel by public transport.

'I'm a human being. I don't consider myself any different from anyone else, so for me to travel on public transport I thought was okay. But I'll make sure I won't in future. It's as simple as that. I can't because it was shown on Sunday what happens when I do. That's the world we live in. I was massively surprised. It wasn't comfortable. I never knock back a request for a selfie, unless I'm racing to somewhere. I try and do the right thing by the fans, but if that happens you've got to have a look at your own safety.'

But not all reaction was sympathetic to Eddie, with some suggesting he had brought the behaviour of the unruly Scottish fans on himself with his regular incendiary comments in the media.

In the lead-up to the Scotland Test former Scottish and British and Irish Lions captain Gavin Hastings had made the point that Eddie's pre-match antics had added a personal element to contests in which he was involved.

'He's just one of those guys that loves to wind the opposition up,' he said. 'I admire Eddie Jones for what he has achieved, but as a supporter of one of his opponents you just want to rub his face in the dirt.'

After the Manchester incident, Eddie referred to Hastings' comments and asked, 'If you're in a position of responsibility, you've got to be careful what you say. Because if you talk about hate and you talk about rubbing people's noses in the dirt, and all those sorts of things, it incites certain behaviours. Are they the behaviours we want to see?'

Respected sports columnist with the *Telegraph* Oliver Brown took a jaundiced view.

'Jones has, when the mood takes him, one of the most lethal tongues in the game,' he wrote. 'When riled up in rugby, his outbursts could blister the paintwork at ten paces.'

Brown then went on to list Eddie's most infamous outbursts: the public humiliation of his Japan captain after the loss to French Barbarians; the targeting of Johnny Sexton and Rhys Patchell; his regular attacks on the media for offering views contrary to his own, and his comment to a New Zealand radio commentator after Hong Kong officials called off a match due to a waterlogged pitch: 'I've had enough of Asian rugby. I'm only going to Hong Kong to shop or eat dim sum. It's a bloody joke.'

Brown finished: 'For all the ugliness of Jones's manhandling we should perhaps be wary of an excess of pious outrage. Yes, he has the right to go about his business unmolested by cretinous drunks, but for Jones to ascribe his dust-up to verbal incitement by his peers represents the height of hypocrisy.'

Typical of anti-Eddie comments by members of the public that appeared online after the incident was one from a blogger signing himself 'Ian y mor'.

'Jones is a man who singles out and rubbishes individual opposition rookie players, such as Rhys Patchell and expects no consequences. His reasons for doing this are that he is hoping to give his England team a big start by destabilizing and intimidating these players. But this could easily destroy players' careers before they begin. Furthermore, he constantly claims opposition teams are cheating and accuses respected players of bad behaviour. These are nasty tactics and are going to create bad feelings. It is one thing to engage in banter and build up your chances, it is quite another when you set about vilifying opposition teams. I would never condone this loutish behaviour by these so-called fans but Eddie Jones needs to tone down his rhetoric because it is sometimes inflammatory and not good for sportsmanship or the game. As Shakespeare once said in one of his plays, "The fragrance of the rose lingers on he that cast it."'

Three men in their early twenties from Edinburgh and a twenty-five-year-old from South Queensferry appeared before Manchester and Salford Magistrates' Court in May charged with using threatening or abusive words over the incident. Eddie did not make a statement, but the driver of the car said he appeared 'quite shaken' and that he felt the incident 'may have become physical' if it had been allowed to escalate. Three of the men pleaded guilty and were fined a total of £365 plus costs of £115 each. The fourth pleaded not guilty and was ordered to face trial in August, but by then Eddie had far bigger issues to worry about.

Within days of the Scotland defeat Eddie and his staff had completed their analysis and begun working on solving the problems that had seen the team come so spectacularly unstuck.

'We've been coming up with solutions to those over the last couple of days. Learning to fix it on the hop is the next step. It's very easy to talk about leadership and how to change things, but it's harder to do.

'It took New Zealand eight years to learn how to fix things on the field. We're trying to do it in four, so everything's a bit more difficult for us. The only way to accelerate the process is not to sleep. That's the only way. It's not easy. We're working round the clock to fix it. We'll get there, but we're going to have these sorts of situations.

'That's the progression of the team, and unless you have these sorts of lessons you don't learn from them, and we've learned a lot. It's a harsh lesson, and a lesson we don't want to have, but the likelihood is we could well have it again.'

Sooner than he might think.

Two weeks after Murrayfield, Eddie and his team arrived at Stade de France needing to win and score four tries to keep any hopes of a third straight Six Nations title alive. They never came close.

Even though a late try would have brought them an unlikely win, it wasn't even the 16-22 loss that was so concerning to England supporters. It was the nature of the loss. England had a majority of possession and territory, but their attack was stilted and their discipline poor. They conceded sixteen penalties, including a penalty try for a high tackle by fullback Anthony Watson. Most worrying of all, they were once again soundly beaten at the breakdown, handing over possession eight times.

'They lost on the floor,' says Chris Hewett. 'No one loses at the breakdown in France. You lose other ways, but not like that.'

After being favourites for a record third consecutive Six Nations title, England were now faced with having to beat new champions Ireland seven days later to avoid finishing fifth, England's worst-ever result.

And to make the task even greater, Ireland was going to be handed the ultimate motivational tool. The good ship Eddie Jones was about to hit the iceberg.

Four days before the match, media outlets in England and Ireland aired the video of Eddie's Fuso Talks speech in which he labelled Wales a 'little shit country' and spoke of the 'scummy Irish'. The timing, four months after the video had been posted, could not have been more pointed. If certain members of the media wanted a chance to get back at Eddie after two years of tongue lashings, he had given it to them.

'I think he would have been angry at himself more than anything,' says Chris Hewett. 'Eddie likes to be the smart-arse, but he doesn't like it when he gets caught out. I don't know how long someone had hold of the "scummy Irish" tape, but the timing wasn't a coincidence. Nothing happens by accident.'

The release of the video proved a major embarrassment to the RFU, Eddie and Fuso.

The RFU announced it would be apologizing to the Welsh and Irish Rugby Unions. Eddie made a brief comment at his pre-match media conference.

'I apologize unreservedly for any offence caused – no excuses, and I shouldn't have said what I did.'

Fuso immediately removed the offending video from its website and replaced it with a written statement.

'The offensive statements made by Eddie Jones in July 2017 regarding the nations of Ireland and Wales run completely counter to our commitment to integrity and our deep respect for all peoples. We do not support or condone such points of view in any way, shape or form. We sincerely apologize for these offensive comments being made and broadcast over a Mitsubishi Fuso-sponsored forum meant to promote learning on leadership through inspiration and positive energy. That said, we welcome Mr Jones's swift apology for his inappropriate language and sentiments.'

It would take more than a few contrite words to erase Eddie's insult from Irish memories. Whether the Ireland players needed added incentive to beat England at Twickenham on St Patrick's Day with a Grand Slam at stake is doubtful, but if they did, seeing the opposition coach refer to them as scum a few days before kick-off would have been just the ticket.

Following Ireland's 24-15 win, the *Sunday Times* led its sports section with a photograph of the jubilant Irish players holding the Six Nations trophy under the headline, 'Not Bad for a Scummy Nation Eh Eddie?'

Minutes after the game, as Eddie had walked onto the field to give his post-match television interview, he had been booed by sections of the Twickenham crowd. Most worryingly for him, he didn't know whether they were Irish supporters or English.

19

BUSTED FLUSH

The day after England's loss to Ireland, *Sunday Telegraph* journalist Paul Hayward gave a lively, colourful summation of the challenges ahead. He said, 'From saviour to busted flush is a road countless coaches have taken, and Eddie Jones has a monumental task to stay off that path.'

It was a common theme in the media over the next few weeks, with commentators questioning whether Eddie's 'use-by date' was well and truly up.

The comment made during England's 2016 tour of Australia by former Wallaby skipper Phil Kearns was regurgitated often. Asked if Eddie would make or break the England team, Kearns had answered, 'I think he will do both. I think in the short term they will be incredibly successful over the next two to three years. The big question is what happens after that?

'He is a very astute coach, but there is a point where the fanatical work ethic goes too far. There's not a lot of people in the world of Eddie Jones. There's one bloke, and that's him. That's his world.

'I've heard a couple of the guys in the Japan team say they would never play under him again because they could not keep up with the workload, it was so intense. It will be interesting to see how over time the Pommies go.

'I actually think he is a good guy, but he is massively intense, massively hard-working, and I have heard he works his team to the point of overtraining them.'

The concept of 'overtraining' is one that Eddie has never seemed to contemplate, but it was one which took on great importance in the media as the RFU announced that a review was being held into England's worst-ever Six Nations result.

Speculation that one of its recommendations would be that the coach be sacked was soon knocked on the head when it was revealed that the man heading the review was one Eddie Jones.

In discussing the review process, RFU chief executive Steve Brown admitted that the only people involved in working out how to right the shaky ship and set the course for the World Cup were Eddie and his staff.

'The first person who puts Eddie straight is Eddie,' Brown said.

And Eddie saw no reason to be calling for the lifeboats any time soon.

'It's just a tough period for us. We were always going to go through this at some stage. Any team that is developing, as we are, goes through tough periods where the game does not love you. I don't think we should get too carried away or too melodramatic about where we are. We are a rugby team, and no rugby team has an aura of invincibility about them. Every team is fallible and every team has a weakness and certain strengths and, at the moment, teams are outplaying us in certain areas of the game, and we have to learn from it.'

He even brought in a professor of human brain research from University College, London, to help the players learn faster.

Brown's continued unqualified support of Eddie was an almighty show of faith in a man whose fractious relationship with the people who paid his wages had seen him either dismissed or walk out of contracts more than once throughout his career. It was also a disappointment to those who had hoped that Eddie's fall from grace in the first half of 2018 might see him reined in by his employers.

The most notable of these were the owners of the clubs.

As Eddie had been so fond of pointing out before he took over as England coach, the RFU was the biggest and best-resourced organization in the game. And they never denied him anything he wanted in terms of facilities or staff. At the beginning of the 2017 season the *Daily Mail* published a list of Eddie's assistants. Starting at the top with lineout specialist Steve Borthwick, defence coach Paul Gustard and scrum coach Neal Hatley and moving down through skills coach Rory Teague, vision guru Sherylle Calder, two analysts, a team doctor, sports scientist, two soft-tissue therapists, two physios, a three-man strength and conditioning unit and kicking coach Jonny Wilkinson, among others, it numbered twenty-four staff in total.

But one thing the RFU couldn't give Eddie was a clear pathway for players from their clubs through to the national team, something that Southern Hemisphere national coaches had enjoyed for years.

While it hadn't always been a smooth transition, the move to professionalism in South Africa, New Zealand and Australia, through the establishment of SANZAR, had seen the season broken up into three distinct phases: Super Rugby, the Rugby Championship Test series and the end-of-season tours. With all players contracted to the unions, there was no overlap in demands for their services and, following the successful New Zealand model, the aim was to have the Super Rugby franchises work hand in hand with the national body to produce the strongest possible Test side.

The England system is very different. The clubs pay the players to play at least thirty matches a season. The RFU pays the clubs to release players for national training camps. All very well in theory, but when players started returning to their clubs suffering the effects of Eddie's rigorous training regimes it caused a major rift.

After RFU data showed that injuries at national training camps had doubled since Eddie took over, he held a meeting with the clubs at the end of the 2016–17 season. Eddie said the outcome was improved dialogue between the parties. By June 2018 the lines of communication had all but broken down.

When front-rower Beno Obano was ruled out for a year following a training-camp mishap – the fifth Bath player and fifteenth in total to be injured on Eddie's watch – Bath owner Bruce Craig called the situation 'unacceptable'.

Eddie retaliated by saying, 'I don't think anyone at a club has the right to tell a coach how to train a Test team.'

And just in case anyone was under the impression that his team's unexpected losing streak had mellowed Eddie's feisty side, he added, 'Bruce is obviously an expert in training-ground injuries, so I'll have to be subservient to his greater knowledge.'

Craig hit back, saying, 'Mr Jones' cynical remarks on an important player welfare issue are inappropriate. If his judgement that fifteen serious injuries in England training and a career-ending injury for Wasps flanker Sam Jones is acceptable and doesn't warrant explanation, apology or some deeper analysis, then that is the problem.

'England training camps are not isolated in our players' conditioning, fitness and well-being throughout the year. Mr Jones also seems to be overlooking the fact that the players are not centrally contracted by the Rugby Football Union and are being released in good faith to

England on the understanding that the clubs feel they will be treated reasonably and with due duty of care.'

Premiership Rugby boss Mark McCafferty said the relationship between the clubs and the national body had 'hit a roadblock'.

'The only way that the English system works is through collaboration. I wouldn't expect a club to say that an English coach has no right to come into our club and see what we're doing.'

In fact, Eddie is a regular visitor to the clubs, says former Leicester Tigers coach Matt O'Connor.

'Eddie has tried really hard to develop a relationship, but there are always going to be issues. The clubs pay the bulk of the players' wages and there is an expectation that when they return from national training they are healthy and in a state to produce optimal performance. It is unacceptable to be breaking blokes at training.

'Eddie is always going to try to squeeze the most out of the time he has with the players, and that doesn't necessarily suit the demands of the clubs. It's a balancing act and both sides have to find middle ground.'

The clubs and the media might have been showing signs of tiring of the Eddie Jones show at the time, but Chris Hewett believed the public still had faith.

'I think he is still a popular figure. He is honest and forthright and he comes out with those clever comments. Sometimes they are too clever, but by and large I think people find him fascinating. They enjoy his style of discourse. Of course, the most important thing is that he gets the team back on a winning path.'

No easy task. Following the Six Nations, there was England's tough three-Test tour of South Africa in June, followed by a punishing autumn schedule, which would see Eddie and his men face the

Springboks, All Blacks, Japan and Wallabies over consecutive weekends at Twickenham.

'When Eddie came in he spun it quite cleverly,' says Hewett. 'He said, "There are some quick-fix issues and some long-term issues." Now that he had that great run he is able to say that he is starting to work on the long-term issues, and there are some endemic problems he has to deal with. One of the biggest is that England doesn't have an open-side flanker.'

As was exposed so painfully during the three losses in the Six Nations, the problems that Eddie had spotlighted during the World Cup, when he labelled England's number seven Chris Robshaw 'a six and a half at best', hadn't been solved in two years. More to the point, coaches of other teams hadn't been sitting still as Eddie had climbed to the top of the world. They had been studying England, identifying weaknesses and working out ways to capitalize on them.

And the biggest weakness of all was the lack of a pilferer at the breakdown; a whippet who would be first to the tackled player and have the strength and fortitude to stay on his feet and secure the ball as opposition reinforcements arrived.

It seemed absurd that such a player wouldn't exist in English rugby, but according to Matt O'Connor it was yet another example of the club–country divide.

'There was no out-and-out seven, because that is not the way the game is played in England. The Premiership is all about size and being dominant at the collision. The clubs that can play the game that way are the most successful. Because there are twelve different clubs there is no collective mandate around developmental pathways into the national team. The clubs aren't developing that type of player so Eddie had to try to mould a player to suit the role.'

Another problem that had been highlighted by the media was Eddie's determination to stick with ageing players.

'Players like Hartley, Haskell, Cole and Brown were all past their best but Eddie hung on to them,' said Chris Hewett.

It was not a new observation of Eddie's coaching style. Former Australian Rugby boss Gary Flowers said that Eddie's blinkered loyalty to certain players played a part in his demise at the Wallabies.

'Post 2003 World Cup one thing that was evident was that he didn't make changes in personnel quick enough. He should have acted sooner.'

Adding to Eddie's concerns, as he embarked on the final stages of preparation for the World Cup, was the loss of defence coach Paul Gustard just weeks before the team left for the South African tour.

Media speculation that Gustard had left the England set-up to take up the role of head coach at Harlequins because he had cracked under the pressure of Eddie's demanding schedule was quickly knocked on the head, but there was no denying that having to bring in a replacement was a setback Eddie could have done without.

It all added to the enormous pressure building on the reigning World Rugby Coach of the Year. If Eddie wanted to produce the number one rugby team in the game, the stretch between June and November 2018 would be the ultimate test of how his plans were progressing. Win the majority of those matches and confidence would be high for the home stretch to the World Cup. The alternative was almost too grim to contemplate.

While Eddie would never admit to feeling the strain, his growing band of critics could argue otherwise. His insistence on rushing New Zealand-born back-rower Brad Shields straight into the touring squad for South Africa despite never having played a game in England was seen by some as smacking of desperation. The selection of the Hurricanes Super Rugby captain before he had even turned out for new club Wasps created a storm. Sir Clive Woodward described it as 'intrinsically wrong' but Eddie was unmoved. As far as he was concerned, Shields' English parentage made him eligible, he could improve the team and that was that. Shields was flown from New Zealand to England to be introduced to his new team-mates, then returned to New Zealand after the tour to complete his contract with the Hurricanes before joining Wasps. It was Eddie at his maverick best.

Other notable selections as Eddie sought to stop the rot were the recall of fly-half Danny Cipriani, three years after his last Test, and the choice of Owen Farrell as captain in the absence of the injured Dylan Hartley.

To those around the rugby world watching Eddie's plight with fascination, the South African tour could be seen as make-or-break. In public at least, Eddie painted it more as a great opportunity.

'This will be the most exciting challenge for us as a group since 2016,' he said. 'We have an opportunity to create history and win the Test series, something no England side has done before. We will need to be physically aggressive and tactically smart against the Springboks who we know will be combative and reinvigorated by their new coaching set-up.'

Heading that new set-up was forty-five-year-old Rassie Erasmus, the former technical advisor to Springboks coach Jake White whose sudden departure prior to the 2007 World Cup had opened the way for Eddie to join South Africa's Cup-winning campaign. Having since met with success at the Stormers and Munster, he had taken over the Springboks following the sacking of Allister Coetzee just twelve weeks before the arrival of Eddie and his men. With South Africa having slumped to seventh in the world rankings under Coetzee, Erasmus was handed the same assignment that the RFU had given Eddie three years earlier: turn things around by the World Cup.

When the first Test kicked off in Johannesburg on 9 June, both men had plenty to play for. Erasmus was chasing his first win as Springboks coach, his team having gone down to Wales 20-22 in his only match in charge a week earlier. For Eddie the stakes were much higher. Including an embarrassing 26-57 uncapped loss to the Barbarians following the Six Nations – the most points ever scored against them at Twickenham – England were facing a fifth straight loss.

If Eddie's men were feeling any pressure they didn't show it early. Their play in the first ten minutes of the match was spellbinding. Throwing the ball wide and attacking with imagination and pace, they raced away to a 24-3 lead as Mike Brown – playing on the wing – fullback Elliot Daly and centre Owen Farrell all crossed for converted tries. It was the kind of rugby that Eddie had spoken about wanting to recreate over a decade earlier – the kind that the Ellas had made famous – but it was short-lived.

The South Africans, at first rattled and mistake-prone, regained their composure and, inspired by livewire Sale halfback Faf de Klerk, worked their way back into the game. At half-time the Springboks led 29-27. England, their legs increasingly heavy at altitude, struggled to keep in touch and despite a brave late rally went down 39-42. To make things worse, Eddie was drawn into a slanging match with a Springbok supporter as he headed down to the field after the match. He made light of it, saying they had only been discussing where best to buy some local wine, but there was no joking about the importance of the second Test in Bloemfontein. Win and the series was still alive. Lose and Eddie's long-term job prospects were looking increasingly shaky.

The second Test started much like the first – and ended the same way as well. Brilliant tries to wingers Mike Brown and Jonny May saw England take a 12-0 lead before a try to rampaging Springboks number eight Duane Vermeulen and goals to Handre Pollard put South Africa ahead 13-12 at the break. In the second half England's discipline let them down badly. There was a penalty try and a yellow card to Nathan Hughes for a blatant professional foul as the hosts won 23-12 to wrap up the series.

The signs of disarray inside the England camp didn't end with the full-time whistle. Mike Brown and Joe Marler had words with South African fans as they left the field and Ben Youngs walked away mid-question during a live, post-match interview with the BBC. Commenting on the performance, World Cup-winning halfback Matt Dawson described it as 'woeful' and voiced publicly what many were saying behind Eddie's back: that his days in the job were numbered.

'The wheels are wobbling, big time,' Dawson said. 'There were a few rumours I heard last week about what's going to happen. Has Eddie Jones lost the dressing room? Has he lost Twickenham?'

Writing in the *Guardian*, journalist Robert Kitson noted: 'The Eddie Jones era has been nothing if not educational for the RFU. The idea was to hire the world's most experienced coach, shower him in cash and then sit back and watch him reel in the 2019 World Cup. The only thing Jones will be catching between now and Christmas, at this rate, is a flight back to Australia.'

Eddie said he wasn't concerned. He'd heard it all before.

'Every coaching job is the same. When you are doing well, everyone pats you on the back and when you are not doing well, you're pulling knives out of your back. That's the reality of it. I've been through it many times. If you coach for a long period of time you have your good periods and your bad periods. These are the great periods. That's what I love doing. I love coaching this team. If someone decides that's not good enough, then they decide. If someone decides I'm good enough then I will keep coaching. That's what I've done with every team I've coached and it's no different now.'

One reporter asked Eddie straight out if he was the right man to be leading England to the World Cup.

'One hundred per cent,' he answered. 'Because I can coach.'

He would have one week to prove it.

It would be overstating it to say that England's 25-10 win over a Springboks side experimenting with four backline changes restored Eddie's stock in the eyes of the fans and his employers, but it was a start. In wet conditions the English forwards were aggressive, decisive and dominant. Far from being tired from overtraining as was reported during the week, they finished far the stronger. Most encouraging of all was the performance of twenty-year-old Tom Curry who showed enough to suggest that he could be the answer to Eddie's dilemma at open-side flanker.

The series may have been lost, but the losing streak had ended and if nothing else, the win had bought Eddie some time.

Just how much time could depend on the outcome of the upcoming horror stretch of Tests in November, with England facing South Africa, New Zealand, Japan and Australia at Twickenham on consecutive weekends. When England had recorded its clean-sweep over the Wallabies in 2016 to move to number two in the rankings, the 2018 showdown with the All Blacks was being billed as an unofficial world championship. After Eddie's stunning fall from grace it was seen by many as the game that would decide whether he even led England to the World Cup.

20

AUTUMN HARVEST

Eddie survived the onslaught of criticism that built up during the 2018 season. His boss and major supporter Steve Brown wasn't so fortunate.

In August, two months after Eddie and his squad returned battered but still upright after the 1-2 series loss in South Africa, former RFU CEO Francis Baron released a damning fifty-page report on the financial management of the organization. According to Baron, the RFU had squandered the £26 million windfall delivered from hosting the 2015 Rugby World Cup on such extravagances as new corporate facilities at Twickenham, which had blown out in cost from the original £53.5 million to £81 million, the £220 million eight-year deal with the clubs to release players for national training and a rise in RFU salaries over three times the national average.

Baron, whose findings were supported by a separate report by former RFU chairman Graeme Cattermole, claimed that the RFU, generally regarded as 'the richest union in the game', had lost £46.6 million over the previous six years and were planning to increase borrowings to £100 million in the lead-up to the World Cup.

The attention placed on the RFU's finances by Baron and Cattermole raised questions over the expense of bringing Eddie on board. Newspaper reports claimed that the England team budget had overshot 'by a six-figure sum' due to the size of Eddie's now twenty-seven-person support staff. There was also an ongoing saga over the hefty compensation demanded by South African franchise Blue Bulls to release John Mitchell whom Eddie brought in to replace departed defence coach Paul Gustard. The Bulls initially asked £500,000 for Mitchell, who had lost his job as All Blacks coach when beaten by Eddie's Wallabies in the 2003 World Cup.

But, ultimately, most damning was Baron's criticism over Steve Brown giving Eddie a three-year contract extension in January 2018. While it seemed like an astute move at the time with the team having won twenty-two of twenty-three games under Eddie, the subsequent slump in England's fortunes made it seem anything but sound business practice. Added to the £200,000 that the Bulls finally accepted to tear up Mitchell's contract, the £100,000 reportedly paid to the Stormers to release Eddie and the £500,000 Bristol demanded and received for Steve Borthwick, it gave the impression of an organization flagrantly throwing money away in pursuit of increasingly unlikely World Cup glory.

The RFU released a statement refuting Baron's claims and he and Cattermole were stripped of their status as 'privileged members' and the free tickets to Twickenham that went with it, but it seemed a tepid comeback. The fact was that large amounts of money were being laid out on the preparation of the England team with high expectations of a return on investment. The pressure on Eddie and the team as they approached the autumn series intensified.

One win in Cape Town hadn't erased the memories of a wretched 2018 Six Nations. If Eddie was to get the show back on the road – maybe even save his job – it would all have to start at Twickenham against the Springboks on 3 November.

His job was not made any easier by an injury crisis in the forwards, with the unavailability of the Vunipola brothers – loose-head prop Mako and number eight Billy – and locks Joe Launchbury and Courtney

Lawes, robbing the side of 400 Test caps' worth of experience. Even so, Springbok coach Rassie Erasmus said he would not be taking the weakened England team lightly, especially as they were coached by the man who had inflicted South Africa's worst-ever sporting embarrassment.

Speaking of Japan's 34-32 win over the Springboks at the 2015 World Cup, he said: 'Any South African can always tell you where they sat, where they were, when they watched that game. Eddie is a sharp coach. He knows a lot about South Africa. He helped us win the World Cup in 2007.'

Not that it seemed to count for much early in the match. For the first forty-five minutes of the Test, Eddie's part in the 'Miracle of Brighton' and the 2007 RWC win were distant memories as it appeared just a matter of time before the Springboks ran away with the game.

The inexperienced England pack, with loose-head Alec Hepburn having his first Test start and the back row of Brad Shields, Tom Curry and Mark Wilson with just ten caps between them, was pushed around early by the big South Africans. After fifteen minutes England lock Itoje was sent to the sin-bin for repeated infringements and South Africa's Sbu Nkosi scooted over for a try, yet somehow, thanks to blown chances by the Springboks and accurate goal-kicking by Owen Farrell, England went in at the break only two points down, 6-8.

At half-time Eddie replaced Hepburn with Test newcomer Ben Moon and a few minutes later Curry went off injured, his place taken by another debutant, Zach Mercer. It was a scenario set up for the Springboks to tighten the screws, but England wouldn't wilt. They hung in, fought their way back into the contest and at the fifty-one-minute mark, fullback Elliot Daly slotted over a long-range penalty to give Eddie's men the lead for the first time. Springbok five-eighth Handre Pollard kicked a penalty of his own to make it 11-9 to South Africa with eleven minutes left.

England had two gilt-edged chances to score but both went begging, Daly ignoring an unmarked Jonny May and Shields spilling the ball forward when tackled a metre from the line. In the end it was left to Farrell to seal the 12-11 victory with a penalty six minutes from the end.

Pollard had a last-minute chance to snatch the win but his penalty attempt hit the upright before a final play that would become the major talking point of the game.

With time up, South Africa kept the ball alive for fifteen phases before replacement centre Andre Esterhuizen picked up a loose pass 40 metres out from the try line and set off on a looping run. As Farrell moved up to meet him, the bigger South African dropped his shoulder and charged. Farrell turned his head to the left as the two men collided heavily and fell to the ground. From the ensuing maul the ball spilled England's way and replacement front-rower Harry Williams kicked it into the crowd as Eddie celebrated with his staff on the sideline.

But the game was not over. The England players and supporters had an anxious wait as Australian referee Angus Gardner reviewed Farrell's tackle on the big screen to rule whether Farrell had used his arms. If not, he would have to award a penalty to South Africa, well within kicking range.

Sky TV commentator Stuart Barnes, who had called the action on first sight as, 'Oh. Was that a shoulder or was that a tackle? That's a shoulder surely,' was not hopeful as Gardner and his touch judge Ben Whitehouse looked up at the screen waiting for the replay.

'From the moment I saw it, from this perspective, it looks like Farrell's gone in with the shoulder,' said Barnes. 'The crowd are booing but the officials are absolutely right to do this.'

When the tackle was replayed even the most one-eyed England supporter would have to concede that things were not looking good for Eddie and his men. The initial contact was unquestionably with Farrell's right shoulder, his right arm hanging by his side. With Farrell turning his head, his left arm was further away from Esterhuizen's body than if he had tried to drive him backwards with a standard front-on tackle. He appeared to make an attempt to wrap the arm around the South African, but it was very late in getting there.

'I'm sorry,' said Barnes, putting into words what most of the 82,000 at the ground and many more watching on TV were thinking. 'It doesn't matter where you are from, that is not an attempted tackle. One shoulder, the other arm's away . . . he'll be very lucky if he gets away with this.'

But lucky he was. Gardner turned to Whitehouse.

'It's a big collision I agree, but I don't think it's a clear shoulder for me. There's enough of a wrap on the far side, yep?'

Whitehouse nodded agreement and Gardner walked over to Farrell.

'I believe there's enough of a wrap on the far side to make it a fair tackle,' he said, as Farrell pumped his fist and the England players and supporters shouted for joy.

At the post-match media conference Eddie was asked what he was thinking as referee Gardner considered his verdict.

'I wasn't really thinking anything, mate, to be honest. I'm not that bright. I was thinking, "I hope he doesn't penalize us." That's pretty natural isn't it? Look, it was a good, solid tackle.'

Not everyone agreed. Wallaby utility back Kurtley Beale, in Wales with the Australian side, made the point that 'a couple of years ago it is a red card'.

Former All Black Craig Dowd didn't hold back in his comments. 'The referees bottled themselves,' he said. 'It was a terrible decision and world rugby should be looking at the referees sideways. There needs to be an explanation to say why that was not a yellow card; at minimum it was a penalty; and how the hell did they not do anything about that tackle, even by citing it afterwards? It was a terrible tackle and the decision was an absolute disgrace and a blight on world rugby.'

Eddie wasn't concerned with what anyone had to say about the Farrell tackle. He had already moved on.

'We've got New Zealand next week and we can't wait, mate,' he told the assembled media. 'They'll be sitting at their camp in Lensbury probably drinking cups of tea and maybe having some scones and cream saying, "We'll take these guys." They'll be confident but we can't wait to get 'em.'

Asked if the performance against South Africa had convinced Eddie that his team could beat the All Blacks he answered, 'One hundred per cent.'

A reporter then made the mistake of asking the under-siege Eddie if the win had been the most important of his time with England.

'Zero, mate,' Eddie snapped. 'The most important thing is what we do next. Look, I don't understand this, guys. We're a bloody good team. We've lost a few games. We played tough today and we won. Why has it got to be the most important game?

'Because you guys want to sack me? Is that why? Well, you're going to do it at some stage. You know that. You know if I stay long enough you're going to get me sacked, so one day you'll be happy, guys. You'll come in and say, "Fantastic. We've got another guy we can terrorize."

'Don't worry about it. This was a good game of Test match rugby today. We're happy, they're not so happy and now we're going to start preparing for New Zealand.'

Many observers would argue that the last thing the English media would want to do was sack Eddie. Who else would possibly feed them so many good lines? But the fallout from Baron's scathing report on RFU management had not gone away. The public and sponsors were demanding a sacrificial lamb and the obvious candidates were either Eddie or Steve Brown. If Eddie was to get his name off the hit list, a good showing against the All Blacks was imperative.

Eddie made two unforced changes to the team that beat South Africa, prop Ben Moon getting the nod ahead of Hepburn and winger Chris Ashton replacing Jack Nowell for his first start in four years. Sam Underhill replaced Tom Curry who was ruled out for the rest of the series with an ankle injury. Aggressive lock Courtney Lawes, returning from a lower back problem, came onto the bench.

The bookmakers had England as rank outsiders but Eddie was as buoyant as ever. With reports of a film being made about Japan's World Cup win over South Africa, he exhorted his players to write their own script against New Zealand at Twickenham. Too often, he said, teams were cowed by the Kiwis' aura and allowed themselves to be mere extras to the men in black.

'They eat popcorn, have a can of Pepsi and they watch the movie. By the time they realize "we can be in this", it's too late. We don't want to sit there and watch, because that's what happens when you play New Zealand sometimes. We want to make the movie; we want to be film directors.'

From the opening scene the Englishmen were the stars of the show. Just as his Wallabies had in the 2003 World Cup semi-final, Eddie's men came out breathing fire and showing intent. After All Black lock Brodie Retallick had spilled the kick-off in wet, windy conditions, England took charge. Following seven phases from the scrum, halfback Ben Youngs sent a long pass to the unmarked Ashton who

377

scored in the corner after just two minutes of play. Farrell's conversion attempt hit the upright but he made amends with a drop-goal seven minutes later. At the twenty-minute mark Elliot Daly gained good ground with a penalty kick for touch, giving England the lineout feed 10 metres out. Itoje took the ball cleanly and the English forwards set up a driving maul. Hartley at the back controlled perfectly as England's backs joined in, the New Zealanders powerless to stem the white-shirted bulldozer. Hartley's try, converted by Farrell, took the score to 15-0 with just under an hour still to play.

The England fans were joyous, but this was the All Blacks and, as Eddie said during the week, the thought of losing was not in their DNA.

'I have never coached against a New Zealand side that doesn't expect to win,' he said. 'It is in their blood.'

The fightback started with less than two minutes left in the half. From a maul on the England line, Kiwi halfback Aaron Smith fed five-eighth Beauden Barrett who put fullback Damian McKenzie over with a neat inside pass. Barrett's conversion and a penalty well into extra-time saw England's lead cut to 15-10 at half-time.

Both teams wasted golden opportunities to score tries in the second half but it was the boot of Barrett, with a drop-goal and a penalty, that put New Zealand in front 16-15 with less than twenty minutes to play. Eddie, with his final throw of the dice, started sending on his fresh players, most significantly Courtney Lawes.

With five minutes left to play, George Ford tackled All Blacks reserve fullback Richie Mo'unga about 35 metres out from the England try line. Four Kiwi forwards pushed over the top and made the ball available to replacement halfback TJ Perenara who attempted a clearing kick. As the ball left Perenara's boot it cannoned off the upstretched arm of the charging 2.01m Courtney Lawes and was then fumbled by Perenara and Scott Barrett before being grabbed by England's Sam Underhill who set off for the line. The only Kiwi within reach was Beauden Barrett but Underhill stood him up with a classic in-and-away before diving over in the corner.

As it had a week earlier Twickenham erupted with roars of joy and excitement, and just as it had then, they turned to boos as referee Jerome Garces signalled to the TMO, South African Marius Jonker.

Garces asked Jonker to check that Lawes was in an onside position when he moved forward and lunged at Perenara.

'Is it onside or offside?'

'From the pictures I have,' Jonker replied, 'as the halfback for black picks up the ball, number twenty white is in an offside position.'

'So it's a try or not a try?'

'It's offside so you must change your original decision to a penalty.'

The England players were shattered but, if anything, the disappointment galvanized them to give one massive, final effort. With two minutes left Jonny May made a good break that took England within drop-goal range but, as Farrell steadied himself for what would have been the match-winner, Lawes threw an unnecessary pass that was spilled forward by Henry Slade and the opportunity – and the match – was lost.

In the post-match interviews Eddie was disappointed by the result but buoyed by England's performance.

'We're obviously devastated but you take the good with the bad. We'll learn a lot from that. We had opportunities to win the game. We didn't take them. They did, so they deserved to win the game. Full credit to New Zealand.

'It's a really good step forward for us because you benchmark yourself against New Zealand. New Zealand are the best team in the world and we'll get a lot of reward for what we've done. You look at it. They've been together three months; we've been together not even three weeks. They had 800 caps out there, we had 400 caps. We've got to work harder. We've got to fix the things we didn't do well today and if we do that we'll be on track to be the best team in the world, which is what we always set out to be.'

Eddie showed that he had already begun implementing the psychological strategy necessary to prepare his troops for the next battle against the New Zealanders, hopefully at the World Cup.

Four years earlier, Wallaby coach Michael Cheika had created a minor ruckus in the lead-up to the World Cup final when journalists noted that he was avoiding calling the All Blacks by their universally accepted nickname, preferring to refer to them as New Zealand or 'the Kiwis'. While New Zealand reporters felt that Cheika was disrespecting the world champions, others believed he was in fact attempting to lessen their aura in the minds of his players. Eddie, never averse to borrowing good ideas regardless of their source, was obviously following Cheika's lead.

'We take enormous confidence from winning the last twenty minutes,' he said. 'That's where the All . . . not the All Blacks . . . *New Zealand* generally run away from teams and they couldn't. They couldn't break us, and in fact I think we finished the stronger. If it had kept going another five minutes then maybe we would have got 'em. We're disappointed but I'll tell you, mate, we're excited about where we're going.'

It was an early shot in a war that wouldn't be fought for the best part of a year and the media let it go through to the keeper. They were far too interested in the major talking point of the match: Underhill's disallowed try.

While non-English supporters were, hardly surprisingly, certain that the TMO had got it right in ruling Lawes offside, those in the England camp were just as adamant that he had not. Leading the charge was outspoken columnist Stephen Jones in the *Times*.

'England had the victory they deserved snatched away from them in the dying moments when Marius Jonker, the television match official, ruled out what would have been a sensational winning try by Sam Underhill,' he wrote. 'The referee awarded the try which means that any decision by the television match official must prove a clear and obvious infringement. The replay clearly showed Courtney Lawes onside, with Perenara taking an age with his clearing kick. There was nothing clear and obvious whatsoever and the referee really should have taken charge.'

Former England forward Ben Kay went so far as to re-enact the incident for his BT Sport television programme *Rugby Tonight*. Using two amateur teams to represent the England and New Zealand players, Kay demonstrated his theory that Matt Todd, the last New Zealand forward involved in the play, was not bound by his shoulder and therefore it was not a ruck, meaning Lawes could not have been offside.

New Zealanders, from All Blacks coach Steve Hansen down, were just as adamant that the TMO had got it right.

'There's no doubt he was offside,' Hansen said. 'He was just about in the halfback's back pocket but what was going through my mind was, "Are they going to be brave enough to make the right decision?" and they were, so it was good.'

As always, Eddie would not be drawn into the debate.

'I think I've said it a number of times. I don't comment on those decisions. I'll leave it up to the TMO. If he can't make the right decision with ten replays then who can? Sometimes the game loves you and sometimes the game doesn't love you. You've got to accept that if you stay in the fight long enough the game will love you, and we're prepared to stay in the fight so we'll get some love from the game further down the track. Don't worry.'

The ones who should be worried, Eddie said, were England's next opponents, Japan. Asked how he planned to prepare for the match he answered with a cheeky smile: 'Sushi. Plenty of sushi, and sake.' And his advice for the Japanese?

'Pray, pray, pray. Go to the temple and pray. Just pray, it's the best thing. We're going to be absolutely ruthless. If I was Japan I'd be worried.'

That might have been the plan, but for the first hour of the match it was Japan who were ruthless and a worried Eddie, up in the grandstand, was doing the praying.

Eddie made eleven changes to the side that had come so close to toppling New Zealand and it showed. The home team looked disjointed and hesitant as the Japanese, inspired by their captain Michael Leitch, took charge early. In Brighton three years earlier, Eddie had told Leitch to follow his heart. The message had obviously endured, and the Japanese followed Leitch. At half-time Japan led 15-10, their enthusiasm and energy upstaging the bumbling English who conceded seven penalties to Japan's one in the first forty minutes.

Eddie made a crucial substitution at the break, bringing on Farrell for Alex Lozowski, and it proved a masterstroke. Farrell's energy and aggression lifted his team-mates and, with formidable Fijian-born winger Joe Cokanasiga scoring on debut, England ran away comfortable winners 35-15.

If Eddie was concerned about the uneven performance of his team, he didn't show it. Instead he thanked Japan for giving England a solid workout and headed for the exit. No doubt he had other things on his mind. England's sterling performance against New Zealand might have ensured his job security, but a head had still rolled at RFU headquarters. Twenty-four hours before the Japan game, Steve Brown had resigned as CEO after just fifteen months in the job. Meanwhile, at the same time as England had been playing Japan, Ireland had beaten the All Blacks 16-9, earning the mantle of unofficial world number one that Eddie had craved for three years. And there was another matter of major personal significance.

England's final game of the season was against Michael Cheika and the Wallabies.

If Eddie and his men were able to prepare for their sixth encounter with the Australians from a position of relative strength and harmony, the same could not be said for their opponents.

England's 30-6 win over the 2015 World Cup runners-up twelve months earlier had been the start of a shocking run for Cheika's team in which they lost ten out of fifteen Tests. The lead-up to the 24 November showdown at Twickenham could not have started much worse for them.

Early in the week Cheika announced that senior players Adam Ashley-Cooper and Kurtley Beale had been dropped from the Test squad because of 'form'. Two days before the game it emerged that they had actually been axed for disciplinary reasons after bringing three women back to Ashley-Cooper's hotel room following the team's 6-9 loss to Wales in Cardiff two weeks earlier.

Pressed to explain, Cheika admitted that the pair had broken team rules but described it as a 'minor matter'. The women were actually friends of Ashley-Cooper from Australia – including his sister-in-law – and their late-night assignation had consisted of pizza and TV.

Of more interest to the media was that Cheika had only learned of the pair's indiscretion when it was brought to his attention by team captain Michael Hooper and other members of the leadership group.

It was a fact not lost on aggressive England front-rower Kyle Sinckler. After a melee midway through the home team's 37-18 win, Sinckler was overheard through referee Jaco Peyper's microphone baiting the Australian forwards with, 'You're all f***ing snitches anyway.'

It was an opinion shared by long-suffering Wallaby supporters. In the days following the match a popular meme surfaced on social media. A photo taken at a Wallaby post-Test media conference, it showed Hooper staring past Cheika at his team-mate David Pocock. The caption reads: 'Hooper wondering if he should tell Cheika he caught Pocock reading after lights out.'

Cheika brushed off questions about Sinckler's sledge. He was more interested in joining the growing list of critics concerned with Owen Farrell's tackling technique.

In the last play of the first half, with England leading 13-10, Australian lock Izack Rodda had set off on a 15-metre burst for the line with no one in front of him. Just as he was about to score the go-ahead try, Farrell charged across from his left and felled him with what could only be described as a copybook shoulder charge. For Sky TV commentator Stuart Barnes, who three weeks earlier had been stunned that Farrell had got away with a similar – if less blatant – body-check against South Africa, it was a case of déjà vu.

'I don't want to go back to the shoulder tackle story again,' he said. 'But that's a penalty, and if it's a penalty, it's a penalty try.'

Referee Peyper disagreed, telling Aussie skipper Hooper that the collision was a 'fair challenge' because both players had lowered their shoulder prior to contact.

Cheika was astounded and barely able to maintain control.

'The justification that Rodda tried to take him on with his shoulder is ludicrous. That's what the referee said. That's what you do when you carry the ball. I went to the referees' meeting they had here in the week before we played Wales and they referred back to the Owen Farrell tackle against South Africa. The referees left Angus Gardner out to dry by saying that that should have been a penalty in front of all the coaches. If that's a penalty, this is three penalties.

'We had three tries disallowed and not one sent for referral. Maybe we need to move Australia to the Northern Hemisphere.'

Once again Eddie wouldn't be drawn into commenting – and why should he?

His team had just won three out of their last four Tests and shown that they could match it with the All Blacks. He had taken his record against the country that had sacked him to 6-0 and his job was as safe as it had been the day he had taken it.

Eddie had stayed in the fight. The game was loving him – and Eddie was loving the game.

21

HOME STRETCH

It wasn't the Wallabies beating the All Blacks in 2003 or Japan downing South Africa in 2015, but it was close.

England's 32-20 win over Ireland in the first round of the 2019 Six Nations championship was arguably England's greatest performance under Eddie and certainly one of the best of his career.

If ever a team went into a match deserving favouritism, Ireland was it. They were the defending champions, they had beaten New Zealand less than four months earlier and they were playing in Dublin where England had won just once in sixteen years.

Eddie tried to stir the pot going into the match, describing Ireland as 'the best team in the world' and saying that all the pressure would be on them. It was a calculated move to mess with Irish minds, but not too many pundits were buying it. It would take more than words to upset the form side in world rugby – and Eddie did have something more than words: he had the Vunipola brothers.

The 180 cm (5 feet 11 inch), 122 kg (19 stone 3 pound) loose-head Mako had missed the autumn series with a calf strain. Younger brother Billy, a 188 cm (6 feet 2 inch), 128 kg (20 stone 2 pound) number eight, had been out with a broken arm. Together with 185 cm (6 feet 1 inch), 114 kg (17 stone 13 pound) centre Manu Tuilagi they brought a level of intimidation and physicality to the England side that Ireland were unable to defuse.

It was following bull-like charges by first Mako and then Billy Vunipola, and a precise cut-out pass from Owen Farrell to slick fullback Elliot Daly, that Jonny May scored after just ninety-three seconds.

Eddie tipped his hand by showcasing the tactics that England would use throughout the tournament and presumably at the World Cup, with halfback Ben Youngs regularly kicking back into the box for speedy wingers May and Jack Nowell to chase. Backed up by an intensity in defence for the entire eighty minutes it was a winning game plan – one that Eddie said he would have employed regardless of the opposition.

Asked if the high kicking had been in order to exploit the inexperience at fullback of Ireland's Robbie Henshaw, who had played thirty-five of his thirty-six internationals at centre, he answered, 'It wouldn't have mattered if they'd had Lance Armstrong playing there. We would have played the same way.'

As if to prove his point England adopted the same kick-and-chase tactics the next week against France at Twickenham with even more devastating effect. The French, whom England would meet in the pool stage of the World Cup, were powerless against the kicking game of Youngs, Farrell, Slade and Daly, and the sheer pace of May.

May scored off a Daly kick after just over a minute's play and had another two by half-time. At the break the England lead was 30-8, with the four-try bonus point already safely in the bank. The second half was almost as catastrophic for France as their back three were continually turned around and inside out by England's guile and speed. And when the visitors did have the ball the English defence was all but impenetrable. Flankers Tom Curry and Mark Wilson pulled off thirty-seven tackles between them, and a solid front-on hit by Courtney Lawes that sat notorious French centre Mathieu Bastareaud on the seat of his pants brought one of the biggest cheers of the day.

The longer the match went the more disrupted and dispirited France became. As one TV commentator put it, 'There's a lot of French oil leaking onto the green surface of Twickenham at the moment.'

The 44-8 final score represented England's biggest winning margin over France for more than a century, and put them on top of the Six Nations table ahead of the crucial game with unbeaten Wales at Cardiff. With England now heavy favourites to win the Grand Slam and leapfrogging Ireland as favourites for the World Cup, it also placed Eddie firmly back in the good books of his employers and the England rugby public.

Typically, he took it all as his due. When a TV reporter noted with excitement that England had scored tries inside the first three minutes of their past five Tests he replied off-handedly, 'It's planned. We train for it.' Ominously he was more impressed with the fact that his team had gone on with the job against France in the second half, scoring two converted tries and keeping their line intact.

'When you get in the position where you've got a bonus point after thirty minutes against a top team you've done pretty well, but I thought our performance in the second half was even better. Even though we didn't score as many points, our focus and our discipline to keep France scoreless was outstanding.'

The one downside to the win was an ankle injury to Mako Vunipola. Eddie was initially optimistic, joking that the damaging prop had left the field only because 'he got a bit tired', but tests the next day proved otherwise, ruling him out for the rest of the series.

Vunipola joined a long list of England players on the sidelines, including fellow key forwards Dylan Hartley and Maro Itoje, but nothing could stem the growing confidence of the England supporters. To them, the derailment of the previous season was now just a minor hiccup. In fact, with the World Cup in mind, it could be seen as an advantage. The tough times had served to harden the team and bring them closer together. The injuries had given some players a break from Eddie's draining training regime, freshening them up for the season ahead, and opened the door for newcomers to be blooded at Test level. He had introduced a style of play that was proving more than effective against Europe's best, and a number of players were rising to the very top of world rugby in perfect time for the team's arrival in Japan.

Of these, three in particular were beginning to stand out. Eddie had copped criticism when he moved Wasps' winger-centre Elliot Daly to fullback for the South Africa tour. He stuck with him through the autumn series, and by the Six Nations Daly's speed and anticipation were a key ingredient of England's attack. After the France game, in which Daly was dynamic, Eddie was asked if he felt Daly was developing into a first-class international fullback.

'I think it was you guys who said he wasn't a fullback,' he said. 'So now he's going to become a top-class fullback? Well okay, I agree. I've agreed all the time. I think he's going to be a top-class fullback. He's got all the attributes. He's got a nice feel for the game, a big left foot and he's got pace. The sort of pace he's got is serious pace so we're really pleased with the way he keeps developing.'

Another member of the team who was developing with every game was twenty-year-old Tom Curry. Thrown in at the deep end on the South Africa tour, Curry had solved Eddie's major problem at open-side flanker. Big, mobile and hardy, Curry was quick to the breakdown, strong over the ball and, at 185 cm (6 feet 1 inch) and 106 kg (16 stone 10 pound), provided bulk in the lineout. Together with Mark Wilson at blind-side and Billy Vunipola at number eight, Eddie finally had a back row that could match any in the world.

But the jewel in the crown for England was Jonny May. Like Wendell Sailor at the Wallabies, May provided Eddie with an attacking weapon on the wing, and laughter on the team bus. Eddie had always been drawn to unconventional characters; those like himself who were a bit different to the run of the mill. May was certainly one of those.

Claiming to possibly have some mysterious Polynesian ancestry, he admitted to enjoying colouring-in books and eschewed listening to the usual pre-match, psyche-up fare of heavy metal or 'Eye of the Tiger', preferring Ed Sheeran and Disney show tunes. Like Sailor, he could break up a room with a one-liner – although not always intentionally. Before the France game in 2017, defence coach Paul Gustard was attempting to add starch to his players' mental build-up by reminding them of the centuries-old history of wars between the two countries.

'And why do you think that was?' he asked.

'Because they fell out?' May answered to roars of laughter from his team-mates.

He was one of the few in the team who could avoid Eddie's ire if he fell short of the coach's high disciplinary standards.

During one team camp Eddie was explaining what was expected under different match situations. May, needing to use the toilet, sneaked out of the room thinking he wouldn't be missed. Unfortunately Eddie chose that moment to discuss a scenario that involved the wingers. May returned to find Eddie talking to his empty chair.

'Luckily he saw the funny side,' he said.

It wasn't always the case, with May admitting that early in Eddie's tenure he felt intimidated by the make-you-or-break-you technique of the new coach who always demanded more.

May was determined that he wouldn't be broken; that if Eddie wanted more from him, he would find a way to give it. While recovering from injury he twice travelled to the high-intensity training camp of four-time Olympic gold medallist Michael Johnson in Texas, practised his skills to the point where Eddie praised him as one of the hardest workers in the team, and clocked a 40-metre time trial that was faster than Usain Bolt's average speed when he set his 100-metre world record in 2009.

After the energy and enthusiasm he showed in his three-try haul against France, Eddie said of him, 'Jonny is like when you go to the park and you see a person with the tennis ball and they throw it and the dog runs 100 miles an hour and chases it and brings it back.'

With England's first-choice players all seemingly at the top of their game and plenty of depth on the sidelines, Eddie could allow himself the luxury of preparing for Wales and beyond from a position of strength. His first move, typically, was to take a snide shot at the opposition.

Wales had been less than convincing in their first two Six Nations matches, coming back from 0-16 at half-time to beat France 24-19 on the bell in Paris after winger George North had been gifted two soft tries, and making hard work of beating Italy 26-15 in Rome. Even so, the two shaky wins made it eleven in a row for Warren Gatland's team, the equal best winning streak in Welsh rugby history – a fact that Eddie jumped on.

Just as he had with the Wallabies in 2017, labouring Cheika's status as 'the best coach in the world' and describing Ireland as 'the best team in the world' before the Six Nations opener, Eddie taunted Wales with double-edged praise.

'We're playing the greatest Welsh side ever,' he said. 'We're going to have to be at our absolute best.'

As is so often the case, Eddie brushed off the inevitable backlash with contrite innocence. Surely no one could have taken umbrage? It was just a throwaway line, a compliment in fact. Those who had followed Eddie's career closely knew better. When it came to Eddie Jones, nothing was unscripted. There was always an agenda.

The description of Gatland's 2019 team as the greatest Welsh side ever was guaranteed to upset. To the proudest of rugby nations, for an outsider to even have the audacity to rate one Welsh side ahead of another was tantamount to sacrilege.

Eddie might have hoped that the sugar-coated barb would put pressure on the Welsh players. It certainly incensed their supporters. After all, this was the country that had produced some of the best players and teams of all time. There was fly-half Cliff Morgan who marshalled Wales to Grand Slams in 1950 and 1952 and a win over the All Blacks in 1953. There was the golden period of the 1970s featuring Welsh legends such as Gareth Edwards, Barry John, Phil Bennett, Mervyn Davies, JPR Williams and Gerald Davies. And there were more recent teams coached by former Kiwi Gatland, which won the Six Nations in 2008, 2012 and 2013 (with Grand Slams in 2008 and 2012) and were desperately unlucky to lose 8-9 to France in the semi-final of the 2011 Rugby World Cup after captain Sam Warburton was controversially sent off nineteen minutes into the match.

Gatland took the bait. 'The only quotes I can see about this being the greatest Wales team are from Eddie Jones. It hasn't come from anyone else so I wouldn't be disrespectful enough to say this was the greatest Welsh team ever. It's a long way off being the greatest Welsh team ever. He's the one talking us up.'

Gatland then upped the ante in the psychological battle, taking a leaf from Eddie's playbook by singling out one of the England players. Kyle Sinckler, whom Gatland had coached on the 2017 British and Irish Lions tour of New Zealand, was one of England's best. If he could be put off his game or, even better, taken from the field early, it would be a huge advantage for Wales, and Gatland knew better than anyone that Sinckler had a reputation for being easily wound up. The fiery Harlequins front-rower, who had called the Wallabies 'f***ing snitches' during the autumn series, had earned headlines for slapping flanker Arthur Iturria on the top of the head after a scuffle in the win over France a week earlier. At his final press conference before the match, Gatland attempted to light a fuse.

'I think the thing with Kyle, there's no doubt he's a very good player in terms of his carrying, scrummaging and work-rate, but there is a challenge with his temperament. He's aware of it. Other players are aware of it. We've already seen in the Six Nations he's been involved in a couple of incidents. Emotionally, he can be a bit of a time bomb. I'm not saying anything that people aren't aware of. Hopefully he goes out and has a good game and keeps his emotions in control because that's a big challenge for him.'

It would prove to be a points win to Gatland in the coaches' pre-game verbal jousting. If Eddie wasn't already unpopular enough in Wales after his 'little shit place' gaffe in July 2017, his latest 'greatest team ever' comments ensured a less than warm welcome when he and his team arrived at Cardiff's Principality Stadium on 23 February.

Both coaches had predicted a tough encounter, and they were right. There would be no opening-minute try for Eddie's men but they did make the first major breakthrough with Tom Curry scoring his initial Test try after twenty-six minutes.

With England leading 10-3 at the break, the Six Nations and probable Grand Slam were just forty minutes away. It might as well have been an eternity. Ten minutes into the second half Wales fullback Liam Williams won a penalty at the breakdown that New Zealand-born fly-half Gareth Anscombe converted to take the score to 10-6.

Four minutes later Sinckler, who had given away the penalty that had led to Wales' first points for a no-arms tackle on lock Cory Hill, was penalized for a high shot on Welsh captain Alun Wyn Jones. Anscombe's kick made it 10-9 as Eddie called Sinckler from the field and replaced him with Harry Williams.

The longer the game went, the more the momentum swung towards Wales. Farrell put England ahead 13-9 after Curry won a penalty, but they never looked like pulling away from the Welsh who were energized by the crowd who smelled blood. With just over ten minutes to go, Wales battered the England line before Cory Hill cut back inside to score. Local hero Dan Biggar, who had received a huge cheer when he replaced ex-Kiwi Anscombe, added the extras to make it 16-13 to the home side. Two minutes from full-time, Biggar kicked cross-field to winger Josh Adams who outleapt Elliot Daly for a spectacular try. Final score Wales 21, England 13.

With twelve straight wins, Warren Gatland's team was now statistically the greatest-ever Welsh side and Gatland would not miss an opportunity to rub Eddie's nose in it, making it clear that he had gone to school on Eddie's kicking tactics of the first two games. His team had worked hard at training on their catching skills and cutting down the time of the England kickers. They had even switched their wingers from their usual sides, with George North playing on the left and Adams the right to upset England's plans.

But it was his answer to the question, 'You highlighted Kyle Sinckler during the week – do you think those tactics worked?' that would prove the most newsworthy.

'He gave away a couple of penalties and I think they identified that in the England coaches' box so they made what they thought was a smart tactical decision,' he said, intimating that Eddie had fallen into a well-planned trap.

'There's no doubt he's a fantastic player, but he's got a few demons he has to deal with.'

Told of Gatland's comments a drained-looking Eddie snapped, 'I didn't know Warren had a degree in clinical psychology, so let me know and I might go and see him as well.'

Just as they had in their previous three losses, twice to the Springboks in South Africa and to New Zealand at Twickenham, England had got off to a good lead only to be run down. It was a problem that Eddie hoped had been overcome with the big second-half performance against France, but clearly not. And it was one that would become even more apparent before the Six Nations ended.

England's dream of a second Grand Slam under Eddie was over, but there was still a slim chance of a third Six Nations championship. For that to happen, Wales would have to lose or draw one of their remaining games against Scotland and Ireland, while England had to beat both Italy and Scotland.

For the match against Italy at Twickenham, Eddie made five changes to the team that had lost to Wales. The inclusion of Joe Launchbury was forced by an injury to Courtney Lawes, but the others were tactical and demonstrated England's great depth with an eye to the World Cup. Most significant was the inclusion of winger Joe Cokanasiga and inside centre Ben Te'o, with Manu Tuilagi moving to outside centre. It was a heavyweight combination that raised conjecture that Eddie was out to punish the Italians for their cat-and-mouse tactics the last time they had played at Twickenham. As Robert Kitson of the *Guardian* put it: 'Rarely has a team been more deliberately picked to dish out revenge, with the Azzurri set to face the heaviest trio of players at twelve, thirteen and fourteen that England have ever selected. Subtlety has left town, at least for the time being.'

Whatever Eddie's motivation, the result was a one-sided 57-14 thrashing with Cokanasiga almost unstoppable. It was England's biggest win over Italy in eight years, but in terms of the Six Nations standings the margin was irrelevant. All that mattered from England's point of view was that Wales beat Scotland 18-11 at Murrayfield to keep the contest for the championship still very much alive.

Eddie called England's upcoming game against the Scots a 'grand final', but in fact it was all academic. Even before the two teams walked onto Twickenham, the Welsh were celebrating after a lopsided 25-7 win over Ireland in Cardiff. The best England could do was finish second and they started off showing that they intended to do just that in style.

Throughout the championship England had been the entertainers and in the first half against Scotland they were at their attacking best, scoring four unanswered tries to Nowell, Curry, Launchbury and May for a 31-0 lead before the Scots finally got on the board after Stuart McInally charged down an Owen Farrell kick. Despite that minor stutter, with a twenty-four-point lead at the break, the England crowd was looking forward to something memorable to end the championship. They got it, but not in the manner they had hoped. Scotland's comeback and England's disintegration was, depending on which side you supported, either an unprecedented display of pluck and daring, or a horror show.

Things began to unravel for England just seven minutes into the half when slick hands from Scottish fly-half Finn Russell set off an interchange of passes that ended with winger Darcy Graham stepping through three defenders before scoring. Three minutes later scrum-half Ali Price chipped ahead, regathered and put number eight Magnus Bradbury over near the posts. At 31-19 after the conversion, what had been looking like a dream England performance was fast becoming a nightmare. Seven minutes later the Scots were in again,

Finn Russell once more the instigator and Darcy Graham the finisher to take the score to 31-24.

As they had when pressured by Wales, Eddie's men lost their composure and began kicking without purpose. Most worrying with the World Cup on the horizon was that captain Owen Farrell, the man England looked to in times of pressure for a cool head and astute leadership, was one of the worst offenders. Just past the hour mark he threw an ill-considered pass in traffic that was intercepted by Russell who scored under the posts. The conversion tied it up at 31-all. When Farrell was penalized for one of his now-signature no-arms tackles on Graham, Eddie had seen enough and replaced him with George Ford.

It proved to be a fortuitous substitution. With five minutes remaining, Scotland's Australian-born centre Sam Johnson beat attempted tackles from Daly, Nowell, Spencer and Ford to score a converted try that looked like being the winner. Then, three minutes into injury time, one of the most bizarre matches in Six Nations history took a final twist, with George Ford dummying and stepping his way through exhausted Scottish defenders to score under the posts. His conversion wrapped it up at 38-all.

In the final reckoning England had avoided defeat and improved from fifth in the 2018 championship to second in 2019, but there was no sidestepping the fact that this was an embarrassment of mammoth proportions. Worse still, in the minds of many supporters it deflated any hopes that had been building for England's chances at the World Cup. After surrendering a thirty-one-point lead and scraping to a draw against a team that had managed only one win – against Italy – surely no one could still have any confidence that England would mount a successful challenge for the greatest prize in the game.

No one, that is, but Eddie Jones.

Epilogue

DESTINATION JAPAN

21 March 2019: Less than a week after the astonishing draw with Scotland, and five months after having read the first edition of this book, Eddie has agreed to an interview to give an overview of where he feels the team is placed six months from the start of the Rugby World Cup in Tokyo.

Maybe he could be forgiven for being a little downcast having just seen his men blow a golden chance of a third Six Nations title on his watch. At the very least, surely he would have to be worried about their second half capitulation to the Scots.

Not Eddie. Not only isn't he the least bit despondent, he seems positively buoyant.

It's fair to say that one should never be surprised when dealing with Eddie Jones but, even so, his first words aren't quite what is expected.

'The Six Nations was good for us,' he says. 'For a team like us going into the World Cup, the current situation is the best situation to be in. We can come in a little under the radar. We've had enough good wins but there is still work to be done.'

Anyone watching England's most recent performances would no doubt suggest that the majority of that work would be in the area of maintaining pressure and closing out a match after getting away to a good start – something the team hadn't managed to achieve in two Tests on the South Africa tour and against New Zealand, Wales and Scotland.

'When you have a recurring problem you can deal with it,' he says.

And the root of that problem?

'I reckon we've been seduced by easiness. We can play. What we can't do is cope with disappointment or easiness. It's like a batsman who can score a great thirty but can't build a big innings. It's all about the thought process.'

To that end, within forty-eight hours of the Scotland debacle Eddie had added yet another member to his off-field support team – a psychologist – and not just for the players.

'We brought someone in to work with the players and the staff. The staff are part of the issue. It is not just about what happens on the field, it is how the whole organization works. She'll work with us going forward. It's very important that we play well for the entire game. Early on we were able to get through the second forty minutes of matches because we had experienced players, but once we were a more inexperienced side that became the most difficult period.'

And according to Eddie, highlighting that problem and other gremlins before the start of the World Cup on 30 September was what lead-up games – including the Six Nations – were all about. Just like he had with the Wallabies in 2003, Eddie was putting his team through a 'Melbourne Cup preparation'.

'We've really been preparing for the World Cup since November 2018, looking at different combinations for different opponents. We really wanted to use that final twelve months to prepare us for Japan. We want to win every game but we want to learn from every game as well. New Zealand have done a bit of that too. This will be Steve Hansen's third World Cup; he knows how things work.'

As does Eddie, which is why he is not too concerned about England's up-and-down form heading into the tournament.

'Looking at the three World Cups I've been involved in, Australia were thrashed by New Zealand and England a few months before it started; in 2007 South Africa lost three of their four Tri-Nations matches, and Japan lost three of their four warm-up matches.

'Australia were beaten in extra-time of the final, South Africa won it and Japan beat South Africa and only just missed the play-offs. That tells me that it doesn't matter what happens before the tournament, as long as you learn from it and use it to your advantage when you get your final squad together and start your preparation. It's the one time you have the players together for an extended period for proper training and coaching, so it's important to use that time to get things right.'

As far as the final make-up of his thirty-one-man squad was concerned, Eddie says he had whittled it down to thirty-six by the end of the Six Nations. It was just a case of seeing who was available before the last cull.

'It's about who is in form and who is fit. How many times do you get to play with a full squad these days? The collisions are so great that all your players are rarely available.'

Many countries arrive at a Rugby World Cup with two distinct sides – their number one Test team and the second-stringers. An A and B side, if you will. Given the success that Eddie had juggling his players in his 'horses for courses' policy during the autumn internationals and Six Nations, would it be more correct to say England would have an A and A-plus side at the World Cup?

'Something like that, but I've got a feeling this World Cup might be a bit different to the others after how Japan went at the last one. Previously some of the tier-two nations would play their B teams against the top sides because they thought they had no hope of winning. They figured they'd save themselves for the other tier-two teams in the hope of getting a win. This World Cup could see the end of the tier-two blowouts. Japan's win over South Africa has given everyone confidence to have a go. Japan only had five or six professional players, the rest were amateurs and yet they beat one of the top teams in the world. The other tier-two countries will see what Japan did and think, there's no reason why we can't do it too.'

So where does that leave England?

'We've got good depth, not incredible depth, but we've been working on it over the past two years. We've been bringing in young players, sometimes forced by injury, in other cases just to give experience. Players like Ben Moon, Tom Curry and Mark Wilson. We took Ellis Genge and Kyle Sinckler with us to Australia in 2016 and we took Joe Cokanasiga to Argentina the next year just to give them experience. In the pack we've got players like Moon, Genge and Brad Shields who've all got less than ten caps. Curry and Kyle Sinckler haven't played twenty Tests yet, but they now know what Test rugby is all about and when you put them together with the experienced players, you've got something to build on.

'Experience is very important. You need guys in these games who can hold things together. These are things you can't be taught. You have to learn. We're fortunate that we've got our senior players Mako Vunipola, Maro Itoje and Dylan Hartley coming back from injury. Mako, Itoje and Billy Vunipola haven't played together in the same side for two years.

'The other two players we've really been missing are Curry and Courtney Lawes.

'Lawes is a modern-day enforcer. When he hits them they don't want to come back into his channel. Curry is very good. He's only twenty years old. He's a hard-working, humble kid. He's getting better all the time. This was the first time he's played in a Six Nations. Until you've played in it you can't appreciate the extent of the pressure they are under. Everything they do is under the microscope. That experience is going to be very important for all of them when we get to Japan.'

Even so, many of England's starters will enter the tournament without a lot of Tests under their belts and Eddie has said on several occasions that a team needs around 800 to 900 caps of experience to win a World Cup. Is he now revising that estimate?

'We won't be right there, but we'll be close, maybe 650–700 and that will be enough to win this World Cup. New Zealand won it last time with 1,000 caps but they'll be a younger team this time. It's part of a cycle that all teams go through. The only older team this time will be Ireland. Their best players like Johnny Sexton, Rory Best and Peter O'Mahony are getting to those tender ages. It's hard for those older guys. The game is so demanding.'

Another theory about winning the World Cup was put forward by Eddie's mentor Bob Dwyer after his Wallabies lifted the trophy in 1991. Dwyer said a winning team needed to have five players chosen in the Team of the Tournament which is named at the presentation dinner held at the end of the event.

'I think we could be close,' Eddie says. 'Itoje, Mako, Billy, Curry, Youngs, Farrell, May . . . they're all capable of making it.'

Of course the most important thing is for England to stay in the fight right up until the final whistle at Yokohama International Stadium on 2 November. There will be no team in the tournament better prepared to achieve that goal. It is as if Eddie has spent his entire professional life preparing for it. No other coach has studied Japan and its customs more; none better understands the idiosyncrasies of the Japanese system. Little things that may confuse or distract other coaches and players will be familiar to him thanks to years of first-hand experience. He learnt early in his time in Japan that there is nothing to be gained from trying to win every skirmish. Pick your battles, he says. Be patient, be calm. They are all lessons he has long been passing on to his players and staff. He has gone so far as to arrange Japanese language lessons for his assistant coaches.

The team will have two training camps in Italy to help them acclimatize to the heat they will encounter in Japan and a final five days in Miyazaki, where Eddie's Brave Blossoms prepared for the last World Cup. There they will continue to train and work on their skills, but the real benefit will be an introduction to the country that will be their home for the next two months; a country unlike any other.

'That will top us up nicely,' says Eddie, who has no illusions about the importance of the World Cup, both to England rugby and his own legacy.

'I'm probably the first and last foreigner ever to coach England so I want to do something good for the game here.'

To that end the rugby gods have been kind, with England enjoying a decent draw. Drawn with France, Argentina, USA and Tonga, Eddie's men are strongly favoured to finish top of Pool C, setting up a quarter-final clash with the team that finishes second in Pool D. With that pool containing Grand Slam champions Wales and a Michael Cheika-coached Wallaby team stumbling from one setback to another, there is every chance that England will have the opportunity to do to Australia what the Australians did to them at the last World Cup – send them packing.

To Eddie, who has relished every moment of the six straight defeats he has inflicted on his former team-mate and his former country since taking the reins at England, the prospect brings a smile.

'That would be a good game, hey,' he says.

It is one that could well determine the future of both coaches. Cheika is not expected to continue with the Wallabies past the World Cup, although a win in the final could see him offered another contract. Likewise, Eddie is contracted to the RFU until the end of the 2021 season but a premature exit in Japan could see an early parting of the ways. The various permutations offer up an intriguing scenario. After England beat the Wallabies in the autumn series, sections of the Australian media began campaigning for Eddie to be appointed as Cheika's replacement.

The support of the Australian press was in stark contrast to the treatment Eddie had received from sections of the British media who had pushed for his dismissal by the RFU. While he did erupt with his 'you know if I stay long enough you're going to get me sacked' outburst following the win over South Africa in 2018, he claims to be uninterested in the media.

'I've got to the age where I don't care,' he says – although there would be many who would find that very hard to believe. 'I try to have a bit of fun. I use them when appropriate to help the team, but I don't read one word.'

Then what about the reports that Eddie's head was on the chopping block several times over the past two years? How close did he come to losing his job?

'I've got no idea. I'm not concerned one way or the other. If they decided I should go, that's their decision, but no one ever brought it up with me.'

Either way it is now irrelevant. There is no question that Eddie is taking England to the World Cup, but what is open to conjecture is what he will do after that. Would he be interested in a return to the Wallabies?

'I don't think I'd ever say never, but it isn't something I've really thought about.'

Then what about the prospect of taking the British and Irish Lions on their 2021 tour of South Africa?

His reply is immediate, but in typical Eddie style there is the hint of a putdown aimed at the man who helmed the previous two Lions tours, outgoing Wales coach Warren Gatland.

'No. The last thing I want to do is spend eight weeks in a blazer. That's an ambassador job. I'm a coach. I'd rather coach the Queensland Sheffield Shield [cricket] team.'

Okay, possibly not the Wallabies and certainly not the Lions, so what then?

He has spoken about following his one-time rival Sir Clive Woodward into the media, or sitting in the West Indies watching cricket. Another time he talked of returning to his first profession: teaching.

'I'd love to be a director of sport at a big private school. You walk around Tuesday and Thursday, games afternoons. You watch the rugby games; you watch the cricket games. That's paradise.'

Asked the question about his future in 2017 he raised an eyebrow, broke into a cheeky smile and gave an answer that could have been a joke. Or not.

'I want to coach England in football. I reckon that would be the greatest job in the world, I really do. I think it would be fantastic. Just give me six months to sort them out.'

But the truth is, there is nothing Eddie Jones wants to be doing other than what he has done for the past quarter of a century: coaching rugby, no matter how hard it might get.

'Sometimes I'm driving the car, going to the game and I think, 'Shit, there must be a better way of making a living than this.' Your stomach is churning, you're worried about a certain player, you're worried about other things, but at the end of the day that's excitement. I know that I've only got a certain amount of time left, and every opportunity is fantastic. To me, as an old schoolteacher, I just love being involved with young people and trying to make them better.

'Look at me. I'm fifty-eight years old. I'm out in the fresh air, I'm wearing shorts, I'm wearing a hat. I've got a whistle.

'It's a good life.'

ACKNOWLEDGEMENTS

From the time I first became aware of Eddie Jones as a feisty player with Randwick Rugby Club in the 1980s, through covering his time as Wallabies and Japan coach and interviewing him about his appointment by the England RFU in 2017, I have found him the most interesting and intriguing of characters.

In the first flush of his enormous early success with the red rose I approached him with my idea of collaborating on an authorized biography. Unfortunately, due to other commitments, Eddie was unable to work with me on the initial project (although he was kind enough to give me an interview for the updated version prior to the Rugby World Cup), but with the support of Allen & Unwin I decided to push ahead regardless.

It was always my intention to write a comprehensive, honest and balanced account of Eddie's life and times. To this end I have relied on the many interviews I have carried out with Eddie and his contemporaries over the years, plus the enormous storehouse of published material provided by the outstanding rugby writers and columnists who have followed his career in such detail. Wherever relevant I have credited these writers in the text.

I would also like to make special mention of Tom Fordyce of BBC Sport whose insightful reports of England matches during Eddie's time in charge were an invaluable source of reference, as were

Eddie's many press conferences and public speaking appearances which are readily available online. Most of all though, I would like to thank the many people from Eddie's past – team-mates, work-mates, players, assistant coaches, employers, reporters, protagonists, friends and foes – who gave so generously in sharing their memories and opinions. While they are all quoted by name in the text it would be remiss not to acknowledge their support. Therefore, in alphabetical order, my sincere thanks to:

Andrew Blades, Neil Breen, Rod Crerar, Bob Dwyer, Gary, Glen and Mark Ella, Rita Fin, Elton Flatley, Gary Flowers, Bernard Foley, Adam Freier, Anthony 'AJ' George, Roger Gould, Richard Graham, Greg Growden, Ian Herbert, Chris Hewett, Tim Horan, Peter Jenkins, Alan Jones, Les Kiss, Stephen Moore, Michael Nethery, Matt O'Connor, John O'Neill, Ben Perkins, Ross Reynolds, Wendell Sailor, Tim Sheridan, Bob Skinstad, Reg St Leon, Jim Tucker and Craig Wing.

I would also like to thank Clare Drysdale and Tom Gilliatt from A&U for making my idea a reality and, as always, pay the most heartfelt yet inadequate tribute to my amazing wife Linda: researcher, proofreader, copy-editor, sounding board, voice of reason and calming presence.

Oh, and last but not least, to Eddie Jones, for giving me and every other journalist who has ever crossed his path so much to write about.

Mike Colman

BIBLIOGRAPHY

Anthony, L, Leros, G, Peters, A, Pressick-Kilborn, K. 2014 *The IGS Story*, Sydney, International Grammar School

Gregan, G. 2008 *Halfback, Half Forward*, Sydney, Pan Macmillan Australia Pty Ltd

Growden, G. 2004 *My Sporting Hero*, Sydney, Random House Australia

Harris, B. 1984 *Ella Ella Ella*, Sydney, Little Hill Press

Larkham, S. 2004 *Stephen Larkham's World Cup Diary*, Melbourne, Penguin Books Ltd

Macqueen, R. 2001 *One Step Ahead,* Sydney, Random House Australia Pty Ltd

O'Neill, J. 2007 *It's Only a Game*, Sydney, Random House Australia Pty Ltd

Smit, J. and Greenaway, M. 2009 *Captain in the Cauldron*, Cape Town, Highbury Safika Media

White, J. 2007 *In Black and White,* Sydney, New Holland Publishers (Australia) Pty Ltd

Woodward, C. 2004 *Winning!*, London, Hodder & Stoughton Ltd

Zavos, S. 2007 *Watching the Rugby World Cup,* Sydney, Allen & Unwin